Controversies in Crime and Justice
series editor Victor E. Kappeler Eastern Kentucky University

Controversies in

Victimology

edited by Laura J. Moriarty
Virginia Commonwealth University

anderson publishing co.
2035 Reading Road
Cincinnati, OH 45202
800-582-7295

Controversies in Victimology

Copyright © 2003
    Anderson Publishing Co.
    2035 Reading Rd.
    Cincinnati, OH 45202

Phone 800.582.7295 or 513.421.4142
Web Site www.andersonpublishing.com

Library of Congress Cataloging-in-Publication Data

Controversies in victimology / edited by Laura J. Moriarty.
    p. cm. -- (Controversies in crime and justice)
    Includes bibliographical references and index.
    ISBN 1-58360-511-8 (pbk.)
    1. Victims of crimes--United States. I. Title: Victimology. II. Moriarty, Laura J. III. Series.

HV6250.3.U5 C56 2001
362.88--dc21

        00-054841

Cover design by Tin Box Studio, Inc.
Cover photo credit: Ryan McVay

EDITOR Gail Eccleston
ACQUISITIONS EDITOR Michael C. Braswell

Dedication

To June A. Hetzel and John M. Moriarty

*"May You Live As Long As You Want,
And Never Want As Long As You Live"*

—An Irish Blessing

Acknowledgments

I wish to thank all the contributors to this reader. I hope it has been a pleasant experience for each of you. What started out as an idea on a long train ride has finally come to fruition. I appreciate each of you working with me on this project and also for participating in the double roundtable session at ACJS in New Orleans where we first presented the information contained in this reader. This product is indeed a labor of love.

A special thanks to Vic Kappeler and Mickey Braswell for supporting this endeavor. Vic provided excellent direction in the conceptualization of this project. Mickey always has an encouraging smile and kind words to say when I see him. Such support is very much appreciated.

Thanks also to my university, Virginia Commonwealth University, and my colleagues in the Dean's Office. Many times I worked on this book - pushing my other responsibilities into another pile. I know you all noticed but no one said anything. Everyone has been so encouraging and supportive of my desire to stay current in the field. I appreciate the support and promise to make up for slacking off in the future.

Finally, I thank my family and friends. Just being able to discuss the contents of this book with others - not necessarily in the field - helped tremendously.

Table of Contents

Introduction   *ix*
Laura J. Moriarty

Chapter 1   Balancing Criminal Victims' and Criminal Defendants' Rights   1
             Gregory P. Orvis

Chapter 2   Victim Blaming   15
             Helen M. Eigenberg

Chapter 3   The Role of Alcohol in Victimization   25
             Richard Tewksbury & Diane Pedro

Chapter 4   The Mass Media and Victims of Rape   43
             Patricia H. Grant & Paula I. Otto

Chapter 5   The Tradition and Reality of Domestic Violence   57
             M.A. Dupont-Morales

Chapter 6   Fear of Crime and Victimization   71
             Elizabeth H. McConnell

Chapter 7   Restoration and the Criminal Justice System   81
             Jon'a F. Meyer

Chapter 8   Victim Impact Statements: Fairness to Defendants?   91
             Ida M. Johnson & Etta Morgan

Chapter 9   Victim Offender Reconciliation Programs   103
             Michael R. Smith

Chapter 10   Reconciling the Controversies: Is Education the Panacea?   117
             Laura J. Moriarty

References   123

Contributor's Biographical Information   145

Index   149

Introduction

Laura J. Moriarty

Whether victimology is considered a discipline in itself or a sub-field of criminology, controversies emerge depending on the emphasis of study. Traditional victimologists study the causes of criminal victimization to explain and prevent it (Doerner & Lab, 1998). The goal being to educate others to avoid general and specific victimization. More modern victimologists focus on "restoring" or making the victim "whole" again. The goal being to restore victims to their pre-victimization state by ameliorating their physical, emotional, and financial suffering (Karmen, 1995). Both perspectives are valid but adhering to one or the other creates conflict.

Traditional victimology is similar to the discipline of criminology with the only difference being the focus of the inquiry. More often criminologists focus on the offender, while victimologists focus on the victim. Neither discipline can afford to be exclusive in terms of the inquiry; moreover, when the focus is only on the offender or the victim, the stage is set to pit victims against offenders and vice versa, resulting in heated debate.

There are many controversial topics in victimology. This reader focuses on 10 specific issues that have been organized into three sections. The issues were selected because they represent, arguably, the most controversial topics in the field. The topics included in this reader should not be viewed as exhaustive for the complexity of the subject matter generates a sizeable number of potential debates. Thus, a number of significant issues are not included in this collection.

The reader is organized into three sections: Part 1, *Foundation Issues*, Part II, *Victimization Issues*, and Part III, *Representation Issues*. Academic experts and professionals in varied fields examine a controversial issue in victimology. Each chapter is organized to provide the reader with an overview of the subject matter, explaining why it is an issue in victimology, presenting both sides of the key factors in the debate, and, when appropriate, including suggestions to attempt to reconcile the controversy.

In the first chapter, Greg Orvis examines victims' rights in relationship to offenders' rights. A common misperception is that offenders have all the rights and victims have none, or that offenders' rights outweigh victims' rights. Orvis, relying on his legal background and his expertise in constitutional law, provides a historical overview of offenders' rights explaining why due process rights are fundamental to our legal system, detailing the decisions of the Warren Court to increase such rights. Orvis simultaneously discusses why victim's rights should not impede on offenders' rights. He discusses the purposes of the criminal and civil courts making the argument that victims can and should seek redress through the civil courts. Orvis concludes with the recommendation that victims' and offenders' rights should be balanced. He advocates for better enforcement of state level victims' rights and admonishes that a federal statute or amendment would tilt the scales in favor of the victims trampling the rights of offenders.

In Chapter 2 the focus is on the concept of shared responsibility. As Helen Eigenberg asserts, shared responsibility is sometimes referred to as victim blaming, victim facilitation, or victim precipitation. She explains the historical trend to blame victims, to some degree, for their victimization. Eigenberg discusses the weaknesses inherent in the concept of victim blaming, including the use of tautological reasoning, conceptual difficulties, placing undue responsibility on the victims, creating culturally legitimate victims, and excusing offenders' behavior. She continues presenting the reasons why the public endorses the concept of victim blaming, and how such a mindset often impedes crime prevention strategies. Eigenberg concludes with the recommendation that victimology should examine the role social structure plays in explaining victimization.

Chapter 3 examines the role alcohol has on criminal victimization. The authors provide a thorough review of the existing literature, establishing the strong linkages between alcohol and criminality, while focusing on college campuses. The authors conclude that not only is alcohol consumption itself a health risk to college students but alcohol consumption can lead to victimization and arrest. When considered together, the authors argue, college drinking becomes the number one health issue for campus administrators.

The second section of the book examines specific victimization issues. In Chapter 4, Patricia Grant and Paula Otto examine the issue of publishing rape victims' names in the print and electronic media. They begin by explaining there is no law prohibiting newspapers or newscasters from publishing victims' names, regardless of the crime committed. Therefore, the only way to actually control the publishing or broadcasting of victims' names is through the ethical standards of the discipline or by having law enforcement block the names from public access. Grant and Otto provide a balanced discussion regarding the value of publishing or broadcasting victims' names versus keeping the names confidential.

Chapter 5 addresses an issue that often creates much controversy - male victims of domestic violence. Some authors dismiss such victimization and few argue that special services are needed for these victims. M.A. Dupont-Morales, however, provides an overview of domestic violence concentrating on male victims. She explains why such a focus is so troublesome and challenges the reader to examine such violence as part of "relationship violence" rather than domestic violence. She maintains that the nomenclature of "domestic violence" is what is problematic. When the term is broadened to "relationship violence," patterns exist which demonstrate that women, men, and even children can be violent. Dupont-Morales argues that the socialization into violence is intergenerational, making violence a lifetime occurrence. With the proper focus, we can begin to strategically address the needs of victims of violence, regardless of gender and age.

Chapter 6 examines fear of crime – perhaps one of the most pressing problems in society. As more and more data sources are reporting the general decline in crime rates, fear of crime is remaining steady or slightly increasing. This is paradoxical. With the crime rate decreasing, fear of crime should decrease as well. What explains this paradox? McConnell reviews the research on the topic, reminding us that if the concept itself is not measured properly we achieve questionable results. She argues that the conceptual and operational definitions of fear of crime are too restrictive or limited and must include an interdisciplinary approach to measuring fear of crime. She argues for biological, psychological, criminological, and sociological perspectives or what would be labeled as a true "interdisciplinary" perspective to fully understand fear of crime.

The last section of the book examines representation issues. How victims are represented in the criminal justice system often results in conflict or controversies. In Chapter 7 the focus is on restoration in the criminal justice system. Providing a historical overview, Jon'a Meyer explains restorative justice, outlining where we have been and where we are going with the concept. She also includes a discussion of restorative justice in relationship to correctional goals. She concludes with a thorough presentation of public support for restorative justice.

Chapter 8 examines victim impact statements. Originally thought to be a good idea, victims are offered a voice in the criminal justice process. But, have these impact statements, without the benefit of cross-examination or challenge by counsel, resulted in unfair treatment of offenders? Do such statements violate defendants' constitutional rights? Ida Johnson and Etta Morgan examine these issues in their chapter focusing on death penalty cases.

Chapter 9 addresses victim/offender reconciliation programs. Michael Smith provides a description of such programs, questioning whether they are good for victims. He does this by examining the cost-effectiveness of such programs and by assessing the programs' impact on recidivism. He also discusses whether the programs are destructive to the Rule of Law and whether or not they punish appropriately.

The final chapter attempts to tie together these controversies in an effort to settle the issues. While there are no simple answers to address the issues, there do appear to be central themes that cross the debates. A broad, underlining explanation for the controversies appears to be a lack of knowledge or misunderstanding of the criminal justice system. Further, some controversies are rooted in and result from too narrow a focus of the discipline.

References

Doerner, W.G. & S.P. Lab (1998). *Victimology*, Second Edition. Cincinnati, OH: Anderson Publishing Co.

Karmen, A. (1995). *Crime Victims: An Introduction to Victimology*. Pacific Grove, CA: Brooks/Cole Publishing Company.

CHAPTER 1

Balancing Criminal Victims' and Criminal Defendants' Rights

Gregory P. Orvis

Criminal Victims' Rights

The 1998 National Crime Victimization Survey found 31 million violent and property victimizations of Americans aged 12 or older. This statistic represents a decline in overall American victimizations; down from 35 million victimizations in 1997, thus continuing a downward trend since 1994 and a tremendous fall from the high peak of victimizations in 1973, which topped at 44 million (Bureau of Justice Statistics, 1999). Despite these facts, the victims rights' movement in the United States has grown as victimization has declined, with victims' rights being at the top of President Clinton's public policy agenda, and culminating with his support for a constitutional amendment guaranteeing victims' rights. President Clinton announced his intentions in the Rose Garden:

> When someone is a victim, he or she should be at the center of the criminal justice process, not on the outside looking in. Participation in all forms of government is the essence of democracy. Victims should be guaranteed the right to participate in proceedings related to crimes committed against them. People accused of crimes have explicit constitutional rights. Ordinary citizens have a constitutional right to participate in criminal trials by serving on a jury. The press has a constitutional right to attend trials. All of this is as it should be. It is only the victims of crimes who have no constitutional right to participate, and that is not the way it should be. Having carefully studied all of the alternatives, I am convinced that the only way to fully safeguard the rights of victims in America is to amend our Constitution and guarantee these basic rights – to be told about public court proceedings and to attend them; to

1

> make a statement to the court about bail, about sentencing, about accepting a plea if the victim is present, to be told about parole hearings to attend and to speak; notice when the defendant or convict escapes or is released, restitution from the defendant, reasonable protection from the defendant and notice of these rights (Office of the Press Secretary, 1996:5-6).

As President Clinton's statement demonstrates, "victims' rights" are the procedural counterparts to the long-standing "due process" rights guaranteed to criminal defendants by the Bill of Rights and, as of the fall of 1999, such a constitutional amendment legitimizing "victims' rights" is before both the Senate and the House of Representatives (National Victims' Constitutional Amendment Network, 1999). Considering that there have been only 26 amendments to the Constitution in its more than 200-year history, a constitutional amendment guaranteeing victims' rights will be quite an accomplishment, if successfully implemented, for a political movement that is not even 20 years old.

Although in 1931 the National Commission on Law Observance and Enforcement noted that the administration of justice suffered because of the great economic and psychological burdens placed on those who testify in court, the first victim/witness assistance programs were not initiated until the mid-1970s, when the Law Enforcement Assistance Administration funded the first 10 programs, and which has expanded to more than 600 programs today (Roberts, 1991). However, it can be argued that the victim's rights "reform" movement did not become prominent until 1982 when California voters adopted "Proposition Eight," which was state legislation that included a victims' bill of rights (Friedman, 1984).

Since that time, the victims' rights movement has been held responsible for Congress passing the Victim and Witness Protection Act of 1982, which makes the granting of victim restitution a norm in federal sentencing. The Victims of Crime Act of 1984 was also passed, which established a federally financed victim compensation fund (Orvis, 1998). Congress also passed a package of victims' rights legislation as part the Justice Assistance Act and the Violent Crime Control and Law Enforcement Act of 1994 (McMurry, 1997).

Today, the federal system and many state systems require that a trial judge read victim impact statements prior to sentencing a convicted criminal defendant (Holman & Quinn, 1996). The federal system and more than 40 states have passed laws requiring victim notification of the offender's trial, sentencing, plea bargain, and parole proceedings. Most states limit these actions to only victims of certain crimes, such as felonies, violent crimes, or crimes specifically enumerated in the law (Tobolowsky, 1999). Twenty-one states grant victims the right to be heard during a hearing on the acceptance of a plea agreement and 31 states give victims the right to attend even the disposition hearing of a juvenile in felony cases. Furthermore, 49 states have laws requiring HIV testing of certain sex offenders and all states require convicted sex offenders to register with public officials, with 48 of these states requiring community notification of the release of sex offenders or to allow community access to sex offender registration information (National Center for Victims of Crime, 1999).

After the vigorous lobbying of state legislatures by victims' rights groups, 31 states have enacted a victims' rights amendment to their state constitutions.* Some of the rights granted to victims by their state constitutions seem to be common courtesy, and are often already provided by victim/witness services, such as Missouri providing its crime victims "the right to information about how the criminal justice system works, the rights and availability of services, and upon request of the victim, the right to information about the crime" (Constitution of Missouri, 1999, art. I, sec. 32-7). Other examples are New Mexico's provisions for the crime victim to have "the right to have the prosecuting attorney notify the victim's employer . . . of the necessity of the victim's cooperation and testimony" and "the right to promptly receive any property belonging to the victim that is being held for evidentiary purposes" (Constitution of New Mexico, 1999, sec. 24-10 & 11).

The vast majority of victims' rights established by state constitutional amendments, however, guarantee the victim active participation in the criminal justice process. Some states take a general approach, such as Indiana's constitutional amendment that provides, "Victims of crime, as defined by law, shall have the right to be treated with fairness, dignity, and respect throughout the criminal justice process; and, as defined by law, to be informed of and present during public hearings and to confer with the prosecution, to the extent that exercising these rights does not infringe upon the constitutional rights of the accused" (Constitution of Indiana, 1999, art. I, sec. 13b). A few states, like Colorado, are more abstract then that, merely stipulating that a victim will be heard at all "critical stages" of the criminal justice process (Constitution of Colorado, 1999, art. II, sec. 16a; Constitution of Florida, 1999, art. I, sec. 16).

Other states' victims' rights amendments have provided specific privileges to crime victims, such as in Wisconsin where victims are guaranteed: (1) timely disposition of the case; (2) the opportunity to attend court proceedings unless sequestration is necessary for a fair trial; (3) reasonable protection from the defendant; (4) notification of court proceedings; (5) the opportunity to confer with the prosecutor; (6) the opportunity to make a victim's impact statement at sentencing; (7) victim's restitution; (8) victim's compensation; and (9) notification about the outcome of the case (Constitution of Wisconsin, 1999). Another specific right sometimes granted state constitutional protection is included in Alaska's provisions on the "Rights of Crime Victims," which is notification about the crime offender's escape or

---

*I.e., Alabama, Alaska, Arizona, California, Colorado, Connecticut, Florida, Idaho, Illinois, Indiana, Kansas, Louisiana, Maryland, Michigan, Mississippi, Missouri, Nebraska, Nevada, New Jersey, New Mexico, North Carolina, Ohio, Oklahoma, Rhode Island, South Carolina, Tennessee, Texas, Utah, Virginia, Washington, and Wisconsin.

release after conviction (Constitution of Alaska, 1999). Arizona's state constitution includes possibly the most rights for victims, including rights to be heard at any post-arrest release or plea negotiation proceeding, to be heard at any post-conviction proceeding when release is being considered, and to read the accused's presentence reports (Constitution of Arizona, 1999). Louisiana goes one step further and allows the victim to comment on the presentence report (Constitution of Louisiana, 1999). South Carolina even goes further with allowing the crime victim "reasonable access after the conclusion of the criminal investigation to all documents relating to the crime against the victim before trial" (Constitution of South Carolina, 1999, art. I, sec. 24-A8). Furthermore, some states, such as Idaho, give the same rights to victims when the offender is a juvenile (Constitution of Idaho, 1999).

The Victims' Bill of Rights in some states evokes change in criminal procedure and evidence laws. California's "Right to Truth in Evidence" provides that, "relevant evidence shall not be excluded in any criminal proceeding, including pretrial and post conviction motions and hearings, or in any trial or hearing of a juvenile for a criminal offense, whether heard in juvenile or adult court" (Constitution of California, 1999, art. I, sec. 28d). Arizona provides a right to victims to have all rules governing criminal procedure and the admissibility of evidence amended to protect victims' rights (Constitution of Arizona, 1999). Mississippi leaves the door open for further "reform" by stating, "The legislature shall have the authority to enact substantive and procedural laws to define, implement, preserve and protect the rights guaranteed victims by this section" (Constitution of Mississippi, 1999, sec. 26A3). It should be noted, however, that some states, such as Alabama and Kansas, limit these victims' rights "to the extent that these rights do not interfere with the constitutional rights of the person accused" (Constitution of Alabama, 1999, amend. 556a; Constitution of Kansas, 1999, art. 15, sec. 15a).

Even the courts have succumbed to the lobbying by the victims' rights movement. Traditionally, interest groups have sought to influence the decisions of the judicial branch through either amicus curiae (i.e., literally translated, "friends of the court") briefs or through the sponsorship of test cases (Epstein, 1991). It has only been in the last decade, however, that cases involving statutes providing victims' rights have reached appellate courts in any great number. Although hesitant at first, state and federal appellate courts have generally upheld statutory provisions allowing greater victim access and participation in the criminal justice process, often balancing them against the defendant's due process rights (Tobolowsky, 1999). The U.S. Supreme Court upheld the statutory right of victims to make impact statements during sentencing unless it was shown that the statements were so prejudicial as to make the process fundamentally unfair (*Payne v. Tennessee*, 1991).

Despite these lobbying successes, victims' rights groups, now about 8,000 strong, continue to press for an amendment to the United States Constitution (Ben-David, 1996). They reason that only a federal amendment would bring into "balance" the scales of justice, which they believe are tipped in favor of the criminal defendant. Furthermore, a constitutional amendment to the U.S. Constitution would guarantee that crime victims' rights would be enumerated and protected like the Bill of Rights protects the rights of those accused of crimes (McMurry, 1997). Thus the joint resolution presently before the House of Representatives for an amendment to the United States Constitution takes the latter approach to victims' rights by proposing specific privileges:

Each individual who is the victim of a crime for which the defendant can be imprisoned for a period longer than one year or any other crime that involves violence shall have the rights—

- to reasonable notice of, and not exclusion from, any public proceedings relating to the crime;

- to be heard, if present, and to submit a statement at all such proceedings to determine a conditional release from custody, an acceptance of a negotiated plea, or a sentence;

- to reasonable notice of and an opportunity to submit a statement concerning any proposed pardon or commutation of a sentence;

- to the foregoing rights at a parole proceeding that is not public, to the extent those rights are afforded to the convicted offender;

- to reasonable notice of a release or escape from custody relating to the crime;

- to consideration of the interest of the victim that any trial be free from unreasonable delay;

- to an order of restitution from the convicted offender;

- to consideration for the safety of the victim in determining any conditional release from custody relating to the crime; and

- to reasonable notice of the rights established by this article (House Joint Resolution 64, 1999).

A similar joint resolution was sent to the Senate floor on September 30, 1999, but it is limited to victims of violent crime and omitted "to reasonable notice of an opportunity to submit a statement concerning any proposed pardon or commutation of a sentence" (Senate Joint Resolution 3, 1999).

Criminal Defendants' Rights

Unlike the history of the budding victims' rights amendment, the four amendments of the Bill of Rights establishing criminal defendants' rights have a long and distinguished history. The debates over ratifying the United

States Constitution soon revealed that there was widespread demand among the colonists for additional constitutional protections of individual rights. Under community pressure, James Madison introduced proposals for constitutional amendments at the first session of Congress and the first ten amendments of the United States Constitution were ratified by the states and went into effect in 1791 (Gunther, 1975).

Almost one-half of these amendments establish protections against arbitrary police and court action by the government. The Fourth Amendment prohibits unreasonable searches or seizures. The Fifth Amendment establishes the requirement that a grand jury indictment is necessary to prosecute a person for a serious crime; prohibits double jeopardy and forced testimony against one's self; and requires "due process" before the "loss of life, liberty, or property" due to federal government action. The Sixth Amendment introduces the crime defendant's rights to a speedy, public, impartial trial with defense counsel and the right to cross-examine witnesses. Finally, excessive bail or fines and cruel and unusual punishment are prohibited by the Eighth Amendment (Wilson, 1986).

Originally, the Bill of Rights was applicable to only the federal government and not to state and local governments. The Fourteenth Amendment came into effect in 1868 and provided, "No State shall make or enforce any law which shall abridge the privileges or immunities of citizens of the United States; nor shall any State deprive any person of life, liberty, or property, without due process of law; nor deny to any person within its jurisdiction the equal protection of the law." The Fourteenth Amendment incorporated at least some of the rights protected in the Bill of Rights so as to make them enforceable against state and local governments as they were against the federal government. The United States Supreme Court rejected the theory of "total incorporation" at the turn of the century, but recognized in later cases that some of the personal rights safeguarded by the Bill of Rights against federal action may also be safeguarded against state action, because to deny them would be to deny due process (*Adamson v. California*, 1947; *Palko v. Connecticut*, 1937; *Twining v. New Jersey*, 1908).

Until the early 1960s, the Supreme Court had adopted the "fundamental rights" or "ordered liberty" interpretation of the Fourteenth Amendment's due process clause, wherein a particular state action could violate the principle without violating a specific provision in the Bill of Rights. The "selective incorporation" approach allowed the court to combine the best of the "total incorporation" approach and the "fundamental rights" approach. It allowed the court to recognize that the Fourteenth Amendment only encompasses rights that are fundamental to the "scheme of ordered liberty," but that not all rights listed in the Bill of Rights are such fundamental rights, and that rights not specifically enumerated could be fundamental (Israel, Kamisar & LaFave, 1995).

By the 1960s, the Supreme Court had selectively incorporated more and more of the specifics of the Bill of Rights and applying them to the state governments to the same extent that they applied to the federal government (Lockart, Kamisar, Choper & Shiffrin, 1986). By the end of the 1960s, the following Bill of Rights' guarantees to those accused of crimes as "selectively incorporated" by the Supreme Court, thus holding states to the same standards as the federal government: (1) the right against unreasonable search and seizure, with the right to have illegally seized evidence excluded from criminal trials (*Mapp v. Ohio*, 1961); (2) the right against cruel and unusual punishment (*Robinson v. California*, 1962); (3) the right to the assistance of counsel (*Gideon v. Wainwright*, 1963); (4) the right against compelled self-incrimination (*Malloy v. Hogan*, 1964); (5) the right to confront opposing witnesses (*Pointer v. Texas*, 1965); (6) the right to a speedy trial (*Klopfer v. North Carolina*, 1967); (7) the right to compulsory process for obtaining witnesses (*Washington v. Texas*, 1967); and (8) the right to a jury trial in a felony case (*Duncan v. Louisiana*, 1968). As Justice Marshall noted in a majority opinion in 1969, "Once it is decided that a particular Bill of Rights guarantee is 'fundamental to the American scheme of justice,' the same constitutional standards apply against both the State and Federal Governments" (*Benton v. Maryland*, 1969:784).

The 1960s decade has also been described as the "due process revolution" because the Supreme Court literally made policy statements governing criminal justice procedure for every court in the nation; often replacing the vague "due process" standard with "specific prophylactic rules," such as the *Miranda* rule governing the admissibility of voluntary confessions:

> Like most Court policies, this one evolved without being formally stated. One likely reason for the sudden concern with such issues was the justices' perception that mere admonitions of due process (i.e., general expression of what was "fundamentally fair") had been insufficient to eliminate or control criminal justice procedures that they found objectionable. A second reason would surely be the philosophical orientation of the Warren Court's liberal majority, what Archibald Cox characterized as the "egalitarianism that has become the dominant force in the evolution of our constitutional law. The broader egalitarianism stirred by the civil rights revolution has already found expression in criminal law decisions" (Grossman & Wells, 1980:739).

Major Arguments for Balancing Victims' Rights with Defendants' Rights

It was apparent to public perception that there was a connection, however fallacious, between the rise of crime in the early 1970s and the Supreme Court's permissiveness towards criminals. Richard Nixon, among countless other politicians, made law and order a top priority of both his 1968 and 1972 presidential campaign platforms, with promises that he would correct the balance between "the forces of peace and the forces of crime" by making more conservative appointments to the Supreme Court bench (Grossman & Wells, 1980). Congress passed several anti-court bills, including a law specifically intended to reverse *Miranda*; a law which is the basis of a test case to overturn *Miranda* presently before the Supreme Court (*Crime Control Act of 1968*; *Miranda v. Arizona*, 1966; *United States v. Dickerson*, 1999).

Nixon kept his word when elected and more conservative justices were appointed by him (and later by Presidents Reagan and Bush), and these new appointees to the court in turn shared a common determination to toughen judicial doctrines relating to crime (Schmidhauser, 1984). In 1971, then newly appointed Chief Justice Warren Burger wrote a majority opinion that significantly weakened the *Miranda* decision, and signaled the beginning of a judicial trend to limit the procedural rights gained by criminal defendants in the 1960s (*Harris v. New York*, 1971). It was this political climate in the 1970s that provided the foundation for the growth of the crime victims' movement in the 1980s and consequently, the movement for a crime victims' federal amendment in the 1990s. Three major arguments support the drive for a federal crime victims' rights amendment: (1) a victims' rights amendment will alleviate the trauma felt by crime victims who have traditionally been forgotten and revictimized by the criminal justice system; (2) a victims' rights amendment will give the crime victim standing equal to the criminal defendant to appeal unjust holdings in criminal cases; and (3) a victims' rights amendment is necessary to counterbalance the rights granted to criminal defendants by the Bill of Rights, so that both are on equal footing in a court of law.

The Forgotten Victim Argument

Further impetus was given to the victims' rights movement in 1982 when then President Reagan appointed a special task force on crime victims and who reported that crime victims were being treated merely as "appendages of a system appallingly out of balance" (Task Force on Victims of Crime, 1982). It was argued that the "unfeeling" system of justice, with its apparent concern only for defendants' rights, "revictimized" any victim who was brave enough to come forward to give evidence in a criminal prosecution (Siegelman, 1988). The criminal justice system "forgot" and subsequently alienated crime victims, and thus the crime victims' movement was born (Cellini, 1997). Early in the movement, victims' rights advocates argued that having such rights would empower crime victims and was therapeutic for their trauma (Adler, Biddle & Shenitz, 1995; Thigpen, 1995).

The retort is that the opposite may be true. Crime victims may neither want such a catharsis, nor get one even if victims' rights are provided by law. Victims may feel even less empowered and more traumatized if offenders get only slight punishments despite victims' best efforts (Thigpen, 1995). Furthermore, one recent study found that there was no effect to a victim's level of satisfaction with the criminal justice system when he or she exercised "victim's rights" (Davis & Smith, 1994). Other studies found that few victims exercised their rights even when they were made available (Kelly, 1990).

The Equal Standing Argument

Some victims' rights activists argue that the reason crime victims fail to exercise their statutory rights is that victims lack the "standing" to enforce those rights in appellate courts. Standing is a doctrine "employed to refuse to determine the merits of a legal claim, on the grounds that even though the claim may be correct, the litigant advancing it is not properly situated to be entitled to its judicial determination" (Wright, Miller & Cooper, 1984:338-339). As their example, these activists point to the problem crime victims have in enforcing their statutory right to restitution. Even when the legislative intent is clear, as it is in granting crime victims restitution, crime victims often have no "avenue of complaint" when a trial court denies them restitution from the crime offender because the appellate courts refuse to recognize the crime victim's standing to enforce the restitution right. These activists argue that crime victims will never have standing absent a federal constitutional amendment guaranteeing their rights (Cellini, 1997).

The rebuttal to this argument is that perhaps the role of restitution enforcer is not a proper one for the criminal courts. Offender restitution, or the idea of transferring money or services from the criminal offender to the victim as damages within the criminal justice system, only dates back as a sentencing option to the 1960s in the United States (Orvis, 1998). The role of assessing and collecting damages was not one that evolved naturally for the criminal courts, and has not been one that they have enforced very successfully (Doerner & Lab, 1995). The civil courts were in fact the institution that evolved in the common law to determine and collect damages when one citizen wronged another, and some scholars argue that the civil courts are the true devices for victim restitution (Orvis, 1998). If this is so, then the judicial doctrine of standing is performing properly when denying crime victims access to appellate courts in these matters.

Counterbalance Arguments

Crime victims' rights, even if established by a state constitutional amendment, will never be on equal footing with crime defendants' rights that are established by the United States Constitution, for the former will always be "trumped" by the latter due to the supremacy clause (Barajas & Nelson, 1997). The supremacy clause of the United States Constitution holds that, "This Constitution, and the Laws of the United States which shall be made Pursuance thereof . . . shall be the supreme Law of the Land; and the Judges in every State shall be bound thereby, any Thing in the Constitution or Laws of any State to the Contrary notwithstanding" (U.S. Constitution, Article VI). Therefore, it is argued by victims' rights advocates that only a federal amendment establishing victims' rights has a chance of balancing the rights already granted to those accused of crimes.

The counterargument questions the foundation of the "counterbalance" position. The Ranking Member of the House Committee on the Judiciary maintains that four questions should be asked, and answered affirmatively, before ever passing a federal constitutional amendment: (1) "Is there a compelling and clearly articulated need to amend the Constitution?" (2) "Will the amendment not have any unintended and potentially undesirable consequences?" (3) "Will the amendment be easily understood and enforceable?" and (4) "Is the amendment consistent with the rest of the Constitution and the Bill of Rights?" The proposed Victims' Rights Amendment fails on the first count, in that there are plenty of state and federal laws already adequately protecting victims' rights and a perusal of the case law doesn't reveal any conflict between these rights and the defendant's due process rights. Thus it is concluded, "Instead of working on finding the funds to place more 'cops on the beat' to actually combat crime, many in Congress prefer to focus their time and efforts on the largely symbolic victims' rights amendment" (Conyers, 1997).

Major Arguments Against Balancing Victims' Rights with Defendants' Rights

Just as there are supporters for the crime victims' rights amendment, there are both academics and practitioners who believe that such an amendment would be detrimental to the criminal justice system. Victims' rights supporters even retort that the existing occupational culture among criminal practitioners "neutralizes" the few procedural privileges gained for victims, such as the right to give victim impact statements (Erez & Laster, 1999). Nevertheless, there is substantial resistance to the federal victims' rights amendment, based on three main arguments: (1) a victims' rights amendment is contrary to the common law tradition of separate criminal and civil law systems;

(2) a victims' rights amendment will make the criminal justice system in general and the courts in particular less efficient and effective; and (3) a victims' rights amendment will diminish the rights guaranteed those accused of crimes in the Bill of Rights.

The Historical Argument

Some argue that when the founding fathers adopted the common law tradition as a pattern for the new country's legal system after the Revolutionary War, they were cognizant of the fact that they were establishing criminal justice as "public justice" wherein the "plaintiff" is the "state" or "commonwealth" (Friedman, 1984). Public law is where the government has a direct interest in protecting society and preserving order, whereas private law is the area which government has only an indirect interest. Criminal law is public law, and has been since the late tenth century when Henry II realized that crimes were acts against society and not to be left to personal vengeance (Gardner & Anderson, 1998). On the other hand, civil law as private law was created to deal with relationships between individual people, including tort actions that might also be a crime (Calvi & Coleman, 1989).

Separate and distinct procedural and evidentiary rules developed for criminal and civil courts under the common law tradition. For example, the burden of proof in civil cases is a "preponderance of the evidence" whereas it is "beyond a reasonable doubt" in a criminal cases. The founding fathers were aware of this difference and further distinguished it in the Bill of Rights by specifically dictating that the procedures outlined in Articles 5 and 6 would apply to "criminal" cases and prosecutions. Advocates of the "historical" argument state that the reasoning behind a victims' rights amendment flies in the face of more than 200 years of legal wisdom. If reform is needed to protect victims' rights, it is better to alter the civil law system and make it more accessible to crime victims than to radically change the two-party adversarial criminal justice system to accommodate a third party, the victim. The result may very well be to do extensive harm to both the civil and the criminal justice systems (Orvis, 1998).

The retort to the historical argument is based on history that predates it. Wrongs done to a person or his property in ancient times were regarded generally as a private matter, with the victim or his family taking appropriate remedial action against an offender and his family. The criminal justice system remained a "victim-centered system" in early Western law until monarchs became more involved in their subjects inflicting harm upon each other as a violation of the "King's Peace," and later, during the Enlightenment period, became philosophically convinced "that criminal prosecutions should serve societal interests of deterrence and retribution rather than interests of individual victims in private redress" (Tobolowsky, 1999:25). Others argue that the public prosecutor concept existed simultaneously with the private criminal prosecution in the early history of the American colonies and predates its establishment in England (Cellini, 1997). Either way, the criminal justice system is finally returning to its roots by becoming victim-centered again.

The Efficiency Argument

The criminal justice system has long been held to be one of scarce resources. One argument widely espoused by criminal justice officials against the enforcement of victims' rights, particularly through a constitutional amendment, is the huge cost to the system. Erwin Chermerinsky from the University of Southern California Law Center notes, "The constitutional amendment is a practical, administrative, and financial burden on institutions trying to dispense justice. It would siphon resources away from essential law enforcement efforts and open the floodgates of claims and differing interests" (McMurry, 1997:13). Beth Wilkinson, a former member of the prosecution team that successfully convicted the Oklahoma City bombers in 1996, actively fights against a federal Victims' Rights Amendment because she believes that if the proposed amendment presently before Congress had been in effect then, they would have lost the case due to the inability to make plea bargains with minor accessories for their cooperation and the divergence of logistical resources into their prosecutions (Wilkinson, 1999). Others argue that the amendment could actually harm victims in that "it could end up subverting just convictions by watering down defendants' rights, fostering lengthy litigation that delays trial, and torpedoing legitimate plea deals devised by prosecutors to obtain testimony necessary to prove other, more serious crimes" (Editorial, *New York Times*, 1999).

Advocates of victims' rights counter that civil code systems in other countries have successfully included victim participation into their judicial processes for years without either disrupting or corrupting the goal of criminal justice (Cellini, 1997). They further retort that, "The most formidable enemy of crime victims' aspirations for getting justice under our Constitution are criminal justice officials - even well-meaning ones such as Wilkinson - who believe that government lawyers know best" (Kight, 1999:A17).

The Due Process Argument

As the victims' rights movement grew, some critics noted that a "contest" of rights was being created between crime victims and crime defendants, with victim concerns being co-opted by crime control fanatics as an excuse to deny bail, abolish the exclusionary rule, establish mandatory sentencing, and eliminate parole (Tobolowsky, 1999). Constitutional scholars worry that the enforcement of victims' rights will infringe on the constitutional rights of those accused of crimes (Reid, 1997; Elias, 1990).

The retort to the due process argument is that our system of criminal justice provides the strongest of rights to those accused of crimes, and must now do likewise for crime victims. Furthermore, interviews with state judges whose laws already provided for victims' rights revealed that such laws have not improperly tipped the "balance" in favor of the victim. In practice, if a victim's right was found in conflict with a defendant's due process right, it was almost always the latter that was enforced by the courts (Barajas & Nelson, 1997).

Summary

The analogy of the Scales of Justice has often been used by both victims' rights advocates and those who would oppose them. Proponents of victims' rights argue that the scales of balance have been tipped away from the crime victim too long, and that the resulting imbalance has only been started to be rectified in the last two decades by legislation and judicial opinions. They argue crime victims have repeatedly been revictimized by their treatment in the criminal justice system. They further argue that crime victims presently lack the legal standing to adequately redress the wrongs done them by both the system and criminal offenders. They also argue that the rights of crime victims will never be in balance with those of criminal defendants until there is an amendment to the United States Constitution specifying the rights of crime victims.

The opponents to the victims' rights movement argue that the common law has already evolved a forum for protecting the rights of crime victims, that being the civil courts. Furthermore, the enforcement of victims' rights in the criminal justice system will tax to the breaking point a system already beleaguered with scarce resources and costly delays caused by enforcing already existing legal mandates considering the state versus the criminal defendant. Finally, it is argued that the protection of victims' rights in the criminal justice system, particularly if done in the form of a federal constitutional amendment, will diminish the due process rights of those accused of crimes, about which the founding fathers who wrote the Constitution were profoundly concerned.

For the victims' rights amendment to become part of the United States Constitution, it must pass both houses of Congress by a two-thirds vote, then ratified by 38 or more state legislatures (U.S. Constitution, Art. V). If this occurs, it can be argued that by passing such a rigorous process, the victims' rights amendment will be demonstrating a clear mandate from the majority of Americans (Cellini, 1997). However, the concern of the founding fathers when they created the Bill of Rights was not for the majority, but for a minority who could be wrongfully accused of a crime and yet have all of the power of the state against them. In fact, one of the founding fathers, James Madison, was profoundly worried about a "tyranny of the masses." Madison wrote of the problems of democracy in 1787, "A common passion of interest will, in almost every case, be felt by a majority of the whole; a communication and concert results from the form of Government itself, and there is nothing to check the inducements to sacrifice the weaker party, or an obnoxious individual" (Madison, 1961:81). One legal scholar captured Madison's concern in a phrase when he described the victims' rights movement as "politics of rights" versus "politics of interests" (Viano, 1987:441).

On the other hand, as many advocates of the victims' rights amendment conclude, it may be true that only a federal amendment will balance the scales of justice for the victim. It may be true that a crime victim will never have the legal standing to redress the wrongs done to him by the criminal offender and the criminal justice system unless there is a victims' rights amendment to the Constitution (Cellini, 1997). Furthermore, it may be true that the only way to guarantee in the long term the participatory rights already granted to victims by statute and long fought for by victim rights' activists is by a constitutional amendment (Barajas & Nelson, 1997; Tobolowsky, 1999).

However, if the victims' rights amendment is passed by Congress and ratified by the states in the near future, the real challenge for the judicial branch will be in finding where the exact balance between victims' rights and the rights of those accused of crimes lays. One legal scholar sees a new model of criminal review arising from the Supreme Court, creating a "good citizen/bad citizen" dichotomy wherein gains for criminals result in losses for law-abiding citizens, and vice versa (O'Neill, 1984). This may not be a totally modern development. It is of historical note that as crime victims' rights in the United States became less protected by the criminal justice system, defendants' due process rights became more protected by the courts. It is possible that the United States has come full circle with crime victims' rights waxing as crime defendants' rights wane.

CHAPTER 2

Victim Blaming

Helen M. Eigenberg

Victim blaming, victim facilitation, and victim precipitation are some of the many labels used to examine the concept of shared responsibility for criminal acts. Generally speaking, victim precipitative behaviors are those which cause victims to bring about their own victimization. For example, "a woman who walks alone toward her car on an unlighted street at night causes her own rape as surely as the man who precipitates his car theft by accidentally leaving his car keys in the car ignition or the man who slaps his wife and brings about his own demise" (Franklin & Franklin, 1976:127). As one might imagine, this type of approach has caused a great deal of controversy.

There is historical tendency to place responsibility for victimization on the victim, at least to some degree. Early victimologists, for example, created typologies which classified victims according to their degree of responsibility. Von Hentig (1941, 1948) was one of the first victimologists to engage in this process. He developed a typology based on psychological, social, and biological factors. He argued there were "born victims" just as there were "born criminals." Born victims were self-destructive individuals who solicited the actions of their "predators" (1941:303). Women, according to Von Hentig, as a group, were born victims because they were weak and easy prey. While he acknowledged that in some cases victims made "little or no contribution" to their victimization, he argued more often there was a "reciprocal action" between perpetrators and victims. As such, the victim was no longer a passive object, but an active subject in the process of criminalization. In other words, victimization was a process of social interaction. This conclusion led other victimologists to study the process of becoming a victim.

Many victimologists followed Von Hentig's example and devised various typologies which categorized the degree of shared responsibility between victims and offenders (Barnes & Teeters, 1943; Fattah, 1976; Karmen, 1980; Lamborn, 1968; Mendelsohn, 1963; Schafer, 1968; Sheley, 1979; Silverman, 1974). This approach tends to divide some finite amount of responsibility

15

between victims and offenders. Victims can be fully responsible, completely innocent of precipitation, or somewhere in between. Proponents of this perspective contend that the victim's actions are important and influence the way the criminal justice system responds to the offender as well as the way in which the public views the crime. Opponents argue that victim precipitation results in blaming the victim and diverts attention away from perpetrators and their responsibility for the crime.

The concept of victim blaming, then, is used to help address several important questions about victimization. Who is responsible for the criminal act? Is it the offender, the victim, or both? Is one more responsible than the other? Is it appropriate to examine the role of the victim at all? Do crime prevention efforts require consideration of victims and any role they may play in their victimization? What role does society play in victim blaming? This chapter addresses these issues. It addresses the development of the concept of victim precipitation, discusses problems with the concept of shared responsibility and examines why the approach is so popular.

Development of the Concept of Victim Precipitation

While the concept of victim precipitation was evident in the earliest literature on victimology, the term itself owes its origin to two classic criminological studies. Marvin Wolfgang (1958) first coined the term victim precipitation in his classic work on homicide and it was further popularized by his student, Menachim Amir, who applied the concept to rape.

Wolfgang examined homicide records in Philadelphia from 1948-1952 and found that victims initially had used physical force against their perpetrators in about one out of every four cases of murder. They may have drawn weapons or physically assaulted the other party who, in turn, then killed the initial aggressor. These cases were deemed to be victim precipitated. Wolfgang also found that these cases often involved victims and offenders who were known to each other and that they had experienced prior altercations with one another. Victims of precipitated homicides were more likely to have been drinking prior to their homicides than victims who had not initiated any violence toward their perpetrators. Most victim-precipitated homicides involved male victims, and most of them were murdered by other males. Few women committed homicide, although when women did murder it was often in response to men who had initiated violence toward them.

Amir (1971) also used Philadelphia police files to analyze rapes reported in 1958 and 1960. He considered a rape to be victim-precipitated when males believed that females had consented to sexual acts, but then rescinded their original acceptance. According to Amir victim precipitated rapes were

> those rape situations in which the victim actually, or so it was
> deemed, agreed to sexual relations but retracted before the act or
> did not react strongly enough when the suggestion was made by

the offender(s). The term applies also to cases in risky situations marred with sexuality, especially when she uses what could be interpreted as indecency in language and gestures, or constitutes what could be taken as an invitation to sexual relations (1971:266).

In other words, it was the offender's interpretation of the events which was crucial to identifying the victim as blameworthy; therefore, a victim's behavior was not as important as the "offender's interpretation of her actions" (1971:20). Thus, if the victim was perceived to be acting provocatively or seductively, or if she had a "bad" reputation, the rape was defined as victim precipitated. This also was the case if she engaged in other "risky" behavior such as drinking, going to bars alone, wearing revealing clothing, or hitchhiking. Despite the very broad definition of victim precipitation used in Amir's study and the focus on the offender's interpretation of the victim's acts (rather than her actual behavior), a relatively small proportion of the rapes qualified as victim precipitated: only 19 percent or about one in five rapes. These "victim precipitated rapes" were more likely to involve white females or teenage girls than adult women or women of color, and these victims were more apt to have met their rapist(s) at bars or parties than were women whose rapes did not involve victim precipitation.

Amir's research was criticized a great deal, in large part because of his focus on the perpetrator's *interpretations* of the victim's actions. This interpretation rendered the actual behavior of the victim meaningless. For example, a woman could have been held down and raped while she was screaming no, but it would have been a victim precipitated rape if the offender believed she had originally consented, if she had a reputation for having multiple sexual partners, or if she engaged in any of the other factors which made her culpable, according to Amir. As Weis and Borges (1973) note, the "only ingredient necessary for constituting a victim precipitated rape is the offender's imagination" (1973:80).

Amir's work and subsequent theorists who use the concept of victim precipitation also apply the concept in ways that deviate substantively from Wolfgang's initial conception. Remember that Wolfgang argued that victim precipitation occurred when a victim first initiated violence. In other words, these victims first committed or attempted to commit a crime. In other words, they were murdered after they attempted to assault or murder someone else. This logic does not flow in the same way in Amir's study. His victims were not raped after attempting to rape someone else. Thus, the original conceptualization of victim precipitation was altered significantly in ways that most contemporary victimologists fail to consider.

Amir's work also was criticized because of his overly broad generalizations. For example, he concluded that "in a way, the victim is always the cause of the crime" (Amir, 1971:258). These statements go far beyond his data and exaggerate the degree of victim precipitation – even when using his own broad definition. Amir, then, was accused of using rape myths to blame victims and giving scientific legitimacy to this practice (see Ward, 1995); however, many other issues also surface when victimology concentrates on the notion of shared responsibility.

Problems Associated with the Concept of Victim Precipitation

The concept of victim blaming has many weaknesses. Some of these weaknesses include the use of tautological reasoning, conceptual difficulties, placing undue responsibility on victims, creating culturally legitimate victims, and excusing offenders' behaviors.

Tautological Reasoning or Circular Thinking

Historically, criminologists have concentrated on identifying the differences between criminals and those who obey the law. Likewise, victimologists have been concerned with studying the process of victimization to determine if there are differences between victims and non-victims; however, these studies have serious methodological flaws. They rely upon samples of victims to determine common characteristics which contribute to victimization, although these studies fail to evaluate the degree to which non-victims in the general population also exhibit similar behaviors. This has resulted in circular reasoning. As Franklin and Franklin (1976) explain:

> The victims' precipitative behaviors lead to the criminal deeds because the victims' behaviors were precipitative. The interrelatedness of the independent and dependent variables "victim precipitation" and "victimization" becomes more apparent when an attempt is made to identify victim precipitation in the absence of victimization. For example, a woman walking alone at night on a unlighted street under present conceptions of victimology can hardly be thought of as engaging in crime precipitative behavior if no criminal act takes place (1976:127-28).

In other words, empirical research has failed to identify any common characteristics that cause one to become a victim other than the process of victimization. The only thing that causes one to be a victim is the process of being victimized and the process of being victimized is the only thing that distinguishes victims from non-victims.

Conceptual Weaknesses

Victim precipitation, by definition, asks whether victims bear some proportion of blame because of their actions? As a result, it creates a continuum whereby victims conceptually can be found to range from totally blameless on one end to fully responsible on the other (Karmen, 1996). Completely innocent victims are not blamed for their victimization and bear no responsibility for their victimization. For example, with respect to property offenses, they took all the actions they could to protect their belongings. They bought and used locking devices, burglar alarms, and other deterrent devices. With respect to crimes of violence, they limited their contact with dangerous people and did not instigate any criminal acts or confrontations with potentially violent people. At the other end of the continuum, victims may be fully accountable and totally responsible for their victimization.

The notion of totally innocent victims is problematic because it implies that all other victims bear some degree of responsibility. With the advantage of 20/20 hindsight, most victims could have "done more" to prevent their victimization which makes the "totally innocent" victim quite rare. It also implies that victims know how to prevent their victimization and ignores that many people in our society face disproportionate risk of victimization. Furthermore, even if it were possible to fully "protect" property, it is even more difficult to image how individuals are supposed to ensure that they refrain from contact with dangerous people. If they were all identified by a scarlet letter, this might be possible. Absent such an identification system, people will clearly associate with individuals without any knowledge that they might be violent. For example, most crimes against women are committed by intimates. How should women conduct themselves to ensure they are not exposed to danger to retain their status as totally innocent victims?

The concept of fully responsible victims is also problematic. As Karmen (1996) notes, a victim can only be totally responsible when there is no offender. In these cases, victims are not victims, but offenders posing as victims for some ulterior motive. For example, a person who has paid someone to steal his/her car and reports it to the police is a criminal masquerading as a victim. The fact that the only totally responsible victim is actually an offender destroys the intellectual integrity of the continuum of victim responsibility. Instead of varying degrees of victimization, the continuum actually represents distinctions between victims and offenders. This conceptual weakness may help explain why the focus of much victimological work has been on creating typologies to classify victims rather than discussing any theoretical rationale for a continuum of blame.

Places Undue Responsibility on Victims

The notion of victim precipitation also is problematic because it places an unwarranted level of responsibility on victims to prevent their own victimization, and many of these actions would require victims to drastically alter their lives. Victims may be able to prevent their victimization by staying in their houses with bars on the doors and windows; however, most people have to venture out sometime, and some people live in neighborhoods where crime is rampant, making it difficult to minimize the risk of harm. Furthermore, many battered women are, in fact, imprisoned in their homes with "criminals" who beat them and lack means to prevent their victimization. And even if it were possible to protect oneself from all victimization, many people do not want to live that way. It may be better to risk a burglary than to feel like one lives in a fortress. It may be preferable to risk being robbed by going out at night rather than feeling restricted in one's freedom to go out in public. Sometimes, risk is incurred because of events beyond the control of individuals. For example, if a woman's car breaks down on the interstate and she does not have a cell phone, she may have to accept a ride from a stranger to get assistance (or risk spending the night on the side of the road waiting for someone to help with no guarantee that they are trustworthy either). Thus, in some circumstances, people have little choice but to engage in "risky" behavior.

Creates Culturally Legitimate Victim

Ryan's (1971) classic work describes the process of victim blaming. He contends that victims first must be seen as deficient in some way; that there is something wrong with them. Victims can be distinguished from non-victims based on their attitudes, behavior, or some basic characteristic. These differences are assumed to be the cause of their victimization. If they were not different, they would not be victimized. Victims are then warned that they must change to become like the non-victim group if they are to avoid victimization, and if they fail to avoid victimization they are to blame. Finally, some governmental bureaucracy or social service agency is assigned responsibility for dealing with "the problem."

An important part of this process, then, begins with defining groups of people as deficient, because they then become culturally legitimate or deserving victims. In fact, the process of creating legitimate victims is central to many crimes. For example, in the Holocaust, definitions of ethnicity were used to demonize Jews and to make it palatable to victimize them. Similarly, gays or lesbians are viewed as legitimate victims of hate crimes because they would be innocent victims if they were heterosexuals. They only need to change their sexual orientation to protect themselves; or at a minimum, go to heroic lengths to ensure that no one knows that they are gay. Prostitutes are blamed for their victimization if they are raped because they engage in sexually risky and promiscuous behavior in the first place. They do not warrant our sympathy or any response by the criminal justice system. The process of creating culturally legitimate victims makes it more acceptable for some people to be victimized and society is less willing to use its resources to do anything about it. As Weis and Borges note,

> some victimologists have . . . turned victimology into the art of blaming the victim. If the impression of a "legitimate victim" is created, then part of the burden of guilt is relieved from the perpetrator, and some crimes, like rape for example, can emerge as without either victims or offenders (1971:85).

This process of creating culturally legitimate victims is harmful to victims. They are further traumatized when society engages in victim blaming. Not only must they deal with the consequences of the victimization itself, but they must cope with the added burden of being told that they are, in some part, to blame. It is no wonder then why some victims of crime are reluctant to reveal their victimization to the police and/or researchers conducting victimization surveys. Many victims use silence to protect themselves from the additional victimization that occurs when they are blamed for their own plight.

Excuses Offenders Behavior and Diminishes Responsibility

If there is some finite amount of responsibility to be allocated for any crime, then, by definition, offenders escape full responsibility for their acts when victims are blamed. "Attention is focused on the behavior and motives of the victim rather than on the offender" (Scully, 1990:45). The concept of victim precipitation provides a cultural framework which offenders can use to rationalize their behavior (Fattah, 1976; Sykes & Matza, 1957; Scully, 1990; Stanko, 1993). According to offenders, victims, then, ask for or deserve what they get; or at the extreme end of the continuum, they deny any harm whatsoever. For example, Scully's study of convicted rapists demonstrated that these offenders used culturally accepted stereotypes about women to create legitimate victims who were blamed for their own victimization. A couple of quotes from the rapists are quite illustrative. For example, one man convicted of a gang rape stated: "I'm against hurting women. She should have resisted. None of us were the type of person that would use force on a woman. . . . I loved her – like all women" (1990:129). Another serial killer and rapist reported that his victims physically "enjoyed the sex [rape]. Once they got involved, it would be difficult to resist. I was always kind and gentle until I started to kill them" (1990:130). A man who abducted his victim at knife point on the street stated "to be honest, we [his family] knew she was a damn whore and whether she screwed 1 or 50 guys didn't matter" (1990:108).

These victim-blaming views affect the way that individual offenders excuse their behavior, but because they are culturally derived, their excuses have a staying power that goes beyond individual rationalization. For example, attorneys use these same stereotypes to try to garner sympathy from judges and juries. Likewise, prosecutors can sometimes be wary of initiating cases against victims who appear culpable or who are viewed as culturally legitimate victims. These actions suggest that society, as a whole, is very supportive of the notion of victim precipitation.

Popularity of Victim Precipitation

This brief overview has demonstrated that there are many problems associated with the concept of victim precipitation and that engaging in blaming victims may be harmful to many (most) victims, then it seems logical to ask why it is that we, as a society, continue to endorse these beliefs? There are several possible answers to this question.

First, victim blaming is consistent with another powerful set of societal beliefs involving a just world (Lerner, 1965). Most individuals believe that people get what they deserve in society. In other words, bad things do not happen to good people. This thinking also allows people to feel a false sense of security. It implies that everyone has control over their lives and that individuals can prevent victimization if they simply take certain precautions and behave in certain ways. It allows people to avoid the alternative conclusion – that crime is often random and unpredictable (Kappeler, Blumberg & Potter, 2000), and that victims can do little to prevent it.

Second, victim blaming perspectives allow for, conceptually, the idea of victim prevention. While this may give people a (false) sense of empowerment as individuals, it also may increase the harm done when people are victimized. Imagine a woman who has attended a rape crisis training session and who has taken copious notes about how to stare strangers in the eyes, to always walk assertively, to carry keys between her fingers to use as a weapon, to scream for help if she is abducted, and so on. This same woman is abducted by a stranger with a knife in a parking lot and is raped. She is so scared she does not scream or resist in any other physical ways. She may blame herself even more than a woman who had not taken any victim prevention courses if she feels that she failed to take the "appropriate" actions to protect herself.

Third, victim blaming helps answer difficult questions about the motivations of offenders and diverts attention from traditional criminology's inability to prevent crime. Traditional criminology has spent most of the twentieth century examining the distinctions between criminals and non-criminals and identifying reasons for criminality, however, it has not made much headway. Thus blaming the victim in some cases is easier to understand than the motivations of the criminal. Furthermore, concentrating on the victims allows us to shift our attention from offenders as a means to prevent crime. The new focus on victims and victim prevention has coincided with the failure of traditional crime prevention techniques. One might argue that the criminal justice system and criminology shifted the focus from offenders to victims out of necessity. Unable to devise strategies to control crime, the attention is shifted to victims and victim prevention. In both instances, however, the focus continues to be on personal accountability and the actions of individuals while social structural examinations remain rare.

Individual level explanations are very popular in the United States. As a society, we tend to endorse the idea that criminals have free will and choose criminality. Victims fail to take sufficient preventative measures and therefore cause their own victimization. Neither explanation examines crime as a social problem rooted in the social structure. For example, poverty causes some offenders to commit crime as a means to secure economic goods necessary for survival. Poverty also makes people more vulnerable to victimization. Poor people are more apt to live in neighborhoods where crime is higher and are less apt to be able to afford security alarms and other types of preventative measures. In other words, both crime and victimization could be prevented by making an effort to reduce poverty. Actions could include changing welfare systems, tax structures, or creating employment opportunities in low income neighborhoods. However, individual level explanations do not require an examination of the social structure.

By failing to examine the social structure, victimology, for the most part, also ignores the ways in which political power affects our understanding of both crime and victimization. For example, a broader definition of victims might challenge social definitions of crime in rather dramatic ways. As Elias notes,

> What if we learned that law enforcement sought to maintain or manage crime, not to prevent or reduce it, or sought social control of certain population groups, not crime control? What if crime waves, media coverage and official crime statistics had little to do with the real victimization level? What if we found our fears and insecurities about crime artificially manipulated for political purposes? Suppose we discovered that most people commit crime, not just certain groups? What if the real career criminals were corporate offenders, not common criminals? What if we found that victims have often been offenders before, and vice versa? What if we discovered that we were as likely to be victimized by a friend or relative as by a stranger (1986:4)?

In other words, victimology has the power to transform our understanding of crime and victimization, although this is not likely to happen unless the field of victimology also changes.

Victimology today tends to concentrate on pitting victims against offenders and ignores the role of social structure. Although victimology, as a field of study, began by examining victims in the broadest sense of the word (e.g., including victims of natural disaster, the Holocaust), contemporary victimology concentrates almost exclusively on victims of street crime (Elias, 1986). This provides Americans with a narrow definition of crime and victimization and creates a "limited social reality of crime" (Elias, 1986:3). Harms such as white-collar crime, consumer fraud, pollution, toxic waste dumping, workplace hazards, police violence, and interpersonal violence generally fail to be defined as crime. As a result, these victims also fail to be defined as victims. The concept of victim precipitation has been central to the study of victimology; however, it has posed many difficulties. Not only does it cause further victimization to some victims who blame themselves or who experience victim blaming by the criminal justice system or others in society, but it affects our very conceptualization of crime and victimization. It keeps us from asking very different questions that might drastically alter our understanding of both crime and victimization.

CHAPTER 3

The Role of Alcohol in Victimization

Richard Tewksbury
Diane Pedro

One of the most well-established facts about crime and criminal vic-timization in the United States is that alcohol is very closely related to the occurrence of crime. The presence of alcohol is perhaps the strongest pre-dictor of criminal events, for almost all types of social settings and situations. While this is a very well-established fact in the study of crime and crime vic-tims, it is not always a popular or well-received piece of information. Among many populations – such as college students – drinking is considered a nor-mative behavior, and those who point out the negative consequences asso-ciated with drinking are dismissed as having a political agenda. The scientific evidence about the role of alcohol in criminal victimization not only shows that alcohol is closely linked to crime, but that there are important differ-ences in the strength of this effect based on characteristics of individuals and settings in which alcohol is consumed.

Throughout the history of the United States, popular attitudes and legal responses to the consumption of alcohol have varied from toleration to a peak of disapproval and back again in cycles for approximately 70 years. By the early 1990s, American attitudes toward alcohol and its use had cycled to a low level of toleration; the amount of alcohol consumed by Americans has declined 20 percent from the 1980s (Musto, 1996). However, recent findings from the 1998 National Household Survey on Alcohol Abuse (SAMHSA, 1999) found that toleration for alcohol use, especially by youth and young adults, is on the rise.

The college years have long been associated with drinking (as well as drug use, sexual experimentation and other dangerous forms of behavior). This may simply be a function of age, or it may be a combination of age and the "freedom" that many college students experience for the first time. For the past 30 years, researchers have shown that anywhere from 75 percent to 96 percent of college students consume alcohol, at least on occasion (Engs,

1977; Gallup Report, 1985; Igra & Moos, 1979; National Institute on Drug Abuse, 1995, 1998). This figure is well above the national population rate of persons who drink. College students have long been known to be more likely than persons in the general population to drink, and to drink both more frequently and in greater quantities.

This pattern may be changing, however. In the 1990s there was a modest decline in the number of college students who drank at least once in the previous year. Although the percentage of college students who report drinking alcohol dropped only four points – from 83 percent to 79 percent – this is an important change in a trend that has been seen for several decades (National Institute of Drug Abuse, 1995, 1998). For some persons, especially college and university administrators, this decline in alcohol use is very encouraging. However, it is important to recognize that this decrease is simply in the number of students who say they drink at all. There has not been any change in the percent of college students who are heavy drinkers and binge drinkers. Furthermore, today's college students (both men and women) are drinking with the intent of getting drunk more than ever before (Wechsler, Dowdall, Maenner, Gledhill-Hoyt & Lee, 1998).

Although a slightly smaller percentage of college students drink today compared to those in the past, those students who do drink tend to have the same or more problems (including criminal activities) related to their drinking (Engs & Hanson, 1994). Thus, these findings suggest that heavy or binge drinking by college students of today is by far the single most serious public health problem confronting American colleges and universities (Wechsler et al., 1998). It is the way that drinking is related to these types of problems, most notably criminal, health and academic problems, that is discussed next.

Scholars have studied the effects and consequences of alcohol use/abuse and dependency for generations. Evidence from the disparate fields of anthropology, criminology, psychology, and sociology indicates that alcohol plays a key role in many acts of aggression and violence in society today (Borsari & Casey, 1999; Bureau of Justice Statistics, 1998; Mustaine & Tewksbury, 1998; Pernanen, 1991; Roth, 1994; Ullman, Karabatsos & Koss, 1999). This includes the fact that a great deal of violence on college campuses is directly related to alcohol use. For each of these acts of aggression and violence that takes place in America today, there are impaired individuals – both men and women alike – who experience some form of victimization (i.e., physical injury, sexual assault, rape, robbery, or homicide).

The purpose of this chapter is to review what is known about the alcohol-victimization link, and to point out how aspects of social structure and lifestyle can have a mediating effect on this relationship. In presenting this, the discussion that follows presents a special focus on the ways in which alcohol has been linked to criminal victimization, and other negative consequences, among the college student population.

This chapter is intended to raise awareness of the role alcohol plays in victimization, especially among young women and men in college. By looking at the scientific facts, the authors' goal is to facilitate a better understanding of how alcohol use can heighten the risk of victimization, and in turn, we also hope to assist students in reducing their future risk of victimization. To accomplish this, we will examine the societal cost of alcohol and its role in crime and victimization, lifestyle and drinking environments, alcohol's role in victimization on college campuses, and the consequences drinking may have on safety and school performance.

Alcohol Use

The 1998 National Household Survey on Alcohol Abuse (SAMHSA, 1999) found that 113 million Americans aged 12 and older reported current use of alcohol. In addition, the survey reports that 12 million Americans self-identified as heavy drinkers (not alcoholic), meaning they had five (5) or more drinks on one occasion five (5) or more days during the past 30 days.

Although the total amount of alcohol consumed by Americans has decreased in recent years, this does not mean that people – across the board – are giving up drinking. In fact, some research suggests that more young adults are drinking today, and actually drinking greater quantities, than in the past. The rates of heavy alcohol use among young adult (18-25 years old) drinkers were significantly higher in 1998 (13.8%) than in 1997 (11.1%). The 1998 percentage means that nearly one in seven young adults in the United States are heavy drinkers, and therefore at risk for serious alcohol problems. Of the young adults (18-25 years old) who report heavy drinking in 1998, 55 percent were men and 45 percent were women (SAMHSA, 1999).

Alcohol use at any level, but especially heavy drinking, has potentially serious consequences. Alcohol use is responsible for more than 100,000 deaths each year in the United States (McGinnis & Foege, 1993). According to statistics from the National Institute on Alcohol Abuse and Alcoholism (NIAAA, 1999), the economic cost to U.S. society for alcohol use/abuse/addiction in 1995 was estimated at $167 billion. Included in this estimate are medical consequences, lost earnings due to premature death, lost earnings due to illness, and automobile accidents, fires, and criminal justice system operations. Obviously these are only the most serious consequences – there are many other possible ways that the use and misuse of alcohol can impose costs on society.

Medical consequences from alcohol use are estimated at close to $16 billion annually. Contrary to popular belief, the costs of medical consequences from alcohol use are nearly triple the cost of medical consequences for other drug use ($6.5 billion). Lost earnings and premature death from alcohol use/abuse/addiction accounted for $35 billion in economic cost, far out-distancing the lost earnings and premature death from other drug abuse ($16 million). Lost earnings due to illnesses related to alcohol use/abuse/addiction cost Americans an additional $77 billion. The total U.S. economic cost from lost earnings due to alcohol-related illnesses is nearly *five times* the amount of the economic cost of drug abuse ($17 billion). Finally, if we put an economic cost on deaths due to drinking and driving accidents we can estimate a cost of at least $25 billion in 1995, as compared to $20 billion involving persons using drugs (NIAAA, 1999). All in all, it is clear that alcohol use/abuse/addiction among young adults has exceptionally high economic costs, as well as physical and social consequences.

Although the use of alcohol can be a pleasant experience for many persons, alcohol use by young adults can lead to serious problems. Whether it be seeking excitement, trying to simply "fit in," or just trying to enhance one's social image, use can lead to serious problems – emotional, physical, and social. When the use of alcohol begins to impact a young adult's life, when the good times associated with drinking turn into negative consequences, he or she may be entering the first phases of dependency (i.e., addiction).

Alcohol Consumption and College Students

Young adulthood is a period of transition in many areas of life. This includes emotional development, educational and vocational activities, living arrangements, and economic status. It is during young adulthood that individuals assume adult roles, take on new and additional responsibilities, and refine their social skills. Additionally, for college students, young adulthood is typically a time when they are no longer under direct parental supervision, are faced with new social and academic pressures, and enter an environment where the use of alcohol is normative, and often encouraged.

Not only do college students drink, but they also commonly drink heavily and frequently. This fact is most clear for males. Men in college are more likely than their female counterparts to drink and to drink heavily (i.e., binge drink). However, the difference in the numbers of male and female students who binge drink appears to be shrinking. In fact, some recent research finds the proportion of drinkers in each gender category is increasing faster among females than males (Hanson & Engs, 1994). And it is not only that more women are drinking, but more women are drinking with the intention of becoming intoxicated. In 1996, the National Center on Addiction and Substance Abuse found that over the past 15 years, the percentage of college women drinking with the intention of getting drunk has more than tripled, from approximately 10 to 35 percent.

While drinking, binge drinking, and intoxication are common across the entire population of college students, there are some groups of students who are most likely to report drinking, binge drinking and drinking for the purpose of intoxication. Perhaps most notable among the heaviest drinking college students are fraternity and sorority members. The Greek system is particularly perceived as providing enhanced opportunities to party, as well as encouraging the unregulated use of alcohol. In addition, students who enter college as low-frequency drinkers are three times more likely to start drinking heavily if they join a fraternity or sorority (Lo & Globetti, 1995). Four out of every five fraternity and sorority members report drinking in binges and frequently drinking with the intention of getting drunk. And, among fraternity and sorority members, those who live in fraternity/sorority houses who are the most likely to engage in binge drinking (SAMHSA, 1999; Wechsler et al., 1998).

The importance of knowing about binge drinking, and being able to identify which students are most likely to engage in such behavior is that such instances of heavy episodic alcohol consumption results in a greater number of and more frequently occurring negative consequences. Simply said, college students who drink more often and who drink greater quantities are more likely to suffer some form of harm from their drinking. These "harms," however, affect not only drinkers (especially binge drinkers) themselves, but also others who interact and encounter such students; these persons often suffer from what are known as "secondhand effects" of drinking. These are the negative consequences that come from drinking, much like the harmful effects of secondhand smoke.

Binge Drinking

The term "binge drinking" became a common phrase across America when *The Journal of the American Medical Association* published the 1993 Harvard School of Public Health College Alcohol Study (Wechsler, Davenport, Dowdall, Moeykens & Castillo, 1994). Based on the results of this study, which showed that large numbers of college students drink frequently and heavily, concerns have been raised about the serious and far-reaching consequences that such behavior may have.

This national survey of 17,592 students at 140 campuses examined the extent of binge drinking by college students and the ensuing health and behavioral problems that drinkers create for themselves and others on campuses. In 1997, the Harvard School of Public Health College of Alcohol Study resurveyed colleges that participated in the 1993 study. The findings revealed few changes in binge drinking: both studies (Wechsler et al., 1994; 1998) concluded that heavy, frequent drinking is widespread on college campuses and is by far the single most serious public health problem confronting American colleges (Wechsler et al., 1994).

The Harvard Alcohol Study provided a definition of binge drinking that was subsequently widely accepted by researchers and scholars (Presley, Harrold, Scouten, Lyerla & Meilman, 1996; Presley, Meilman & Lyerla, 1996; SAMHSA, 1999). As now recognized, "binge drinking" is:

heavy episodic alcohol use. For males to "binge" they must drink *five* or more drinks on the same occasion in the past month (includes heavy use). For women, drinking *four* or more drinks on the same occasion in the past month (includes heavy drinking) is considered binge drinking. In addition, if men/women binge drink three or more times in a two week period this behavior is defined as "frequent" binge drinking (Wechsler, 1998:58).

It is this type of drinking that is considered the most problematic, both for individuals and society as a whole. What raises the most concern, however, is that as the Harvard studies show, among college students binge drinking is a fairly common event. Consequently, problems arising from drinking are also common among college students.

Consequences of Binge Drinking

The problems associated with heavy episodic or "binge" drinking on college campuses has caused college and university administrators nationwide to define binge drinking as their number one campus life problem, and research about the effects of drinking clearly support this view. Forty-seven percent of binge drinkers on college campuses report more and more serious consequences stemming from alcohol-related incidents than students who do not binge drink. Students who binge drink report a variety of problems, including engaging in unplanned and unsafe sexual activity, being victims of physical and sexual assault, suffering unintentional injuries, higher rates of all forms of criminal victimization, increased frequency of interpersonal problems (poor relationships, loss of friends, etc.), physical or cognitive impairment, poor academic performance, greater likelihood of being involved in fatal automobile accidents, and increased rates of suicide (Wechsler et al., 1998). Clearly, the consequences of binge drinking are serious, lasting, and potentially fatal.

Problems arising from binge drinking have effects that reach much wider than the experiences of the individual drinker. Binge-drinking students also create serious problems for others, both students and non-students. Those who suffer at the hands of binge drinkers are individuals who usually are not binge drinkers. This leads to the labeling of these problems as "secondhand binge" effects (Hanson & Engs, 1992; Wechsler et al., 1998). Such problems, one-step removed from the binge drinker, are both the same and different from the negative consequences experienced by binge drinkers themselves. Secondhand binge effects include increased risks of physical assault, sexual harassment, date rape, property damage, and impaired sleep and study time – problems that threaten the quality and safety of the college experience for millions of non-binge-drinking students. Clearly, binge drinking is a problem for entire campuses and communities. It is not only the binge-drinking student who suffers the consequences, but is the social groups, organizations, networks and communities in which the student lives, works, studies (and drinks) that suffer.

Binge Drinkers Underestimate Their Behavior

Many students who binge drink do not believe that either (1) they drink at problematic levels, or (2) that their drinking produces serious problems for themselves and others. In simple terms, most college students who binge drink see themselves as "normal" drinkers, and therefore do not believe they "have a problem."

Only a very small proportion of binge drinkers consider themselves to be heavy drinkers or problem drinkers, despite the fact that researchers have shown binge drinking to be fairly common among college students. In some ways this makes sense; when considering whether they drink more or less than others, most binge drinkers compare their drinking habits to that of their friends. These tend to be the people with whom they drink. College students are prone to have friends that drink (or "party") in similar ways and at similar levels as they drink themselves. Women who compare their drinking to men's drinking are especially apt to underestimate their drinking. Wechsler and colleagues (1994, 1997) found that 91 percent of the women and 78 percent of the men who were frequent binge drinkers considered themselves to be only moderate or light drinkers. This means that even the heaviest drinkers perceive their drinking to be within acceptable limits, which in turn means that heavy drinkers do not see their drinking as problematic (for themselves or for others). Therefore, such perceptions may seriously compromise an individual's willingness to accept that he/she may have a serious alcohol problem. This means such persons will continue to drink (most likely heavily), will have recurring problems resulting from their drinking, and may continue to bring harm to themselves and others around them.

Women, Bingeing, and Secondhand Binge Effects

Our understanding about binge drinking by women, and the effects that binge drinking may have on women specifically, are not as well developed as are our understandings about binge drinking among men. Most research on drinking behaviors and the effects of drinking, especially research conducted before the 1980s, has focused on men's behaviors and the consequences of men's drinking. However, during the last two decades this focus has broadened, and has begun to draw increasing attention to the drinking habits of women and the consequences of their drinking. The early lack of attention to women was based on the belief that few women drank, and those who did, did not drink to the extent to cause significant problems (for either themselves or others around them). This may be most clearly seen in the fact that one post-World War II study of college drinking suggested that drinking by women was such a minor problem that the researchers defined five different levels of quantity and frequency for men but only two for women (Monahan & Murphy, 1999). Today, while women are still less likely to be binge drinkers than are men, the gender gap has closed. As a result, today we know that women do drink, frequently drink heavily, and suffer many of the same consequences as men as well as some problems unique to women.

One important area where women's use/abuse of alcohol differs from men is in regards to the increased level of risk for women to be victimized by unwanted or unprotected sex when intoxicated. Compared to a sober woman, a drinking woman is often considered by others (both males and females) to be less sexually inhibited and more sexually available (George, Gournic & McAfee, 1988). This misconception can put a woman at risk for unwanted advances or unprotected sex. In fact, one of the best established facts about women and drinking is that alcohol use (and the amount consumed) is one of the most important distinguishing factors between women who are and are not sexually assaulted. Alcohol, then, has important, and sometimes gender-specific, consequences, especially when it concerns binge drinking.

Alcohol and Crime

The link between alcohol use – especially heavy or binge drinking – and crime is one of the most serious consequences that points to the acute nature of the problem of alcohol on college campuses. For decades, the two most consistent research findings about crime show that crime is (1) directly related to alcohol use, and (2) the vast majority of crime, especially violent crime, is committed by young adults. We should not be surprised, then, that when college students binge drink, crime is a common result. College students who drink heavily are more likely to be both criminal offenders and victims of crimes.

The concern about the relationship between alcohol use and crime is based on a long history of criminological research producing strong evidence. This relationship remains strong today, as reflected in the latest findings from the U.S. Department of Justice (1998) and the National Incident-Based Reporting System (NIBRS) of the Federal Bureau of Investigation (1998). The NIBRS indicates that a large percentage of incidents described by investigating officers are alcohol-related and involve perpetrators acquainted with their victims. In addition, nearly four in ten violent victimizations – murder, rape, sexual assault, robbery, aggravated assault, and simple assault – are committed by a perpetrator who reported drinking prior to committing the crime (FBI, 1998). It is not only young adults who commit crimes while drinking, however. Alcohol is an important factor in crime at all ages, although the effects may be most pronounced during the young adult years.

The 1980s and 1990s saw a dramatic surge in the number of persons incarcerated in the United States. Between 1985 and 1998, the number of men in prison or jail more than doubled (going from 694,881 to 1,665,659) and the number of women in prison or jail tripled (going from 40,373 to 139,187) (U.S. Department of Justice, 1999). Even more overwhelming, on an average day in the late 1990s, correctional authorities supervised between five and seven million offenders. Approximately one in three (36%) of these incarcerated offenders had been drinking alcohol when they committed their offense and had blood alcohol concentration levels (BAC) well above the legal intoxication level. Female offenders actually report higher levels of intoxication at the time of their offenses than male offenders. It is not just that offenders drink, but rather that large proportions of criminal offenders have serious abuse and dependency problems. According to one national study, 58 percent of incarcerated offenders are alcohol abusers and 32 percent are alcoholics (U.S. Department of Justice, 1998).

Victims' Use of Alcohol

The relationship between alcohol and crime is not restricted to individuals who commit crimes. There is also a well-established, and fairly strong, link between drinking and being a crime victim (see Lasley, 1989; Mustaine & Tewksbury, 1998). Some data suggests that smaller percentages of victims than offenders report drinking at the time of crime. However, there is still a significant number of crime victims who are drinking when they are victimized. The relationship between victimization and alcohol use holds for practically all types of crimes, but is especially strong for serious violent crimes (as discussed below). However, it is not simply the act of drinking alcohol that makes someone more likely to be a crime victim. It is important to also look at how much and how frequently someone drinks and how alcohol affects an individual's behavior to fully understand the relationship between drinking and victimization.

Understandings about the effects of quantity and frequency of drinking are clearer than understandings about alcohol's effects on behavior leading to victimization. In simple terms, as the use of alcohol increases, so does the likelihood of being a victim of criminal violence (Collins, 1981a; Collins & Messerschmidt, 1993; Lasley, 1989; Lasley & Rosenblaum, 1988; Mustaine & Tewksbury, 1998). This is a straightforward relationship. As both the amount of alcohol consumed and the frequency of drinking increases, so too does the chance of being a crime victim (U.S. Department of Justice, 1999a; 1999b).

The second issue, how alcohol affects one's behavior and increases risk of victimization, has less obvious answers. There may be several ways to explain the alcohol-victimization link. For one, individuals who have been drinking may be seen by offenders as very vulnerable (i.e., attractive) targets. Alcohol decreases a person's awareness of the environment and lessens abilities to avoid or ward off an offender. Alternatively, individuals who drink are well known to have their inhibitions lowered. This may mean alcohol can lead us into situations, places, and interactions that we might otherwise avoid. Some of these situations, places, and interactions may include offenders looking for vulnerable victims. Lowering of our inhibitions may also mean that our own behavior – especially what we say – may be affected. Many individuals find that when they drink they say things that may insult or offend others. Such situations often lead to arguments, fights, assaults, or other violent actions. These are crimes that some criminologists have referred to as "victim-precipitated" (Wolfgang, 1958). Although the victim is not necessarily to blame, the behavior of the victim may have set in motion the events that ended with the victimization. [For a more thorough discussion of victim-blaming, see Chapter 2 of this text.]

Relationship Between Alcohol and Violent Crime

Several decades worth of effort have been put forth by researchers and practitioners alike seeking to better understand the relationship between alcohol consumption and violent crime. These efforts have been fruitful, as several "facts" about this relationship have been established. We have continued, however, to raise new and more challenging questions about how alcohol is related to crime. Beyond simply knowing that the use of alcohol is related to both criminal offending and being a crime victim, scholars and practitioners also find it important to further specify our knowledge, focusing on how, when, specifically for whom, where and perhaps most importantly, why the consumption of alcohol and the commission of crimes are so strongly linked.

At the foundational level, we know that both the physiological and social effects of alcohol are associated with increased risks for criminal violence to occur (Collins & Messerschmidt, 1993; Testa & Parks, 1996). This appears to be largely tied to the effects alcohol has on our perceptions of stimuli and physical abilities. Alcohol leads to "significant impairment of information processing and motor performance, . . . a specific set of physical sensations, general improvements of mood, and . . . increase(d) aggression" (Hull & Bond, 1986:347). Alcohol, more than any other psychoactive substance, causes increased levels of aggression as well as substantially contributing to crime and victimization as evidenced by the measured results on the prevalence of alcohol involvement and crime by the U.S. Department of Justice in 1998.

This means that alcohol, not illegal drugs, is more likely to be linked to crime. This may come as a surprise to many people. This also appears to go against what many consider "common sense." But, it is this type of misunderstanding that contributes to the ongoing nature of the problem. If we do not recognize that alcohol is so critically tied to crime we are likely to focus our attention, energy, and resources elsewhere (i.e., illegal drugs), but fail to see any real results of our attempts to fight crime. Meanwhile, alcohol use continues at high levels.

But, remember it is not just the fact that an individual drinks alcohol that increases the likelihood of violent behavior or the risk of victimization. A great deal of our advances in understanding the how, where, by whom and why of the alcohol-crime link has come from the area of criminology known as routine activity theory (Cohen & Felson, 1979). Research produced by scholars in this area has shown that the location in which one drinks, as well as the other contextual factors (i.e., with whom one drinks, when drinking occurs, how much the individual consumes, and drinkers' age and gender) are all important in mediating the role of alcohol on criminal (especially predatory) victimization risks (Collins, 1981b; Fillmore, 1985; Lasley, 1989; Mustaine & Tewksbury, 1998; Parks & Miller, 1997; Roncek & Maier, 1991; Sampson, 1987).

One of the main areas of research addressing the alcohol and violence relationship has focused on examining the settings and contexts in which each is present (Collins, 1981b). For instance, Lasley (1989) showed that drinking in public places is significantly associated with increased risk of being robbed or assaulted, and Lasley and Rosenbaum (1988) have shown as individuals spend more time in bars their likelihood of being a victim of violent crime increases. Similarly, Fagan (1993) has noted that violence occurs more often in bars than in any other social-drinking context. Or, as reported by Roncek and Maier (1991), this relationship extends from bars themselves out into the neighborhoods in which they are located. As they report, city blocks with bars have a 17.6 percent higher crime rate. Thus, being in or near locations where alcohol is consumed increases the likelihood of being a crime victim, even if one is not drinking themselves.

In addition to the contexts in which drinking occurs, some characteristics of individuals who drink are significant for predicting those who are more or less likely to yield increased likelihoods of being a victim of violent crime. It is not simply the act of drinking, nor even something as simple as where one drinks and how much one drinks that alone affects an individual's chances of being a victim of violence. There are also demographic characteristics that are associated with the likelihood of violent victimization when alcohol is involved. The two most clearly established – and perhaps most obvious – are the variables of gender and age. Very simply, men are more likely to be victims of violent crime, in all situations. This fact continues to hold true when alcohol is involved. Similarly, young adults and adolescents are more likely than older persons to be victims of violence. Just as the case with gender, this relationship holds across almost all situations, but is even stronger when we look at instances where alcohol is involved (Lasley, 1989; Mustaine & Tewksbury, 1998). It is important to interpret these research findings correctly; this does not mean that *only* males and young adults are at risk of being victimized when drinking. In fact, there is some research that suggests that the risks of victimization for women who drink are closing in on the level of risk experienced by men who drink. One recent study (Parks & Miller, 1997) has shown that when a woman drinks in a public place (such as a bar), she significantly increases her chances of being a victim of violence. This occurs for two general reasons: (1) drinking in public exposes her to potentially dangerous environmental circumstances associated with the bar environment (e.g., intoxicated individuals, perpetrators of crime, etc.) and (2) the chances of being a victim increase because of enhanced vulnerability associated with the drinking woman, due to impairment (both hers and others') arising from the use of alcohol (i.e., reduced ability to perceive risk or avoid aggression). Plainly said, when drinking in public (especially when drinking heavily), individuals are exposed to others who may be intoxicated (and therefore more likely to be aggressive) *and* when an individual is perceived by others to be intoxicated/impaired, he or she is seen as less likely to be able to fend off an aggressive attack (or, are easier targets).

An additional characteristic that some researchers have identified as associated with increased victimization risks is marital/relationship status. Individuals who are single (i.e., not married or in a long-term, intimate relationship) have consistently been shown to have increased risks of violent victimization, especially when they are drinking (Sampson, 1987). This is clearly related to lifestyle differences between single and married persons. Single persons are presumed to spend more of their free time and socializing time in the company of multiple other people, and to participate in more social activities in public places. These are exactly the settings where heavy alcohol use is more common, and where we are more likely to find more young persons, many males (some of whom are likely to be intoxicated) and other factors that have also been shown to be linked to violence. These characteristics are obviously common to college students as well.

The personal characteristic that is consistently shown to be the most significant predictor of violent victimization is age. We know that the ages at which one is most likely to be a victim of a violent crime are during the teen and early-twenties years (U.S. Department of Justice, 1998). The implication for college students, once again, is clear. It is during the late teenage and early to mid-twenties when individuals typically consume the most alcohol. These ages are especially related to heavy or binge drinking (Johnson, O'Malley & Bachman, 1997; Quigley & Marlatt, 1996; Wechsler et al., 1998; Wechsler, Dowdall, Davenport & Rimm, 1995; U.S. Department of Education, 1997).

Alcohol and Victimization on College Campuses

Based on the frequency and intensity of drinking by college students and the characteristics of individuals who are likely to be victims of crime (especially violent crime), it should come as no surprise that college students who drink have fairly high rates of victimization. Criminal victimization is especially common for students who drink heavily or binge drink. At the base level, just as is the case for the population in general, it has been well established that when college students are involved in crime – either as victims or offenders – alcohol is very likely to be present (Abbey, 1991; Koss, Gidycz & Wisniewski, 1987; Pezza & Bellotti, 1995). The relationship between criminal victimization and alcohol use is as strong, if not stronger, for college students as it is for Americans in general.

The one form of violence and victimization involving college students that has received the most attention over the past two decades is sexual assault. Numerous researchers have looked at the association of alcohol and sexual assault offenders and victims. Again, the research is fairly conclusive: alcohol is associated with the prevalence of both rape and lesser forms of sexual aggression among college students (Commission on Substance Abuse at Colleges and Universities, 1994; Koss & Dinero, 1989; Meilman, Riggs & Turco, 1990; Muehlenhard & Linton, 1987). A relationship between drinking alcohol and being either a victim or an offender of sexual assault is shown in numerous research studies. In fact, more often than not it is both the perpetrators and victims of sexual assault that have been drinking prior to an assault taking place. Most frequently the perpetrator and victim have been drinking together (Abbey & Ross, 1992; Koss & Oras, 1982; Miller & Marshall, 1987; Ullman & Knight, 1993).

Clearly, the risk of being sexually assaulted – as well as experiencing more severe sexual abuse and physical injuries – is greatly increased when one or both parties has been drinking. Psychological research clearly shows that the consumption of alcohol is related to aggression (Abbey & Ross, 1992), and a lowering of behavioral inhibitions. This does not only apply to students who would be perpetrators of sexual assaults. Alcohol use by potential victims is common; this may be due to less forceful victim resistance and therefore, a greater chance of an attempted rape being completed. Or, it may be that drunken students are seen as more sexually available, more sexually approachable, or simply less likely to say "no."

The relationship between alcohol and sexual assault holds true for college students in nearly all types of settings and situations, including completed and attempted rape and regardless of whether the victim and offender are strangers, casual acquaintances or dates (Abbey & Ross, 1992; Ullman & Knight, 1993). However, it is not only drinking that ties into sexual assaults; also (and perhaps even more) important for predicting sexual assault likelihood is where and with whom one drinks. This line of research has also been very productive; there are a number of factors researchers have identified that influence the likelihood of sexual assault in instances where alcohol is present. Just as with some of the relationships discussed above, personal characteristics of students may intensify – or increase the likelihood of – the relationship between alcohol use and sexual assault.

Alcohol is involved in one-third to two-thirds of rapes; most of the rape victims are acquainted with their assailants (Abbey, 1991; Pernanen, 1991). One in eight college women is the victim of rape during her college years, while one in four is the victim of an attempted rape. A majority of these women (84%) knew the men who raped them and 57 percent were on dates. Additionally, researchers have also shown that certain types of college men are more likely than others to be involved in sexual assaults. This is a point that has some serious political implications, and is often very unpopular with many students. However, rape (and in fact all forms of sexual aggression) is more likely among men who are members of fraternities where alcohol is used (Koss & Gaines, 1993; Schwartz & Nogrady, 1996). And, women who attend and drink at fraternity parties are among the most likely women on campuses to be victims of rape/sexual assault.

Among male college students, whether or not an individual belongs to a fraternity has been frequently, and strongly, associated with both heavy alcohol use and sexual aggression. Much of the socialization and drinking in the Greek system occurs in a fraternity house. As a result it is often the site of the heaviest drinking on campus. One of the more consistent findings in research concerning college drinking has been that residents of fraternity houses are more likely than other students to be heavy and binge drinkers (Engs & Hanson, 1994; Wechsler et al., 1998). When there is heavy or binge drinking at fraternity houses there is also a much greater likelihood of fraternity men being sexually aggressive or assaultive (Frintner & Rubinson, 1993; Garrett-Gooding & Senter, 1987). One of the most popular arguments found to support the alcohol and sexual aggression connection is the position that the fraternity environment encourages antisocial behavior such as drinking and the abuse of women (Martin & Hummer, 1989). Fraternities are seen as providing an atmosphere where sexual prowess, sexual activity, and "scoring" are encouraged, permitted, and reinforced (Martin & Hummer, 1989).

Drinking and Driving

One of the most dangerous aspects of college students' use and abuse of alcohol is related to drinking and driving. Sadly, this is a common activity for college students (McCormick & Ureda, 1995). The dangers involved in drinking and driving are well known in American society. Drinking and driving accounts for more than 16,000 deaths every year in the United States (U.S. Department of Transportation, 1998). Persons most likely to be killed while drinking and driving are those between the ages of 21 and 24 – typical ages of American college students (U.S. Department of Transportation, 1998). The good news here is that the number of alcohol-related traffic deaths, and the percentage of all traffic deaths attributed to alcohol, have been decreasing in the past two decades, but they still remain high. As recently as 1988 more than 23,000 persons were killed annually in drinking and driving accidents, with fully one-half of all traffic fatalities linked to drinking and driving. Despite the fact that the annual number of alcohol-related fatalities is decreasing, the fact remains that more than 16,000 persons lose their lives every year due to drinking and driving.

In addition to physical injury and death, drinking and driving also presents a significant potential legal problem: the possibility of arrest. The risk of being arrested is much greater than the risk of being killed in an alcohol-related traffic accident. The most recent national statistics show that just shy of one million persons are arrested every year for drinking and driving in the United States (U.S. Department of Justice, 1998). And, persons most likely to be arrested are those between the ages of 20 and 24 (U.S. Department of Justice, 1998). Once again, we see that these are typical college-aged persons. Whereas the number of traffic fatalities due to drinking and driving has been decreasing in recent years, so too has the number of persons arrested for drinking and driving. But, even so, driving under the influence (or, driving while intoxicated) remains the second most common offense (behind drug abuse violations) leading to an arrest in the United States (U.S. Department of Justice, 1998). Therefore, even though "progress" is being made in curbing drinking and driving, it still remains a major problem in our society.

Despite the clear and obvious physical and legal dangers involved in drinking and driving, college students largely disregard the risks and frequently do drink and drive. In fact, according to the U.S. Department of Health and Human Services (1998), individuals most likely to drink and drive are those who are between the ages of 21 and 25, have at least some college education, and are single/never married. Yet again, these are characteristics that describe most, or at least, the "typical" college students.

However, it is not only that students themselves drink and drive that puts them at risk. Not surprisingly, students who are heavy drinkers are more likely to report dangerous driving behaviors or driving while intoxicated (Canterbury, Gressard & Vieweg, 1992; Sarvela, Taylor, Drolet & Newcomb, 1988). A large number of students will frequently ride with another individual who has been drinking instead of driving themselves home from a party or a bar (McCormick & Ureda, 1995). What this means is that many college students are at serious risk of being injured, killed, or arrested because either they have chosen to drink and drive or they have taken a ride with another drinker.

This is not to suggest that college students do not use designated drivers; some researchers have shown that the use of designated drivers is "a well established strategy for avoiding impaired driving" (DeJong & Winsten, 1999:151). However, not all research on this topic comes to the same conclusion. Others (Glascoff & Knight, 1994) have shown that students who serve as designated drivers often do not abstain from drinking. What this means is that even when some students attempt to be more cautious about their drinking, their situation is not necessarily any safer than if they had not tried to institute precautions.

Health-Related Consequences

Engs and Hanson (1994) found that students who drink had become involved in fights after consuming alcohol, and had engaged in ill-advised behavior, such as damaging property or sending false fire alarms. Wechsler and colleagues (1994, 1995) found that the consequences reported more often by binge drinkers included having arguments with friends, getting hurt or injured, damaging property, and engaging in unprotected sex. What makes these facts a bit more concerning is that these are situations that have the potential to become serious; college students who drink more – especially those who binge drink – are more likely than other students to carry weapons with them (Presley, Meilman & Cashin, 1997). This clearly shows that alcohol use and abuse can have serious and lasting effects on the health of young adults.

Alcohol use/abuse may also have an indirect effect on students' health by impacting their sexual activities. As discussed above, there is a well-established link between alcohol and sexual assault, but so too does alcohol influence decisions about consensual sex. Among adolescents and young adults who drink, a majority report engaging in sexual activities when, or immediately following, drinking (Strunin & Hingson, 1992). The health risks presented by sexual behavior paired with alcohol use are, not surprisingly, greatest in instances of abusive levels of alcohol use. In simple terms, students who drink heavily and who binge drink are less likely to practice safe sex (Parker, Harford & Rosenstock, 1994; Prince & Bernard, 1998; Sigmon & Gainey, 1995), and therefore more likely to experience negative consequences of sexual activity. Some researchers have even documented the fact the young adults who drink moderately (not heavily or bingeing) have a lower likelihood of practicing protected sex (Keller, Bartlett, Schleifer, Johnson, Pinner & Delaney, 1991). When an individual does have unprotected sex they may be at risk for two major types of serious health consequences: pregnancy and infection with sexually transmitted diseases.

Both males and females who drink more frequently and more heavily can be expected to have higher rates of infection with sexually transmitted diseases, because of the lowered likelihood of practicing safer sex and the greater likelihood of having multiple sex partners. Researchers have consistently shown that college students who drink are more likely to report multiple sex partners, and failing to inform current sex partners about past sexual partners (Desiderato & Crawford, 1995). Similarly, students who drink report a lower likelihood of using condoms for sexual intercourse (Desiderato & Crawford, 1995). This is especially true for male college students (Noell, Biglan, Berendt, Ochs, Metzler, Ary & Smolkowski, 1993). However, both males and females suffer from sexually transmitted disease infections stemming from alcohol-related sexual activities. Women who drink at abusive levels are four and one-half times more likely to contract sexually transmitted diseases than women who do not drink at an abusive level (Ericksen & Trocki, 1992). Men who drink heavily also have a higher risk of sexually transmitted disease infection, although not as great as for women.

For women the practice of unprotected sex has the additional potential health consequence of pregnancy. Logically, we can expect females who drink more and more frequently to have higher rates of pregnancy, due to the fact that women who drink are less likely to practice safer sex. Although pregnancy and sexually transmitted diseases are not direct consequences of drinking, it is through the effects of alcohol on students' decisions about sex that they may have their health seriously and lastingly affected.

Secondhand Binge Effects

The effects of alcohol use and abuse on college campuses goes far beyond the direct and indirect consequences for students who drink. Through the effects that alcohol has on the behaviors of students who drink, the lives of others – other students, faculty, administrators, and the general public – are likely to be affected. It is no longer possible to view heavy or binge drinking solely as the binger's problem; a wide range of other persons and institutions experience negative effects as well. Of course, most prominent among these are the victimization experiences suffered by those whom binge drinkers target for offenses.

Secondhand effects of binge drinking are common. They may range from relatively minor nuisances – such as having to contend with a drunken neighbor's noise – to serious, harmful events. Serious secondhand binge effects may include destruction of one's property by a binge drinker, physical or sexual attacks, or in the most extreme case, death. The Harvard studies (Wechsler et al., 1994; 1995) show that two-thirds of college students reported experiencing at least one adverse effect as a result of another student's drinking during the most recent school year. These included verbal harassment or humiliation, being confronted with unwanted sexual advances, being drawn into a serious argument or quarrel, being physically assaulted, having repeated interruptions to studying or sleeping habits, having to "babysit" a drunken student, having one's property damaged or destroyed, and being sexually assaulted. These are serious, harmful, and almost always unnecessary experiences that detract from the educational experiences and quality of life of these other students. However, these are experiences over which the victims have no control. In this way it is clear that alcohol has a direct effect on victimization.

Conclusion

The role alcohol plays in the occurrence of crime in the United States has been well established. In addition, alcohol use by perpetrators and victims alike has been found to be the strongest causal link to criminal victimization. A large proportion of the murder, rape, sexual assault, robbery, aggravated assault, and simple assault occurrences in the United States are committed by men, women, and young adults, in all types of social settings and situations, who had been abusing alcohol at the time they committed their offense. Thus, the many men and women housed in the jails and prisons in this country have serious alcohol abuse and dependency problems which directly impact the criminal justice system and in turn, society as a whole.

Although alcohol use in the United States has declined over the past decade, alcohol use and abuse by youth and young adults – particularly college students – is on the rise. Thus, our discussion has focused on the effects of alcohol on college students. We have clearly shown that an overwhelming number of college students, many of whom are below the minimum drinking age, use alcohol and that the pattern of heavy or binge drinking is widespread among college campuses. Binge drinking is of particular concern, not only because of its risks to the drinker but because of the problems it causes for those around the drinker. The prevalence of this episodic, heavy drinking behavior has brought the issue of undergraduate alcohol abuse to the forefront, making it the number one health hazard for college students.

Alcohol use and heavy binge-drinking behavior has clearly been shown to increase diverse negative consequences among youth and young adults, including violent crime offending and victimization; accidents and fatalities; destructive behavior, such as damaging property and being involved in arguments or fights; and engaging in unplanned sexual activity. Excessive drinking has also been linked to students' missing classes and falling behind in classwork. Heavy alcohol use adversely affects the drinker as well as the students who must share the same college environment. These adverse effects range from having their studies interrupted to sexual assault.

Alcohol abuse remains one of the biggest social problems facing all facets of society today. Alcohol is perhaps the most strongly related variable associated with criminal victimization, including both minor and major forms of offenses. Because of this, our attention must be directed to the role alcohol plays in human suffering and the social contexts in which alcohol use is accepted and glorified. With this heightened awareness, a better understanding will emerge as to the numbing toll that alcohol takes, especially among young women and men in college today.

CHAPTER 4

The Mass Media and Victims of Rape

Patricia H. Grant
Paula I. Otto

According to the Uniform Crime Reports (UCR), 96,153 females in the United States were victims of attempted rape or forcible rape in 1997 (FBI, 1998). Defined by the UCR as the "carnal knowledge of a female forcibly and against her will" (FBI, 1998), rape is a violent and traumatic act that significantly redefines quality of life for victims. Often isolated and ostracized by members of society, as well as their families and social networks (Davis & Brickman, 1996; Estrich, 1987 as cited by Ullman, 1996a), victims of rape face societal stigma and distrust regarding their claims of sexual assault (Estrich, 1987 as cited by Ullman, 1996b). Rape victims are also subjected to "victim blaming" by family and friends who are having difficulty understanding or accepting the victims' innocence and may therefore behave inappropriately or emotionally withdraw from the victim (Cuklanz, 1996; Thornton et al., 1988 as cited by Davis & Brickman, 1996; Symond, 1980 as cited by Ullman, 1996a). Although family and friends may appear to be supportive, they may also be seeking to diminish personal feelings of guilt and/or inadequacy, which may represent a "second injury" for rape victims (Cuklanz, 1996; Thornton et al., 1988 as cited by Davis & Brickman, 1996; Symond, 1980 as cited by Ullman, 1996a). Blaming the victim by suggesting that they are somehow responsible for the crime, and thus creating feelings of rejection and lack of support may further isolate the victim while denying her an opportunity to openly discuss the psychological and emotional effects of the crime (Davis & Brickman, 1996; Symond, 1980, as cited by Ullman, 1996a). Consequently, the re-victimization and dehumanizing treatment experienced by the victim when dealing with the criminal justice system, as well as the possibility of victim identification by the media, only succeeds in keeping the voices of rape victims silent, while perpetuating increased feelings of distrust and fear (Cuklanz, 1996).

While recognizing the quandary these and other issues pose for victims of rape, this chapter is predominately concerned with the struggle between the media's right to publish the identity of rape victims versus the victim's right to privacy.

History of the Media's Treatment of Rape Victims

Crime began to be a mainstay for news stories in the 1830s as new technologies allowed for less expensive printing of newspapers, literacy in the country was growing, and urban population centers were expanding, thereby increasing potential readers. Known as the "penny press" era for the one-cent-a-copy price of newspapers sold on the streets, the era marked the beginning of the media's reliance on reporting violence and crime to sell newspapers (Benedict, 1992). However, it was not until the 1930s that crimes involving sex began to be written about regularly (Harris, 1932, as cited by Benedict, 1992). After World War II, the rate of violent crime, including rape, rose in the country (Hall, 1983, as cited by Benedict, 1992) and the practice of naming the victim became commonplace throughout the 1940s, 1950s and 1960s. Although there was increased media coverage of these stories, the focus was generally on those crimes that involved a white female victim and a black male as the accused. With the civil rights movement of the 1960s, however, the media became more aware of the racial bias in their stories and began to make changes in reporting habits. With the women's movement in the 1970s came a greater understanding of rape. Susan Brownmiller's book titled *Against Our Will* (1975), a feminist history and analysis of rape, brought women's issues to the forefront. The media began examining the way it was portraying the crime, the victims, and the rapists. During the late 1970s, the media began focusing on whether victims' names should be included in news stories (Benedict, 1992) and by the early 1980s, most media outlets, including newspapers, wire services, radio, and television stations, voluntarily began excluding rape victims' names from news accounts. This practice has continued until today, with some notable exceptions in the past 10 years.

Notable Exceptions

The *Winston-Salem Journal* has been printing the names of rape victims since 1971 (Haws, 1996) and identifies both the victim and the assailant after the arrest has been made. Although this had been the policy of the newspaper for 25 years, a 1996 study indicates that overall knowledge of the policy was not commonplace among victims (Haws, 1996). In this study, 18 victims who had been named by the *Journal* were interviewed. Of those interviewed, 15 of the 18 reported that they were not aware when they decided to report their rapes to the police that their names would appear in the newspaper. Thirteen of the 18 women said the publicity increased their embarrassment and heightened their feelings of shame. In defense of the *Journal* policy, the Managing Editor, Carl M. Crothers stated, "We believe reporting rape cases should be done fully and with care and sensitivity. We are not untouched by the emotional pain suffered by victims, but we feel strongly that we are making a statement in this community that rape should no longer carry a stigma for the victim and be a source for shame and embarrassment" (Haws, 1996:3).

In 1989, a female executive was brutally raped while jogging in Central Park. The suspects were a group of black and Hispanic teenage boys, six of whom were found guilty in three separate trials, lasting into 1991. Although most newspapers and broadcast outlets did not identify the victim, some minority publications in New York did – noting that the mainstream press guarded the identity of a well-to-do white woman while stigmatizing the lower-class black youths by naming them before they were indicted (Benedict, 1992).

In what is often cited as a turning point in modern media coverage of rape issues, the *Des Moines Register* ran a five-part series in February 1990, about a 29-year-old woman who had been abducted and raped. The victim, Nancy Ziegenmeyer, allowed the *Register* to use her real name, saying she hoped to focus attention on this underreported crime and thereby prevent other women from being raped (Elson, 1990). The *Register's* editor, Geneva Overholser, in a 1990 interview stated that when society refuses to talk openly about rape, it weakens our ability to deal with it, and further, the media participates in the stigmatization of rape victims by treating victims of rape differently (Elson, 1990).

Perhaps the best known case is that of Patricia Bowman and William Kennedy Smith. Bowman, a single-mother, met Smith one evening in a Florida bar in the spring of 1991 and later accompanied him to the Kennedy compound, where Bowman said she was raped. Bowman's identity was broadcast on NBC without her consent and newspapers across the country, including the *New York Times,* soon carried the story with the victim's name (Thomason, LaRocque & Thomas, 1995). Although Smith was eventually acquitted in December 1991, in the months leading up to and during the trial, Bowman found herself and her actions at the center of intense media scrutiny and public debate.

The Media, Victims, and the Criminal Justice System

Criminal trials allow for the resolution of controversial subjects that are pertinent to society in general, yet, for victims of rape these trials are more likely to result in further victimization by the judicial system (Benedict, 1997; Dworkin, 1997; O'Toole & Schiffman, 1997; Cuklanz, 1996). Rape trials are often considered as dehumanizing and may lead to additional trauma for the victim, thereby forcing many rape victims to forego reporting the incident for fear of embarrassment, further humiliation and revictimization by the system (Benedict, 1997; Dworkin, 1997; O'Toole & Schiffman, 1997; Cuklanz, 1996). Thus, the adversarial nature of the trial, which allows for the introduction of insensitive and graphic testimony and prior sexual history may further impede and discourage victims from reporting the rape (Benedict, 1997; Cuklanz, 1996).

The issue of privacy is addressed by the Court in *Whalen v. Roe* (1977), which stated that "Rape is an act of physical violence which by its very nature is an affront to privacy. It represents forcible exposure of aspects of oneself that are protected by conventions of limited access. These conventions are normally adhered to out of regard for well-being and respect for personal privacy" (*Bloch v. Ribar*, 1998:10). Citing *Roe v. Wade* (1973), the Court in *Whalen* established that although the Constitution does not explicitly mention any right of privacy, the law does currently recognize two distinct forms of privacy, which are that "(1) constitutional privacy protects an individual's freedom (fundamental right or one implicit in the concept of ordered liberty) to make choices regarding personal, intimate aspects of life; and, (2) the government's interest in disseminating the information must be balanced against the individual's interest in keeping the information private" (*Bloch v. Ribar*, 1998:10).

While stopping short of prohibiting the identification of rape victims, in recent years, the courts have attempted to balance the privacy rights of victims against the rights of the media to publish the names. Acknowledging that the Constitution does not guarantee the right to privacy, the courts have sought to balance the rights of the victim against the media's First Amendment right to freedom of the press (*Bloch v. Ribar*, 1998). The Court acknowledges the "negative social stigma that is attached to victims of rape," and postulates that rape victims are "subjected to a different level of victimization that exceeds the impact of other types of victimization" (*Bloch v. Ribar*, 1998:11). At issue in *Bloch v. Ribar* was whether the sheriff, in response to comments made by the Blochs to the media, acted inappropriately when releasing the intimate details of the assault. In response, the Court addressed the derogatory and negative connotations associated with rape imposed by society, as well as the stigma society places on rape victims. Additionally, the Court confirmed the consequential and detrimental impact imposed when the media subsequently names victims and observed that "a historical social stigma has been attached to victims of sexual violence. In particular, a tradition of 'blaming the victim' of sexual violence sets these victims apart from those of other crimes. As a result, releasing the intimate details of rape will not only revive a particularly painful sexual experience, but often will subject a victim to criticism and scrutiny concerning her sexuality and personal choices regarding sex." Subsequently, the Court ruled that "a rape victim has a fundamental right to privacy in preventing government officials from gratuitously and unnecessarily releasing the intimate details of the rape where no penalogical purpose is being served" (*Bloch v. Ribar*, 1998:11).

In two important cases relevant to the news media's right to publish names, the Supreme Court attempted to balance the important privacy concerns of the sexual assault victim against the legitimate interests of the news media in reporting newsworthy events. In the first case, *Cox Broadcasting Corp. v. Cohn* (1975), the rape victim privacy statute for Georgia was tested by the father of Cynthia Cohn, a victim of gang rape who was killed by her attackers. Cohn brought a civil suit against Cox Broadcasting, the television station that broadcast his daughter's identity. In this case, the Supreme Court ruled that the protection afforded the press through the First and Fourteenth Amendments ". . . forbids civil liability for the publication of lawfully-obtained truthful information." Writing for the Court, Justice Byron White expressed that "the interests of privacy fade when the information involved already appears on the public record" (1975:20). Consequently, the Court overwhelmingly supported the views of the media over those seeking penalties for the disclosure of the victim's identity.

However, in the case of the *Florida Star v. B.J.F.* (1989), while the Court moved away from punitive sanctions against the media for publishing names, the decision left open the distinct possibility of valid state sanctions against those officials who disclose the names of sexual assault victims prior to trial. In this case, the *Florida Star* newspaper published an assault victims' full name in the "Police Reports" section. A reporter-trainee for the newspaper obtained the name by copying the Duval County sheriff's report provided in the media information area. Initially, the plaintiff was awarded compensatory and punitive damages, however, the Supreme Court later ruled that imposing damages on the *Star* for publishing the full name violated the First Amendment. Further, the Court ruled that although the sheriff's department failed to fulfill its obligation under the Florida Statute, the *Star* could not be held liable for publishing truthful information that was lawfully obtained.

Partly in response to *Florida Star v. B.J.F.*, the Florida Legislature in 1995 addressed the "victim-identity question in favor of privacy by criminalizing the publication of rape victims' names" (Berlin, 1995:1). Specifically, the law states that "if a newspaper lawfully obtains truthful information about a matter of public significance then state officials may not constitutionally punish publication of the information, absent a need to further a state interest of the highest order" (1995:1). However, Section 92.56 of this Statute mandates that "All records, including testimony from witnesses, which contain the name, address, or photograph of the victim of the crime of sexual battery, etc., should remain confidential. These records could not be made public or a part of the public record and violation of this statute by a public officer or employee is punishable as a second-degree misdemeanor." In addition, at about the same time as the Florida legislation was passed, Georgia enacted a rape victim privacy law that now prohibits all forms of "public dissemination [of] the name or identity of any female" rape victim (Berlin, 1995:12).

Rape Shield Laws

Many states have created rape shield laws designed to provide further protection for victims of rape. Based on the 1974 Michigan statute (O'Toole & Schiffman, 1997), and impacted by the disillusionment that many women experienced in the process of having their cases heard and adjudicated by the judicial system, eight states – Florida, Georgia, Massachusetts, South Carolina, South Dakota, Washington, Wisconsin, and West Virginia – passed legislation making it unlawful to publish or broadcast identifying information of adult sexual assault and/or child abuse victims, and Colorado and Pennsylvania, through legislative proclamation mandated that the media use restraint (Beatty, 1999). These laws represent a reversal of legislators and the judicial system from victim blaming to providing fair and compassionate treatment for victims of rape and were also designed to prohibit the introduction of a victim's past sexual history in court except in specific circumstances (O'Toole & Schiffman, 1997), while advocating against the publication of the names of rape victims. Additionally, Alaska, Arkansas, California, Colorado, Connecticut, Florida, Indiana, Kansas, Louisiana, Massachusetts, Montana, New York, Rhode Island, and Virginia protect the identity of crime victims by requiring that records for adult sexual assault victims remain confidential, and place the responsibility for keeping these records confidential and anonymous on law enforcement and court officials (Beatty, 1999).

How Does the Media Decide?

In the absence of laws prohibiting the publication of the names of rape victims, the media is often left to decide what to do and to enforce its own codes of ethics and guidelines. Before examining the media's dilemma of weighing the public's right to know against the victim's right to privacy, it is instructive to determine what functions the media has in our society. Mass communications scholars define the media's role as one of surveillance: gathering news and information. With about 90 percent of the American public reporting that they receive most of their news from the media (Dominick, 1998), the media assumes the responsibility of gathering information that is not readily available to society at large.

In examining the role of the media in relation to government, Dominick (1998) summarizes the *Four Theories of the Press*, which were first categorized in 1956 as the *authoritarian, communist, libertarian* and the *social responsibility* theories. The authoritarian theory, which arose in sixteenth-century England about the time that the printing press emerged, states that the ruling elite should guide the masses, who were believed to have limited intellectual ability. Under this theory, public dissent and criticism were considered harmful and not allowed. The communist theory states that the media are "owned" by the people, and their purpose is to support the Marxist system and to achieve the goals of the state. The libertarian theory assumes human beings are intelligent and capable of making their own decisions if given the appropriate information and that the media is free from governmental interference.

The social responsibility theory takes libertarianism a step further. Based on this theory, the media is free, but the freedom is not absolute. While the media has the right to criticize government and other social institutions, it also has the responsibility to respond to society's interests and needs. On the other hand, the government often regulates the media to some extent. For example, the United States requires the licensing of radio and television stations. In addition to the United States, Britain, Japan, and many western European countries also follow the social responsibility model.

How does this role of social responsibility impact the media's decision to identify or withhold the names of rape victims? Jay Black in a 1995 article "Rethinking the Naming of Sex Crime Victims" states that "news coverage of sex crime victims has become as much of an ethical as a legal issue, and the media are not sure how to handle the options before them" (1995:97). Black contends that while the distribution of information about sex crime victims may aid in the apprehension of the perpetrators, and may even help society better understand and deal with significant and broad social questions, including the destigmatization of rape (Gartner, 1993), the identification of victims could lead to personal anguish and potential revictimization of individuals who are already in a state of crisis (Benedict, 1992; Black, 1995).

Black further states that some have perceived the issue as a question of weighing the rights of vulnerable individuals to avoid needless and public revictimization and the right or desire of the public to satisfy its "prurient curiosity" along with the news media's desire to sell papers, get good ratings, and keep profits high (1995:97). In this case, Black states that the decision is easy: the media should not identify victims. On the other side are those who seek to guard the First Amendment, which they define as the media's constitutionally guaranteed right to print anything, versus anti-democratic censorship and prior restraint (prior restraint occurs when an entity gets a court order to prevent the publication or broadcast of certain information). In this debate, Black states, journalists would say "let the chips fall where they may" (1995:98).

There are currently no state or federal laws that prohibit the media from using the names of sexual assault victims, although many states have laws to limit the media's access to that information. Instead, the media must often rely on its own judgment, newsroom policy or professional code of ethics for guidance.

The following is a brief overview of the guidelines, codes of ethics, and a sample newsroom policy currently in place for journalists. The Society of Professional Journalists' code of ethics states that journalists should "Be cautious about identifying juvenile suspects or victims of sex crimes, [and] only an overriding public need can justify intrusion into anyone's privacy" (*www.RTNDA.org*).

The Society of Professional Journalists and the Poynter Institute for Media Studies have outlined three fundamental principles underlying ethical journalism:

1. to gather and distribute truthful, accurate information;

2. to do so free from extraneous forces;

3. to minimize the harm caused by the process (Black, Steel & Barney, 1995).

Media ethicist E.B. Lambeth (1986b) suggests that journalists should first consider the humanity of people involved in any story and act humanely.

The Associated Press Managing Editors Code (Lambeth, 1986a) states that newspapers "should respect the individuals right to privacy" (1986a:34).

The Radio Television News Directors Association (RTNDA) code of ethics states that broadcast journalists "should respect the dignity, privacy, rights and well being of people with whom they deal" (*www.RTNDA.org*). Although shortly after the William Kennedy Smith rape trial in which NBC decided to use the victim's name, David Bartlett, then president of the RTNDA, said "If the name is relevant in the story, then we should have no hesitancy about using it. I agree entirely with [NBC News President] Michael Gartner that we are in the news dissemination business and not the news repression business. I am very impatient about the journalist as sociologist" (*www.RTNDA.org*).

Cooper and Whitehouse (1995:11) suggest a series of questions journalists should ask before publication:

1. Is the victim in danger? The victim shouldn't be identified if the attacker hasn't been arrested.

2. What is the social value in identifying rape victims? Does the good gained outweigh the harm publication may cause?

3. What are the community expectations? What impact would publication have on the community? What community mores would have an impact on the victim if her name were published?

4. Is the victim particularly vulnerable or will the victim refuse to prosecute?

5. Is the victim a public figure in her own right? Traditionally, public figures and elected officials sacrifice a certain amount of private life. Identifying the public figure as a victim does not place the same stigma as it would on a private individual because the public knows her in other contexts.

6. If this is a departure from normal policy, what is the motivation?

7. Has the case been published elsewhere? Are they credible media outlets?

8. If the victim has granted permission for her name to be pub-
    lished, is she aware of the consequences?

9. Is the news story written in a way that myths concerning rape are
    perpetuated?

The *St. Louis Post-Dispatch's* crime policy (Offen, Stein & Young, 1999)
evolved after a September, 1987 robbery of a St. Louis supermarket in
which seven store employees where shot, five fatally. The paper ran grisly
photographs of the crime scene and printed the exact address of the victims.
After protests from the community, the victims, and their advocates, the
paper created its "Crime News Privacy Policy." The *Post-Dispatch* policy
begins with three broad principles. The first is most instructive: "The perceptions and perspectives of reporters and editors on the one hand, and
readers and other members of the public on the other, are different. The
news professionals are motivated chiefly by a desire to get the news and publish it. The others are more likely to react personally, imagining how they
would feel as the subject of a story. In weighing matters of privacy, perhaps
some effort should be made to bring that personal perspective into the equa-
tion" (Offen et al., 1999:3-12). The policy states that names of victims of sex
crimes will not be used except for: (1) When they voluntarily identify themselves in the belief that publicity will lead to some public benefit; (2) When
the victim files a civil lawsuit, making no effort to conceal his or her identify; and (3) When a husband is charged with raping his wife or former wife,
if the fact of the relationship is integral to the story.

The National Center for Victims of Crime in its "Crime Victims and the
Media" publication endorses a code of ethics for the media that includes
"The media shall not . . . print facts about the crime, the victim or the criminal act that might embarrass, humiliate, hurt or upset the victim unless there
is a need to publish such details for public safety reasons" (1990:26).

The National Organization for Victim Assistance (NOVA) believes that
well-informed reporters and editors will treat crime victims in a way that pre-
serves the victims' integrity and dignity in telling what happened to them
involuntarily (Offen, et al., 1999). Media treatment of victims comes from
policies voluntarily adopted by their employer, by interest groups most
affected by their behavior and by the laws under which they operate. NOVA
offers recommendations for a sensitive interview, including accepting a
refusal to be interviewed; acknowledging the crime and its impact on the
victims; and, not minimizing the crime. NOVA also implores, "Remember the
motto, 'Do no harm'."

The "*Do nots*" outlined by NOVA includes (Offen et al., 1999:3-12):

1. Do not print or broadcast facts about the victim or the criminal act
    that might embarrass, humiliate, or hurt the victim unless there is
    a compelling need, such as an interest in the public safety, to
    publish such facts.

2. Do not engage in any form of sensationalism in reporting crimes, its investigation or prosecution, especially erring on the side of restraint with any victim or witness who was not previously a public figure or who has evidenced a desire not to become one as a result of the crime.

What Does the Media Think?

Several studies have been conducted to gauge the opinions of newspaper editors regarding the government's role in protecting rape victims by not publishing their names, with somewhat conflicting results. A 1995 study of newspaper editors found that nearly 72 percent of the 589 editors polled believed that victims' rights laws which restrict access to public information are contrary to First Amendment rights and should be repealed, 12 percent were neutral, and 14 percent disagreed or disagreed strongly (Thomason, LaRocque & Thomas, 1995). However, only 24 percent agreed or strongly agreed that withholding the names of rape victims interferes with the public's right to know, while 58 percent disagreed, and 15 percent were neutral. [Two percent did not respond.] When asked if newspapers identified rape victims by name would help to remove the stigma of rape, nearly 23 percent agreed or strongly agreed, whereas, 54.5 percent disagreed or strongly disagreed, and 22 percent were neutral (Thomason et al., 1995). [Three percent did not respond.]

An April 1993 phone survey by the Roper Center (1993) at the University of Connecticut of 1,040 newspaper editors for the American Society of Newspaper Editors asked:

> Do you feel the media should be protected all the time, protected under certain circumstances or not protected at all when journalists report the name or identity of a rape victim?

Fifty-four percent of the editors said the media should not be protected at all; 22 percent said the media should be protected sometimes; 22 percent said the media should be protected all of the time; and two percent said they don't know.

While these data reveal that the majority of editors responding to the survey believe the laws designed to protect the names of victims should be repealed, a significant number also indicate that the media should not be afforded protection when reporting those names.

Public Perception

There were many polls taken in the early 1990s in the wake of the William Kennedy Smith and the Central Park jogger trials to gauge public opinion on the issue of publishing the names of rape victims. A Gallup Poll (1991a) sponsored by Newsweek asked 761 adults:

Do you think the names of rape victims should be reported by the news media just like the names of other crime victims, or not? Seventy-seven percent of the respondents answered no; 19 percent responded yes; and 4 percent said they didn't know. [Two percent did not respond.]

Some people feel that reporting the name of a woman who has been raped indicates that society does not attach a special shame to being a rape victim, and treats male and female crime victims equally. Others say it is a special hardship for women. Which comes closer to your view? Nine percent said equal treatment; 86 percent said it creates a special hardship; and 5 percent said they don't know.

Another Gallup Poll (1991b) asked 1,005 adults:

Do you approve or disapprove of the decision by most news organizations to keep the name of the alleged rape victim (in the William Kennedy Smith trial) confidential – or do you think her name should have been released? Sixty-four percent of the respondents said they approved of keeping the victim's name confidential; 33 percent said it was okay to release it; and 3 percent said they didn't know.

In a more recent study, the Newspaper Research Journal (1999) asked respondents to react to four stories about rapes (some of which included the victims' names). The study findings indicated that individuals were not affected by the identification of rape victims and were neither more sympathetic nor more blameful of victims, thus suggesting that the details of the crime and the way the crime is reported probably has a more powerful impact on readers' perception than the use of the victim's name. From these data, one can conclude that the majority of the public believes that the media should not release the identity of rape victims.

Why Withhold?

Advocates and critics of victim naming advance a myriad of reasons for and against identifying rape victims. Advocates are generally most concerned with protecting the rights of the victims, while critics tend to be most concerned with the rights of the media.

The reasons purported by advocates for withholding the names of victims are directly related to the harm that may be inflicted on the victim as a result of the publication of her identity by the media. Rape victims who are identified in news stories that relate the specifics of the crime are forced to relive the traumatic experience each time the story is broadcast (Dworkin, 1997). This form of revictimization, perpetuated by the media, increases feelings of humiliation for the victim, who may be ridiculed by friends, family, co-workers and the community at large and may result in a second assault on her privacy (Dworkin, 1997; Davis & Brickman, 1996).

Advocates for withholding the identity of rape victims also suggest that reporting the names would continue to hamper efforts that encourage rape victims to report the crime (Dworkin, 1997). As stated by Dworkin, "Now, thanks to *The New York Times* and NBC News, both of which identified by name the victim in the William Kennedy Smith rape trial, there will be a third rape – by the media. If a woman reporting a rape to the police means she will be exposed by the media to the scrutiny of voyeurs and worse, a sexual spectacle with her legs splayed open in the public mind, reporting itself will be tantamount to suicide" (1997:55).

Furthermore, advocates contend that rape survivors have already suffered enough and that releasing their names would heighten the feelings of powerlessness that occur during the assault. Victims feel a stigma and a sense of shame attached to the experience, and the consequences of publishing their names will only increase the feelings of guilt and loss of control (Cuklanz, 1996; O'Toole & Schiffman, 1997). As stated by Benedict, "To name a rape victim is to guarantee that whenever somebody hears her name, that somebody will picture her in the act of being sexually tortured" (1992:15).

Finally, advocates suggest that naming victims in most crime stories is meaningless to the vast majority of readers (as indicated by the above-mentioned data), and thus of no great significance to the integrity of the story. Publication of the names of rape victims is harmful to the victim, as well as the family and only serves to increase the psychological and emotional devastation (Davis & Brickman, 1991) that began with the initiated assault.

Why Not Withhold?

The arguments for critics of not withholding identities center primarily around the issues of censorship; enhancing the credibility of the story; providing the victim of rape a protection that is not guaranteed to other victims; and removing the stigma that society places on rape victim by providing a forum that will facilitate the healing process.

When addressing the issue of legislative policies related to censorship, critics contend that any form of censorship is a violation of the First Amendment. Charles Gay, whose Washington state newspaper prints rape victims names regularly contends that because the Constitution gives the defendant the right to a public trial and to meet his accusers in public, they believe it is important that accusers are named in the paper (Stein, 1986). By not allowing the media to make independent decisions, critics assert that legislators are intruding on the right to freedom of the press, which should be deemed unconstitutional. As noted previously, the courts have supported the media on this issue, especially in the case of privacy, thereby negating efforts by state legislators to prohibit the media from publishing the names of rape victims.

Critics suggest that naming the victim in the news report promotes credibility. According to Gartner, ". . . names and facts are news that make readers better informed. The more we tell our viewers, the better informed they will be in making up their own minds about the issues involved" (Gartner, 1993). Readers want to know who was victimized, as well as where the crimes are occurring, and by providing this information, the media is performing the service that is expected by society.

Any restriction that would not allow the media to publish the names of rape victims provides a protection of nondisclosure that is not afforded any other victim (Berlin, 1995). Other than juvenile delinquents, whose names are withheld (by law) from the media to diminish the possibility of future stigma and labeling, and possibly victims/offenders whose identities may be protected for security reasons, rape victims are the only victims whose names are not provided to the media. Therefore, critics suggest that this "protection" extends special privileges to rape victims, while diminishing the sense of fairness for the accused.

Others purport that like advocates, the media is also concerned with the well being of rape victims. Citing reasons ranging from deconstructing the myths associated with rape victims to educating the public, critics suggest that naming the victims would dilute the negative connotations and facilitate the healing process (Berlin, 1995). By identifying rape victims, the media could educate the public of the stigma attached to rape thereby, minimizing victim-blaming and the stereotypes associated with this particular form of victimization, while pulling off the veil of shame (DeCrow, 1990).

Conclusion

As outlined by Brownmiller (1975) and Benedict (1992), there are many myths in society regarding rape, including the myth that rape is a natural sexual act, rather than an aggressive act. Benedict argues that this myth "encourages people to not take rape seriously, nor consider it as a crime, which may continue to promote the practice of victim blaming" (1992:14). In addition, Brownmiller and Benedict discuss the myths that women provoke rape by their looks, sexuality, and the way they dress, and that only "loose" women are victimized. Unfortunately, these myths are so pervasive that we often find lawyers, police officers, victims, perpetrators, and the media perpetuating them (Benedict, 1992:16).

Society continues to struggle with these myths, as evidenced by the attention given to "Why Men Rape," by Thornhill and Palmer. These evolutionary biologists contend that rape is not an act of violence, but a sexual act that they believe occurs because of the natural urges of men to procreate. In addition, they suggest that how a woman dresses and her behavior impacts her chances of being raped. They alone are decelerating 20 years of feminism research and grassroots efforts to educate society about the true causes of rape. Rightfully so, Brownmiller, rejects Thornhill and Palmer's assertions, stating once again that rape is a crime of violence. It is the result of young male aggression and cultural attitudes promoting the acceptance of young men forcing themselves on women" (Brownmiller, as quoted by Rosenfeld, 2000).

It is the authors' belief that the benefits of protecting rape victims' identities far outweigh the arguments for making victims' names public. Women whose names have been made public by the media report embarrassment, concerns about safety, a sense of revictimization, and acknowledge that they would be less likely to report the crime if they know their name would be made public. Additionally, most in society agree that rape is intrinsically a very different sort of victimization, the trauma of which lingers for many years. Unlike other types of victimizations, rape victims are subjected to continued emotional, psychological, and oftentimes physical degradation that is not easily remedied and is not improved by victim naming. Consequently, identifying these victims under the auspices of the public's right to know may only succeed in denying the victim her right to privacy, as well as hampering her ability to heal.

It is apparent from *Cox Broadcasting Corp. v. Cohn* and subsequent cases, that it is unlikely legislation barring the media from publishing names will ever pass a constitutional test. However, many states have tightened the flow of information to the media by making it illegal for law enforcement agencies to disclose victim's identities. Although this is perhaps not a complete solution, it does provide some protection for victims of rape.

Current media codes of ethics, such as those of the Society of Professional Journalists and Radio Television News Directors, as well as individual newsroom policies, have generally assisted journalists in making the right choice. When journalists have strayed from the practice of keeping victim's names confidential, the public outcry has been loud and clear. Therefore, it should be apparent to journalists that if their goal is to report what people want to know, and in keeping with their professional codes of ethics, they will continue to refrain from reporting the names of rape victims.

CHAPTER 5

The Tradition and Reality of Domestic Violence

M.A. Dupont-Morales

Introduction

In October 1999, the National Resource Center (NRC) on Domestic Violence compiled a booklet for social, legal and educational agencies detailing a "combination of activities and events . . . solicited over the past two years from sponsoring organizations . . . recognizing Domestic Violence Awareness Month" (NRC, 1999). The slogan for the 1999 campaign was "*Domestic Violence—It IS Your Business*." The packet included some of the following facts:

Did you know that . . .

- 82 percent of Americans say that they would do something to help reduce domestic violence if they know what to do (Lieberman, 1995).

- One out of four American women report that a husband or boyfriend at some point in their lives has physically abused them (Lieberman, 1996).

- Among all female murder victims in 1995, 26 percent were known to have been slain by husbands or boyfriends. Only three percent of the male victims were known to have been slain by wives or girlfriends (FBI, 1995).

- In a national survey of more than 2,000 American families, approximately 50 percent of the men who frequently assaulted their wives also frequently abused their children (Strauss & Gelles, 1990).

- Children (from violent homes) are more likely to be involved in violent criminal activity in the future than their non-abused peers (Widom, 1992; 1996).

- Eight percent of teenage girls age 14 to 17 report knowing someone their age who has been hit or beaten by a boyfriend (Kaiser Permanente, 1995).

. . . the costs of domestic violence reaches every person's pocket?

- A study at Rush Medical Center in Chicago estimates an average charge for medical services to abused women, children, and older people as $1,633 per person per year, excluding psychological or follow-up costs (Laurence & Spalter-Roth, 1996).

- An estimated 50 percent of the 256,000 children in foster care are victims of abuse. Those of us who pay taxes spend $2.5 billion in Federal foster care expenditures under Title IV-E (Laurence & Spalter-Roth, 1996).

(NRC, 1999)

While these compelling facts force us to recognize domestic violence as a major social problem, the concept itself is somewhat limited in terms of its conceptualization, resulting in a narrow understanding of the problem. While it is true domestic violence affects many psychologically, physically, or financially, the term, with its narrow focus, is applied inadequately. We must question the application of the terminology to comprehend the vast number of violent acts occurring in society that could be labeled as domestic violence. There is some controversy regarding what violent acts should be listed as domestic violence. A more limited definition focuses on the relationship between the offender and victim often ignoring relationships that are not heterosexual or sexually intimate. Relationships can be gay or lesbian, two-parent, single parent, adoptive parent, and/or kinship and all can be violent. The purpose of the chapter is to explore our definition of domestic violence. It examines the context of domestic violence in the traditional sense and the reality of relationship violence in a broad sense. Beginning with traditional definitions of domestic violence the chapter provides a framework for the construction of linkages concerning violence, that is, its initiation, its modeling, its consequences, and the manipulation of these distinctions. The chapter concludes with specific definitions of physical assault and aggression as applied to female-on-male violence.

Definitional Issues

Historically, many terms have been used to characterize the actions and behaviors defined as "domestic violence." More descriptive terminology increases the awareness of violence within relationships and how such violence is perpetrated. Investigating violence within relationships that should be nurturing is of international concern. While it may have begun with violence against women, today's research and policy implications have expanded the concept to include "family relationships" and how these relationships perpetuate violence in general.

A review of the literature finds the following definitions for battering, dating violence, domestic violence, and family violence. For example, Dasgupta (1999) defines *battering* as "acts that intimidate, isolate, and deny victims personal power and establish the abuser's control over them. Historically, violence is a recognized strategy used to resolve conflicts" (1999:200-201). Sugarman and Hotaling (1989) define *dating violence* "as the perpetration or threat of an act of physical violence by at least one member of an unmarried dyad on the other within the context of the dating process (1989:5)." Utah defines **domestic violence** as "any criminal offense involving violence or physical harm or threat of violence or physical harm, or any attempt, conspiracy, or solicitation to commit a criminal offense involving violence or physical harm when committed by one cohabitant against another. Victim means a cohabitant who has been subjected to domestic violence" (Utah ,77-36-2.3). Wallace (1999) defines *family violence* "as any act or omission by persons who are cohabitating that results in serious injury to other members of the family (1999:3)." Wallace includes spousal abuse within family violence. And, Goodyear-Smith and Laidlaw (1999) write:

> New Zealand defines *family violence* "as encompassing a range of behaviors, including physical, sexual, and psychological abuse, perpetrated by partners and former partners, family members and household members, and within other close personal relationships. Psychological abuse includes intimidation, harassment, damage to property, threats of physical, sexual or psychological abuse and (in relation to a child) causing or allowing the child to witness the physical, sexual, or psychological abuse of another person" (1999:285-286).

The witnessing of such violence by a child is an important concept in comprehending and combatting future violence.

Physical assault and the witnessing of such assaults have become commonplace within violent families and violent relationships. Comprehending aggression and physical assault within relationships challenges tenets long held by legal, social, and medical institutions. Under the umbrella of "domestic violence," physical assault embodies the infliction of physical injury that may include physical, sexual, and psychological abuse. Physical assault is the intentional infliction of pain, bodily injury and emotional harm, while aggression is a series of behaviors primarily intended to cause emotional harm that may escalate to physical acts of violence. Aggression and physical assault are not mutually exclusive and are often paralleling violent behaviors used to control individuals or groups.

Emotional harm is not to be minimized in that threats, stalking, destruction of property, interruption of employment activities, and verbal aggression are significant markers of intimate, family and acquaintance violence (DuPont-Morales, 1998). The emotional harm from these violent acts is devastating to those abused and to those who witness the abuse. Often witnessing abuse is traumatic and confusing and may model future reaction to conflict. This is of particular importance for children who grow up in aggressive and physically assaultive homes.

These concepts and definitions are vital to the reformation of domestic violence to "relationship violence." To refine the concept, reflecting a more accurate measurement of such violence, other characteristics of the violence must be captured including the gender of abusers, the age of abusers, the role of abusers, the impact of witnessing abuse, and the linkages between aggression and the physical assaultive acts. Such advancements – namely labeling the violence appropriately (that is, "relationship violence" rather than "domestic violence") – will broaden social scientific research, policy design, and intervention and prevention programming.

Female-on-Male Violence: Reality, Myth, or Contradiction?

When the focus of inquiry expands to "relationship violence," the first area of inquiry is female-on-male violence. What are the dynamics of such violence? How are such incidents reported? How do such incidents result in policy implementation?

Cate, Henton, Koval, Christopher, and Lloyd (1982) reported that both genders engage in premarital abuse during the dating and courtship phases of a relationship. Gwartney-Gibbs, Stockard, and Bohmer (1987) found that courtship aggression is a learned response engaged in by both parties often because of the family's use of aggression, the tolerance level of peers toward the use of aggression in relationships, and previous experiences with aggression in personal relationships.

Both young men and women equally engage in the use of violence during dating; however, women appear to use violence that is less physically debilitating (Makepeace, 1986). This is not to negate the impact of psychological abuse or the fact that "Men's experience of emotional and physical abuse from their partners deserves attention . . . [and that such abuse] leads to psychological distress and depression" (Simonelli & Ingram, 1998:681).

Strauss and Sweet (1992) researched the differences between physical aggression and verbal/symbolic aggression. Partners, to inflict psychological pain, use intentional verbal/symbolic aggression. The authors found that in a sample of 5,232 American couples, both genders engage in about equal amounts of verbal aggression. Further, verbal aggression may lead to physical aggression, and substance abuse increases the likelihood of all aggression (Strauss & Sweet, 1992:346-348).

Steinmetz (1978) first introduced "The Battered Husband Syndrome" to criticism by scholars, feminists, and family violence researchers. The claim that women may abuse men more often than the traditional perspective touched off serious criticism of Steinmetz's research and professional standing. The article reported this concept without fully delineating the characterization of such violence. Saunders' (1986) article was more important because it reported the use of violence by women in context, called for relevant research in family violence, and advocated "the application of a feminist perspective to reduce bias in such research" (1986:47). He noted that female violence might be a function of the relationship and not always a reflection of the woman. He noted that mutual combat, self-defense, and fighting back are important concepts within relationship violence.

Positioning these important pieces of research in the evolution of relationship violence is important for a full comprehension of relationship violence. Steinmetz and Lucca (1988) followed up Steinmetz's 1978 research by providing more depth to the forms of violence wives perpetrate on husbands and concluded that a society which glorifies and tolerates violence requires prevention and intervention programs for both genders, rather than holding to traditional views. A context for female violence was unfolding.

Giordano, Millhollin, Cernkovich, Pugh, and Rudolph (1999) found "that women bring to their adult intimate relationships [a] backlog of previous experiences and a view of self that is either consistent or inconsistent with the expressions of violence" (1999:32). A woman might or might not be abusive in a relationship. Giordano et al. cautioned "Feminist theories that emphasize issues of male dominance and control could be more comprehensive to the extent that they also factor in other social dynamics influencing women's lives. Giodano's et al. research reflects issues requiring stronger linkages within relationship violence. What formulates the use of aggression and physical violence by women in relationships?

The preliminary findings of a survey of college students by Hendy, Eggen, Freeman, and Gustitus (2000:1) found no significant differences in the frequency of verbal aggression or violence between partners:

> For college men, having a violent mother and a non-violent father was most associated with violence toward their current partner. For a college woman, having witnessed reciprocal violence between her parents and now receiving violence from her partner was most associated with violence toward her partner. Taken together, the present results suggest that the mother's pattern of violence appears to be the most consistent "model" for violence in the romantic relationships of both college men and women.

This survey continues to formulate the linkages important to understanding female violence.

Myopia or Ignorance?

Irrespective of this research, legal and social institutions have collapsed aggression within any relationship into "domestic violence" without enhancing statutory definitions or funding resources to address the causes and corroborate the span of relationship violence. Commensurate with this omission is the charge that the *lace curtain* - the anti-male/pro female bias has resulted in ". . . virtually no coverage of male victims of domestic violence. A computer search of over two million articles appearing in the nation's largest newspapers revealed 112 that focused on battered women and one focused on battered men" (Brott, 1994:1). While Brott made the same claim for magazines and journal articles, the irony is that numerous articles focus on both. How do we account for the discrepancy in Brott's claims and the published research? Perhaps what Brott was noting was the preference by reporters to focus on the traditional definition of domestic violence, as acts against women, rather than the reality of such violence where both victims and offenders engage, to some degree, in violent acts.

Cavanagh (1994) addressed how "myths" associated with relationship violence often misdirect the intervention of ministers and pastoral counselors (1994:48-49). His recommendation of "zero tolerance" appears ignored. Kelman (1995) wrote about family violence perpetrated by women and the extent of such violence. Her article is important because of her stated incredulous attitude toward violent women within the family. When she had documented traditional violence committed by women, it needed a perspective and an explanation. Violence committed by men did not need either.

By 1998, women abusing men was being called the "ignored violence" by Higgins of the *Boston Globe*. Higgins wrote, "Judges don't buy the concept that women are violent. What they don't realize is that violence is a societal-based problem, not a gender-based one" (Higgins, 1998:1).

Goldberg of the *New York Times* (1999) reported that in Concord, N.H., "this year nearly 35 percent of domestic arrests have been of women, up from 23 percent in 1993. In Vermont, 23 percent of domestic assault arrests this year were of women, compared to 16 percent in 1997 (1997:1). Goldberg reported that the numbers might be high because of mandatory arrest laws requiring police to arrest anyone found to have engaged in aggressive behavior. Mandatory arrest laws, intended to support female victims of domestic violence, leave little discretion about arrest to the police according to those who are concerned about mutual arrests, dual protective orders, and the increase in female arrests.

All research concerning relationship violence clearly state that male batterers generally commit substantial physical violence consistently while female violence ranges from verbal aggression, to hitting, spitting, scratching, kicking, and throwing of objects. Although males are injured by female violence, they report that their injuries are less serious and generally do not seek medical attention; however, women report their injuries as serious and tend to seek medical attention (O'Leary, Barling, Arias, Rosenbaum, Malone & Tyree, 1989). The general fear held by female advocates is that any coverage of battered men might seriously deplete the paltry amount of money allocated to medical treatment and shelters for women and their children (Brott, 1994).

The contradiction between the lace curtain and the misconception about the evolution of violence within relationships is that it is politically unwise to address such violence without engaging in gender bias. Feminists, politicians, and legal institutions incur political capital by characterizing the domestic violence scenario with the perpetrator as male and the victim as female. Such a formal practice within these institutions results in a substantial failure to prevent violence while teaching violence to future generations. What costs does society incur by minimizing violence committed by women against men? The point is that female violence is not limited to adult males. The inclusion of children as victims of relationship violence, of noting the need for victim services because of the future impact of witnessing such violence, and the funding of such services out of victim compensation programs reflects the reality and context of relationship violence. If relationship violence is reconstructed into a societal issue rather than a gender issue, then prevention might be concentrated on the acts of violence and the results of that violence.

Violence committed by women within the family institution has not been aggregated and published by mass media in the same manner as that committed by men. While scholarly journals are replete with articles on domestic violence committed by men, there is disparity when reporting domestic violence committed by women. To study this phenomenon would mean concentrating on a sample whose data is not easily generalized to the population, is possibly best illuminated using qualitative research, and includes risks to the researchers such as that faced by Steinmetz. However, the aggregation of such research might provide an impetus for policy and program development.

Children raised in violent families bring their reactions and conditioning to aggression and physical violence into other relationships. Further, statistically, women engage in aggression toward and physical abuse of children of both genders at a greater rate than males; however, males engage in sexual abuse of both genders at a greater rate. Sibling abuse that includes aggression, physical abuse and sexual abuse is probably the most common form of family violence yet it receives little research, funding, and intervention and prevention programming (Bard, 1971; Goodyear-Smith & Laidlaw, 1999; Hotaling, Strauss & Lincoln, 1990; Steinmetz, 1971).

It is clear that aggression and physical violence witnessed and received as a child determines present and future reactions to conflict, stress, and aggression irrespective of gender. Children, adolescents, college students, and adults recognize that aggression and physical assault controls other's behavior if they were controlled by such behavior themselves or witnessed the controlling of others through such behaviors.

How do we begin to study such violence? How do we formulate the same victimization statistics for the victims of female violence?

Formalizing the Data

Researchers study phenomena based on facts and observations about a topic or theme. If knowledge is to be current and relevant, information, data, and facts must be re-synthesized to include new observations. What methodology documents information about female violence in relationships that will influence future research and public policy?

In order to answer this question, statistics about female violence were attempted to be collected. Students were assigned the task of collecting such data as part of a "Women and Criminal Justice" course. Students surveyed the National Resource Center on Domestic Violence and specific cites to determine how many female-on-male violent incidents resulted in the issuance of protective orders (e.g., protection from abuse orders, protective orders, or restraining orders). Dual orders as well as permanent and temporary orders were included in the data.

The National Resource Center on Domestic Violence located in Pennsylvania did not have information on the incidence of protective orders filed by male victims nor on the number of dual orders filed between 1997 and October 1999. A telephone survey of major cities about relationship statistics on female violence produced some startling results. District Attorneys' offices, domestic or family courts, magistrates, domestic units in law enforcement, attorney generals' offices, state supreme courts, and /or domestic coalition resource centers were contacted for the information. The following sites did not keep statistics according to gender, did not know where to find such statistics, or refused to cooperate with the request.

Salt Lake City-Utah Domestic Violence Cabinet Council	4 calls
Boston-Suffolk County, MA	10 calls
San Diego-San Diego County, CA	35 calls
Phoenix-Maricopa County, AZ	3 calls
Albuquerque-Bernalillo County, NM	1 call
Los Angeles-Los Angeles County, CA	15 calls
Manhattan Borough-New York County-NY	8 calls
Philadelphia-Philadelphia County, PA	15 calls

However, statistical information was found in other counties. For example, in 1997, Miami-Dade County [Florida] reported 1,092 male petitioners with 672 repeat petitioners. Further, in 1998, the Domestic Violence Gender Report included reporting from four governmental units in Miami-Dade County. Male petitioners rose to 1,333 with repeat petitioners increasing to 688.

In Cook County (Chicago, Illinois) the issuing of protective orders from 1994 to 1997 indicated that there was a 69 percent increase for wives, a 111 percent increase for ex-wives, and a 143 percent increase for female friends. Further, the incidence according to ages of the male victims for the same categories and period indicated that under age 18 experienced a 256 percent increase with age 65 experiencing a 217 percent increase. From 1994 to 1997, males went from 601 to 1,405 protective orders, which is an increase of 134 percent.

Durham-Wake County [North Carolina] provided statistics solely on domestic violence homicides by male and female perpetrators. The victim-offender relationship for this homicide includes current or former husband or wife, parents, children, siblings, or boyfriend and girlfriend. In Dallas [Texas] during 1998, 93 males applied for a protection from abuse order and accounted for 5 percent of the applications in 1997 and again in 1998. Six percent of the time, husbands, common-law husbands, and ex-husbands were victims of family violence. In 1997, 21 percent of offenders involved in family violence in Texas were females. Lastly, Delaware County [Pennsylvania] reported that out of 602 protection-from-abuse orders, males requested 19 and four were dual orders.

It is of consequence that individuals, agencies, and associations, who should know the statistics and where to find them, did not. If the primary resource agencies could not provide such information then how is the broad context of relationship violence and zero tolerance for such violence going to be achieved? The goal is to end relationship violence, not to limit the definition and study of such violence.

Utah provided a very important factor for consideration that has an impact on the issue of dual protective orders and dual arrests. Utah has taken the concept of "primary aggressor" and redefined it as "predominant aggressor" which is key to determining the roles within relationship violence. Usually a primary aggressor is the first of the two to engage in a particular physical assault. However, the Utah concept of predominant aggressor allows for the full extent of the situation, past and present, to be considered. Law enforcement may use this concept to consider issues of self-defense, likelihood of future injury, relative severity of injuries inflicted on each person, and prior complaints of domestic violence (Utah 77-36-2.3).

The effectiveness of this concept and the move toward mandatory arrest based upon evidence of physical assault relies on the training of law enforcement regarding defensive wounds, progression of bruises, and gender differences in inflicting, sustaining, and reporting physical injuries. Law enforcement may decide to arrest and leave this decision to a prosecuting attorney or magistrate. Such a decision results in the inappropriate arrest of an individual who engaged in self-defense and not primary aggression. This also requires law enforcement to comprehend that males are far more reticent to report abuse or injury from their partners. The medical profession has not been able to delineate the full impact of such violence because of this attitude and the fear that such information would take away from the importance of services for abused women (DuPont-Morales, 1999).

It is the contextualization of female violence in relationships be it family, dating, intimacy or marriage, that proves the most difficult for determining what is data and how to report that data. For instance, consider the contextualization of an abused male in terms of the Uniform Crime Reports, the National Crime Victimization Survey and the National Family Violence Survey. How does such a victim get counted? Further, if it is the person engaging in the contextualization of the violence who determines how the data get reported, then we have to educate the masses that such violence is criminal. It is no less of a crime because the offender is female.

Utah and California, among others, extend the issue of relationship violence to include family violence. When children witness the violence, when children are part of the relationship, and when children live in violent homes, child protective agencies and the state include the children among the victims of the violence. Thus, children witnessing such abuse are provided psychological treatment as well as emotional support and intervention to enable them to learn appropriate responses to conflict. The children's welfare is monitored so that ill-advised parental visitation orders are prevented. This is another essential concept to intervene in the formation of violent and aggressive behavior in male and female children that may be exhibited in their future relationships if not addressed.

Emotional Harm and Violent Relationships

Research indicates that female-on-male violence and female violence within the family has been a subject of inquiry and concern for those who study family violence. It must be said that not all children victimized by aggression and physical violence become violent. There appears to be stronger findings that these children more often end up being victims and in adulthood engage in victimizing. Numerous surveys state that women who have used shelters, crisis hotlines, and other emergency services reported witnessing violence in their childhood. Children, however, exhibiting aggressive behavior in the shelters, irrespective of gender, often grow up to use aggression during conflict, and their mothers claim the same history (Maxwell, 1994; Goodyear-Smith & Laidlaw, 1999). It appears that children exposed to aggression and physical violence exhibit violence throughout their lives – consider school violence, dating violence in middle school, high school, college, and through adulthood. We have little research to characterize the transition of children from being victims of violence, witnessing violence, or engaging in violence in response to conflict while maturing into adulthood.

Emotional Harm Within Relationship Violence

Verbal aggression, the demeaning of a person's worth, when persistent, produces emotional harm that may be exhibited in a number of ways. One form of aggression often ignored and documented in both genders is bullying, which grows into aggressive conduct. The tormenting of another through taunts, surveillance, and encouraging others to join in or devalue the emotional harm of such conduct is another use of aggression to control an individual or a group of individuals. Such behavior in the schoolyard, the classroom, and with peers is highly disruptive.

In adulthood, this behavior is termed stalking and it has followed a course similar to domestic violence. The misconception that males do not become stalking victims or should somehow ignore the stalking behavior is parallel to males who receive aggressive and physical abuse by females. This violence is trivialized, minimized, or ignored by legal and social service agencies who could address the deviant behavior. Stalking is a form of predatory violence engaged in by teenagers as well as adults. As with relationship violence, it is a gender-neutral act where legal, social and medical services preconceptions about who the perpetrator is and who the victim is has exacerbated the problem.

Similar to relationship violence, stalking is a long-term, ongoing predatory behavior affecting the victim's life and self-esteem. Such misconceptions hamper the study of the act and the comprehension of the antecedent linkages that form the predatory behavior.

About 27 percent of all stalkers are females. When males or other family members are the victims, law enforcement and the courts have substantial difficulty in addressing the recalcitrant behavior. Males are routinely the stalkers in non-stranger, intimate, and acquaintance stalking; however, stalkers are not exclusively male. Female stalkers within the same categories usually come from dysfunctional families, often exhibit aggression and physical violent behaviors in the family or relationship in question, and may abuse substances (DuPont-Morales, 1998). Stalkers are often acquaintances who have become obsessive about the victim. The victim, to activate the criminal justice system, is referred to as an "intimate" under the "domestic violence" statutes. Often traditional statutes and law enforcement attitudes reformulate stalking behaviors into simple harassment, nuisance behavior, or a lovers' quarrel. They appear to have even more difficulty when the behavior is between family members, same-sex victims, or acquaintances. The reality is that stalking takes place in a number of contexts, and the reluctance of the legal system to address the reality of the scenarios increases the impact and duration of the victimization.

Incessant phone calls, unwanted contacts, notes and gifts, unwanted surveillance, threats, destruction of property, and signature acts that can only be attributed to the stalker cause serious emotional harm. The victim impact of stalking can be recognized by comprehending the aggression within the act, the potential for physical assault, and the resulting post-traumatic stress syndrome resulting from the act.

Discussion and Summary

Relationship violence is learned, used, and perfected over a lifespan. Violence begins in the family setting, caused by parents or siblings, and continues as a long-term reaction to conflict. While domestic violence is substantially researched, family violence, relationship violence, and sibling violence appear to be categorized within a limited context. What is the long-term impact of receiving and perpetrating violence from childhood and within the most formative relationships of life? It seems it is a consistent, prevalent continuation of such violence in all intimate relationships. Perhaps that is why relationship violence falls so easily into lifespan violence. It is simply the next step – the next relationship.

The following recommendations provide a research agenda that reflects the broader context of relationships, particularly female-on-male violence. The call for and the funding of a national survey to determine the incidence, gender, and role of bullying behavior, family violence, sibling violence, aggression, physical violence, sexual violence and stalking can form the basis for the research agenda. There should be an expectation that agencies funded to report such violence readily have the information available regardless of gender. All of these behaviors are a part of the formation or are a result of relationship violence. The recognition that violence within relationships is not about domestic violence – it is more than that. It includes the cascading impact from numerous forms of relationship violence that presents current and future risk to society.

We know from numerous surveys that we are far more likely to be at risk for violence in our homes and in those relationships most close to us. That includes the violence perpetrated by females within their relationships and their roles as daughter, sister, spouse, mother, and/or significant other. When research began to illuminate female violence within relationships, why did politics, policy, and funding persist in recognizing only male on female violence? Any form of violence must be chronicled, exposed, and detailed, irrespective of the gender of the perpetrator.

Research, policy, and government funding for programming need to recognize that relationship violence often includes mutual violence. Longitudinal studies of those in violent relationships may provide important information about reactions to conflict irrespective of the initiator. Long-term monitoring of the use of aggression and physical assault in both partners might contribute to comprehending the antecedents, which increase, decrease, and cease violence within relationships. Why is it that some move from one violent relationship to another? It is likely that they take acts of aggression with them that will move toward more physical violence? While it is sad for the adults, it is a catastrophe for children, their peers and their future relationships.

Prevention is not about attributing the battering role to a specific gender; rather it is about intervening in the cycle of violence.

CHAPTER 6

Fear of Crime and Victimization

Elizabeth H. McConnell

Why Is Fear of Crime Important in a Discussion About Victimization?

One could argue that fear of crime is an outcome of victimization. The fear we feel as a result of being victims of crime may make us give up activities in which we would normally engage. For example, people may decide that specific areas in the community pose too many risks for jobs, recreation, or shopping. People may feel compelled to spend monies for protective products, monies that they could have spent to enhance other aspects of their lives rather than on security. Fear can result from either direct or indirect victimization. An example of direct (actual) victimization would be fear of crime that people experience due to having been actual victims of crime. Baumer (1978:258) acknowledges the "ripple effect" that vicarious victimization has on people. This happens when fear of crime spreads as a result of hearing about others' criminal victimization. It is believed that fear which results from indirect victimization is more common, as this is the more likely form of victimization (Elias, 1986; Riger & Gordon, 1981; Skogan & Maxfield, 1981). Moriarty (1988) acknowledged the vicarious nature of victimization when she found that 12 percent of her research sample's fear of crime was explained by their perceived fear of crime level of spouses, other family members, best friends, co-workers, organizational co-members, and neighbors. One can conclude from these findings that opinions of "significant others" are important in shaping individuals' attitudes. For example, if one perceives "significant others" to be fearful about crime, then the individual might also develop these same fears.

How Pervasive Is the Fear of Crime?

Fear of crime is an element of daily life in American society. The degree to which it exists has been measured by many studies. According to a 1975 Harris poll, 55 percent of the adults responding to the crime survey reported that they were apprehensive when walking in their own neighborhoods (see Research & Forecasts Inc., 1980). In a later poll (Gallup, 1981) researchers found that 45 percent of the sample was afraid to walk alone at night while Garofalo, in a 1977 study, found that 45 percent of his sample limited their activities because of the fear of crime. In another study conducted throughout the state of Michigan similar results were found when it was determined that 66 percent of the respondents avoided what they perceived as high-crime areas because of their fear of crime. In a Texas study, Teske and Powell (1978:19) examined fear of crime on the basis of serious versus non-serious crime and found that more than 50 percent of their sample was fearful of becoming a victim of a serious crime within a year. Two years later, in *The Friggi Report on Fear of Crime: America Afraid*, researchers concluded that two-fifths of the national sample reported that they were extremely fearful of being victimized by a violent crime (Research & Forecasts Inc., 1980). In a more recent national survey, 43 percent of Americans participating in the 1991 General Social Survey reported being fearful of criminal victimization (National Opinion Research Center, 1991). As recently as 1995, 80 percent of Americans surveyed in a public opinion poll reported a general fear of crime (Sourcebook of Criminal Justice Statistics Online, 1997). In fact, 29 percent reported that they were "somewhat concerned," while 51 percent indicated that they were "very concerned" about becoming victims of crime (1997:156).

Is Fear of Crime a Social Problem?

The acknowledgment of fear of crime by social scientists as an important social issue is usually traced to the mid or late 1960s (Baumer, 1985; Garofalo & Laub, 1978; Smith, 1987). Concern about fear of crime gained national prominence on February 6, 1967, when President Johnson, in an address to Congress, warned legislators that "crime – and the fear of crime – has become a public malady and that it is the duty of legislators to seek a cure" (Harris, 1969:17). This message was also echoed by former Attorney General Nicholas B. Katzenbach when stating that "the fear of crime is a reality in the United States today" which is "genuine" and is "strongly felt by rural America, blue-collar white America, those who live in modest suburbs and the majority of black Americans who live in the ghetto" (Harris, 1969:1, 10-11). Katzenbach further stipulated that rural America, blue-collar white America and those who live in modest suburbs have the least to fear while black Americans who live in American ghettos have the most to fear as they are the most likely victims of crime.

In the early 1970s, researchers began to take note of a "national" fear of crime when it was recognized that the fear of crime was no longer a matter of local concern (Silver, 1974:1). Crime and fear of crime had gained such recognition that "by the end of the 1960s, some polls ranked it as the most serious problem facing our society" (Furstenberg, 1972:601).

The recognition of fear of crime as a social problem stems from the destructive effects that it has on our quality of life. For example, it makes people feel vulnerable, so much so that they may employ crime precaution measures that isolate them from society. They may refuse job offers that would require them to work in or travel through areas that are perceived as unsafe because of crime. Skogan provides one of the best discussions of the fear of crime, as a serious social problem, when he explains the infectious nature of fear. He says that:

> Fear . . . . can work in conjunction with other factors to stimulate more rapid neighborhood decline. Together, the spread of fear and other local problems provide a form of positive feedback that can further increase levels of crime. These feedback processes include (1) physical and psychological withdrawal from community life; (2) a weakening of the informal social control processes that inhibit crime and disorder; (3) a decline in the organizational life and mobilization capacity of the neighborhood, (4) deteriorating business conditions; (5) the importation and domestic production of delinquency and deviance; and (6) further dramatic changes in the composition of the population (1986:215).

Fear of Crime – Is it Sociology, Psychology, Criminology, Biology, or What?

A review of the research literature leads one to believe that fear of crime is interdisciplinary in scope, even though many researchers approach its study from a single disciplinary perspective. For example, Garofalo (1981:840) recognized the psychological dimension in the following definition, "fear is an emotional reaction characterized by a sense of danger and anxiety." Watson (1924) proposed a theory of fear where it was suggested that fear stimuli are learned, with the exception of innate fear stimuli associated with loud noise, loss of support, and pain. He believed that all other stimuli, which can produce fear, is acquired through a form of learning known as classical conditioning. According to Friedberg (1983), behavioral psychologists divide fear into three categories that are based on the origins of fear. They are (1) innate fear, that with which we are born, (2) maturing fear, that which results from physiological aging, and (3) learned fear, that which is acquired through life experiences in one's environment.

Biologically, fear involves a series of complex changes in bodily functioning that alerts an individual to potential danger (Ferraro & LaGrange, 1987). A bodily change associated with enhanced fear levels is the body's increased production of the hormone adrenaline. It is reasoned that the hormonal increase occurs because adrenaline is a power enhancer that facilitates a fight or flight response to the fear inducer. In comparison to the activities of everyday life, potent forms of fear involve intense emotional and physiological reactions to potential danger.

Scruton explains fear from a sociological perspective (1986:9). He says that human fears are most efficiently understood as social phenomenon since "fearing is an event that takes place in a social setting and it is performed by social animals whose lives and experiences are dominated by culture." In Scruton's opinion, to fully understand human fearing, for example, how fear happens in the individual, how it is expressed both to self and to others, how it is received and acted to by others in the community, it must be treated as a feature of the cultural experience; a dimension of human social life. For Scruton, learning to fear is learning what it means to understand a situation, label it accurately, feel the significance of it, express it accurately to others, and act upon it. Accordingly, "fearing is an act of interpersonal communication and, as is true of other such human transactions, this communication conveys significant cultural meaning" (1986:33).

In subsequent research, it was found that fear of crime is learned. In a test of social learning theory Moriarty (1988) determined from an analysis of six social learning variables that each were significantly related to respondents' fear of crime levels. This held true for the sample regardless of gender, age, race, or marital status.

Smith (1987) points out the interdisciplinary nature of the fear of crime by recognizing that there is an anthropology, sociology, psychology, and geography of fear. The anthropology of fear is found in studies (e.g., Merry, 1981; Smith, 1983) which indicate that fear is not discreet or clearly bounded. Smith points out that the "anxiety of crime is not so much an event as a persistent or recurring sense of malaise" (1983:235). As a sociological phenomenon, fear extends beyond the population of victims and impinges on more general aspects of well-being. The locus of the psychology of fear, Smith suggests, is within the individual, while the geography of fear concerns itself with physical characteristics of the environment such as urban or rural areas. This interdisciplinary model seems a more prudent approach in the conceptualization of fear of crime.

What Is the Definition of Fear of Crime?

Prior to measuring fear of crime, one must come to terms with its conceptual definition. According to Dubow, McCabe, and Kaplan (1979:1), "*fear of crime* refers to a wide variety of subjective and emotional assessments and behavioral reports" which are characterized by "a serious lack of consistency and specificity." Ferraro and LaGrange (1987:71) suggest that "a casual review of the literature, indicates that the phrase *fear of crime* has acquired so many divergent meanings that its current utility is negligible."

Riger and Gordon (1981:74) report that "the heart of the conceptual problems in the study of fear of crime is the definitional ambiguity surrounding the construct *fear*." Yin (1980), in a review of fear of crime literature, reports that only one study (see Sundeen & Mathieu, 1976:55) reported a definition for fear of crime. Miethe and Lee (1984:398) suggest that "the disparate findings of past studies are likely due to a lack of standardization of measures of fear." Taylor and Hale (1986) agree with Garofalo and Laub (1978) that the basis for the ongoing debate concerning the meaning or construct validity of fear of crime is measurement of fear of crime that is intermingled with other fears. Even though conceptual problems with the concept of fear have been examined by many researchers (see Baumer, 1978; Clemente & Kleiman, 1977; Ferraro, 1995; Fowler & Mangione, 1974; Garofalo & Laub, 1977; McConnell, 1989; Moriarty, 1988; Williams & Akers, 1987), consensus has not been reached regarding a precise definition or measurement. A general view is that what is broadly being tapped is an emotional response to a threat, an acknowledgement that crime is intimidating and a sense of concern about being harmed. This might more appropriately be labeled fear of anticipated criminal victimization rather than fear of crime.

Another major problem with the conceptualization of fear of crime as noted by Ferraro and LaGrange (1987:73) is the "generic reference of the term *crime*." They suggest that crime refers to a wide variety of activities and that fear of being victimized varies by the type of crime considered. They suggest that to obtain the most valid and reliable indicators of the fear of crime, "it is best to specify the type of crime to the respondent rather than leave it up to the respondent's own inference" (1987:74).

Is Fear of Crime the Same Thing as Risk of Victimization?

According to Clarke and Lewis (1982:51), "Furstenberg made a contribution to conceptual clarification by drawing attention to the important analytical distinction between concern about crime and fear of victimization." Furstenberg (1971) suggests that fear of crime can be measured by a person's perception of one's own chances of victimization, whereas concern is based on the individual's estimation of the seriousness of criminal activity in one's locality or society. Elias (1986:118) suggests that fear of crime and concern about crime are different and can be distinguished in that "fear seems to imply a much more immediate danger – and a much more intense psychological response than concern." Lotz (1979) differentiates between fear of crime and concern about crime by suggesting that low-income people express greater fear of crime, perhaps because they risk victimization more, yet the other income groups show more concern about crime.

Furstenberg (1971) criticized the Harris Poll surveys and the President's Crime Commission studies in America for using two concepts interchangeably, that is, fear of crime and risk of victimization. And even though he found the methodology for the studies lacking, Furstenberg (1971:602) suggests that the research results provide the "best and virtually the only source of information on public reaction to crime up until 1970." The Commission's findings, summarized in *The Challenge of Crime in a Free Society* (President's Crime Commission Law Enforcement and Administration of Justice, 1967), reveal fear of crime to be most intense among residents of ghetto areas, especially low-income blacks. Furstenberg's (1972) re-evaluation of the original data suggests that those concerned about crime often have comparatively little to be concerned about, yet they usually employ more crime precaution behaviors than those who are the most likely victims of crime.

Is Fear of Crime the Same Thing as Worry About Crime?

Garofalo (1981) and Maxfield (1984) define fear as a sense of danger and anxiety produced from the threat of physical danger. The researchers suggest that fear is linked to violent crime and physical harm and that worry is associated with the emotional responses to property crimes. Levy and Guttman (1985:251) attempt to differentiate the interrelations among feelings of worry, fear, concern and coping under a general situation of stress. From a review of the literature they found that "no generally accepted technical definitions existed for distinguishing among worry, fear, and concern." Their findings indicate that "to worry does not coincide with fear but rather that fear is a sufficient but not a necessary condition of worry" (1985:258). This finding of an asymmetric relationship between worry and fear provides evidence that fear must generally be accompanied by worry, but worry can take place without fear. They further recognize that fear is expressed cognitively (mental reactions) and that worry is expressed effectively (emotional reactions). Eve (1985) concludes that Sundeen and Mathieu (1976), Eve and Eve (1984), and Warr (1984) acknowledge the confounding problems associated with fear of personal victimization and concern about crime whereas most other fear of crime researchers, prior to 1985, confound fear with concern in their operationalizing of fear of crime.

Fisher (1978) suggests that in the conceptualization of fear of crime one should keep in mind the distinction between actual and anticipated fear. Accordingly, Garofalo (1981) suggests that a person walking alone in a high-crime neighborhood is experiencing something different than the person who is telling an interviewer of would be fear in an area at night. Garofalo does not discount the importance of anticipated fear, but only suggests that conceptually the two are distinct and that the operationalization of fear of crime should reflect these differences.

Is Fear of Crime the Fear of Strangers?

Garofalo and Laub (1978:245) recognize that "what has been conceptualized as the *fear of crime* has its roots in something more diffuse than the perceived threat of some specific danger in the immediate environment." They indicate that one factor other than actual fear of crime which may be involved in respondents' attitudes is anxiety about strangers. Baumer (1978:259) concludes that since the President's Commission first suggested the phrase "fear of strangers" it has become commonplace to pronounce that "the fear of crime is a fear of strangers." McIntyre (1967) and Ennis (1967) indicate that the precautions people take to protect themselves against strangers, even though the proportion of violent crimes committed by strangers is relatively small, supports the view that fear of crime is fear of strangers. Other researchers have recognized the conceptual dilemma of fear of crime and fear of strangers (Baumer, 1978; Brooks, 1974; Conklin, 1975; Hindelang, Gottfredson & Garofalo, 1978; Hunter, 1974; Hunter & Baumer, 1982; Merry, 1981; Reiss, 1967; Riger, Gordon & LeBailly, 1978; Smith, 1987). Baumer argues that "although fear might be directed towards strangers, it is probable that only certain types of strangers, perceived to be potentially dangerous are likely to evoke fear" (1978:257).

Are Fear of Crime and Vulnerability the Same Thing?

Another problem in defining fear of crime is the possibility of confounding fear as general anxiety about crime and vulnerability, see for example, Miethe and Lee (1984), Lawton and Yaffee (1980), and Yin (1980). Yin suggests that although vulnerability might be a dimension of fear, it appears necessary since vulnerability reflects one's perception of particular physical or environmental circumstances rather than subjective anxiety about crime per se (1980). Hansson and Carpenter (1986) report that fear of crime among the elderly may be more related to what an individual brings to the situation, i.e., personality and personal competencies rather than actual factors such as crime rates or victimization experiences. Normoyle and Lavrakas (1984) support this view through research in which fear of crime is strongly related to perceptions of predictability and control and not related to previous victimization experience. Fuentes and Gatz (1983) also found fear of crime in older adults to be unrelated to actual neighborhood crime rates, while it was related to one's sense of personal mastery or self-efficacy.

Ferraro and LaGrange (1987:71) indicate that "a major problem in conceptualizing fear of crime is the confounding of fear with risk or vulnerability to crime." Yin's (1980:496) research supports this finding when he concluded that "[al]though fear of crime is almost never explicitly defined by researchers, their measurements suggest that such fear is implicitly defined as the perception of the probability of being victimized." Other researchers have examined fear of crime, risk for crime, and vulnerability to crime. For example, some researchers have examined the safety assessment of one's environment as *fear of crime* (Dubow et al., 1979; Silberman, 1980), while another examined fear as a general tendency to be fearful (Erikson, 1976).

What Is the Best Measure – Single Item Or Multiple Item Indicators of Fear of Crime?

In a review of the fear of crime research, Ferraro and LaGrange (1987) focused attention on fear of crime indexes when they noted the use of single-item versus multiple-item indicators of fear of crime. They found that "40 percent of the 46 studies they reviewed relied solely upon a single-item indicator of fear of crime while 28.3 percent employed more than one *fear* measure, yet analyzed them individually rather than as a multiple-item construct" (1987:74). As a result they suggest the use of multiple-item indicators when measuring "abstract theoretical constructs such as fear of crime" (1987:74-75). They also recognize other problems inherent in the use of multiple-item indicators, such as proper construction and testing of indices and scales to assure that they possess "appropriate psychometric properties" and "the publication of reliability coefficients to substantiate the reliability of test instruments." They report (1987:75) that only two of the 13 studies that utilized a fear of crime index reported reliability coefficients for their indexes (see Lee, 1982; Miethe & Lee, 1984).

Ferraro and LaGrange (1987:76) recognize that "much of the fear of crime research is characterized by measurement problems." They argue that the most common measure of fear of crime, "How safe do you feel walking alone at night in your neighborhood?" is more a measure of judgment about possible victimization in one's neighborhood. It is their contention that what should be measured is the emotional reaction of fear rather than judgment about victimization. Garofalo (1979:82) also recognizes this dilemma and suggests that the National Crime Survey (NCS, now called the National Crime Victimization Survey, NCVS) measure "How safe do you feel or would you feel being out alone in your neighborhood?" mixes actual with hypothetical assessments of safety and fails to discriminate risk judgments about crime from emotional fears of crime. Ferraro and LaGrange (1987) suggest that measuring fear of crime might best be achieved through analysis of life experiences such as assessments of fear associated with specific victimizations.

Is Victimization an Appropriate Fear of Crime Measure?

According to Gates and Rhoe (1987:427), "fear of crime is the affective experience associated with the perceived personal risk of victimization." Fear of crime has been more often defined in the literature as "an emotional reaction characterized by a sense of danger and anxiety about the potential for physical harm in a criminal victimization" (Garofalo, 1981:839); thus the predilection of some to use victimization as a measure of fear of crime. Sundeen and Mathieu (1976:55) define fear of crime as "the amount of anxiety and concern that persons have over being a victim." Agnew (1985:236) reports that much research "in this area tends to treat the individual as a 'black box,' assuming that victimization leads directly to fear."

Yin (1980:496) reports that most measurements of fear of crime implicitly define fear as "the perception of the probability of victimization." He argues that although victimization is important, it is not a sufficient measure in that it does not incorporate the "frightful elements" of fear of crime such as serious physical injury, property loss, or ability to recuperate. A more comprehensive utilization of victimization as a fear measure is the analysis of fear on the basis of specific-offense victimization. Several researchers (see for example Lalli & Savitz, 1976; McConnell, 1989; Sundeen & Mathieu, 1976; Warr, 1984; Warr & Stafford, 1983) measured fear of crime through examination of victimization associated with specific offenses. This approach according to Ferraro and LaGrange (1987:82) "provides better measures of fear of victimization than most other studies" and "are good baselines for further analyses." Similarly, Williams and Akers (1987) compared measurement approaches in fear of crime research and concluded that the best instrument for measuring fear of crime is a specific-offense victimization-chance scale.

In attempts to discover the relationship between victimization and fear of crime, researchers have divided victimization into distinct categories; (1) direct and indirect victimization, (2) actual and vicarious victimization, (3) traditional and nontraditional victimization, and (4) property and violent crime victimization (see for example Conklin, 1975; Hindelang, 1975; Taylor & Hale, 1986; Toseland, 1982). Believing that time between victimization and measurement impacts measurement outcomes, several researchers incorporated the element of time in their assessment of victimization. For example lifetime, recent, remote, vicarious, and anticipated victimization were examined by Williams and Akers (1987) and McConnell (1989). However, the previous researchers generally agree that the key focus of the victimization perspective is to specify the crime-fear linkage. They also acknowledge that the connection between criminal victimization and fear of crime is not straightforward. Several studies have been reported which tend to support the victimization perspective (see Balkin, 1979; Lindquist & Duke, 1982; Lurigio, 1987; Skogan & Maxfield, 1981; Stafford & Galle, 1984; Tyler, 1980). Even though there appears to be some support for the victimization perspective, numerous researchers conducting quantitative studies found that at best there is only a weak relationship between victimization and fear of crime (for example, Agnew, 1985; Dubow et al., 1979; Hindelang, Gottfredson & Garofalo, 1978; Reiss, 1982; Rifia, 1982; Sparks, Glenn & Dodd, 1977; Taylor & Hale, 1986).

Conclusion

One can conclude from the foregoing review of fear of crime research that validity and reliability problems are considerable in the measurement of fear of crime. One of the most elementary problems is the lack of a generally accepted definition of fear of crime. The definitions used in past operationalizations of the variable seem almost as numerous as the researchers. As long as researchers continue to measure fear of crime through assessments of variables such as any of the diverse types of victimization, risk, vulnerability, or avoidance behaviors, one can expect questionable outcomes. It appears that measuring fear of crime requires a much broader array of indicators, certainly multiple-item measures such as indexes. One of the better attempts to incorporate many of the indicators of fear of crime is Ferraro's (1995:18) generic model of fear of crime that he based on individuals' interpretation of risk. Components of the model include ecological variables such as crime prevalence and community traits that include incivility and cohesion, and personal variables such as victimization, status and residential traits and perceived risk. He points out that both fear and behavioral adaptations, such as constrained and defensive actions, can result from individuals' interpretation of risk. Even though Ferraro's model for assessing fear of crime is one of the more inclusive models proposed to date, it does not reflect comprehensive indicators for predicting fear of crime. He acknowledges this dilemma when suggesting that "although the personal variables may still well explain the bulk of the variance in fear of crime, other ecological variables merit consideration" (1995:121). What is needed is a means of measuring individuals' thoughts, emotions, perceptions, symptoms, and behaviors that are associated with fear of crime.

The most important consideration in the development of valid fear of crime measures is the acknowledgement that fear of crime is an interdisciplinary phenomenon. As a result, researchers cannot let their disciplinary biases limit their conceptualization and operationalization of the fear of crime. What is required are measurements based on an integration of the relevant disciplinary perspectives, for example, sociology, psychology, criminology, anthropology, and geography.

CHAPTER 7

Restoration and the Criminal Justice System

Jon'a F. Meyer

It was not the first time she had injured her little brother, but it may have been her last. Glenda was certainly tired of Gene's refusals to cooperate when she tried to teach him how to ride a bicycle. He kept freezing on her as though he were frightened. Knowing that the path was safe, she told him to stop acting like a "sissy" and to start pedaling. Alas, the poor boy clenched the handlebars and refused to pedal, requiring her to support the moving bicycle so that it would not teeter. Furious that he was not performing up to her expectations, she angrily pushed him and the bicycle to the ground and ran home. Gene showed up later with a conspicuous ring around his right eye where the handlebar had struck him during the fall. His eye was swollen shut and was watering. He had sustained numerous scratches and bruises all over his body. Glenda's mother was angry and immediately "sentenced" her to take care of Gene's wounds. Glenda waited on him hand and foot until he recovered.

Somewhere between his injury and recovery, Glenda began to view Gene as someone who had suffered due to her actions. She could not easily dismiss his winces as she dressed his wounds. He could no longer help her with her homework because his vision was affected by the patch he wore over his eye, and she missed his assistance. As she did his chores in addition to her own, she saw how much work he really did at their family home to care for the family's livestock. She came to view him as an equal, someone who deserved better treatment. Glenda was truly sorry she had deliberately caused such damage. Of interest, she never struck or hurt him again.

The ideas behind this sanction were not entirely invented by Glenda's mother. Had Glenda been Tlingit (a Northwestern native peoples), she would have had to attend to Gene until he recovered (de Laguna, 1972:511), similar to what her mother required her to do. Had she been a member of Mi'K-maq Nation of Nova Scotia (Canada), she would have been ordered to make restitution to Gene in addition to caring for him: "In this way the child is very much aware of his wrongdoings and usually will never forget that incident or the events that led up to it" (Marshall, 1991:6). Had she been traditional Navajo, she would have been held responsible, even as a child, for the injuries she had caused, by first apologizing to and then somehow compensating Gene for the harm she caused him (Vicenti, Jimson, Conn & Kellogg, 1972:147). In other words, Glenda's sanction was not some peculiar invention of an eccentric mother who wanted to transfer her own motherly nursing duties onto her daughter. Instead, Glenda's mother wanted her to learn a lesson while simultaneously making Gene "whole" again. Glenda had been held accountable for the wrongs she caused.

From Restoration to Retribution and Back Again: The History of Restorative Justice

Some may find it interesting that Glenda's sanction, despite its lack of easily identified severity (e.g., she could have been threatened with a spanking or ordered to spend time in a corner or in her room as these punishments were common in her family), seemed to have reduced her chances of mistreating her little brother. The likely reason is that Glenda began to view her brother as someone who had been harmed by her actions. Working to restore him to his pre-crime status lead Glenda to reanalyze her actions toward him, making this penalty effective in "curing" her of her tendency to abuse Gene.

Despite its effectiveness, it is unlikely that this sanction would have ever been applied to Glenda in a modern American criminal court. Had Glenda been charged with the battery of Gene, she would probably be fined or put on probation and ordered to attend anger management counseling. If the judge thought she needed a stronger lessen (e.g., if this was not her first time abusing Gene or if the injuries were very severe) she might even be jailed. These sanctions are considered to be retributive (e.g., punishing offenders because they deserve to be penalized for their actions), incapacitative (e.g., jailing offenders to protect future victims from harm), rehabilitative (e.g., putting offenders on probation to ensure that they get services and programming they need to prevent future criminality), or deterrence-based (e.g., punishing an offender because doing so demonstrates what happens to lawbreakers and deters that offender and/or others from committing crimes in the future). While these sentencing philosophies are admirable for their ability to prevent crime, none of the four appreciates the central role played by the victim in the criminal justice drama. There is a fifth philosophy that both reduces crime and focuses on the victim: restoration.

Restoration, also called restorative justice, is a sentencing philosophy in which the goals are to restore both the victim and offender to their pre-crime status. During this process, the community in which the offense took place is also returned to balance. The basic idea is that offenders try to make up for the harm they have caused through apologies, financial payments to victims, work service, and other restorative-based concepts. While the criminal justice system cannot feasibly order offenders to "undo" every one of their crimes, it can provide structured settings in which offenders may attempt to repair the harms they have caused to others. Many such programs are being operated in jurisdictions around the world.

Although it may seem like a new approach, restorative justice is actually a very ancient form of justice. In fact, restoration was around long before prisons and other forms of punishment. About two thousand years before the birth of Christ, the Babylonian Code of Hammurabi ordered that victims receive compensation from those who had harmed them (Hammurabi circa 1750 BC). Flood damage incurred by neighbors due to careless irrigation, for example, meant certain restitution to those neighbors for the damage to their own land. Many criminal injuries resulted in specific monetary payments made to the victims, as in the restitution of 10 shekels if a "freed man strike the body of another freed man." Almost ironic by today's standards, this ancient code dictated that unintentional injuries resulting from a quarrel should not be criminally punished if the offender paid the victim's physician's fees. It is clear that one purpose of the Code of Hammurabi was to use restitution to "undo" the harms caused by others.

Another ancient system that used restoration was Islamic law, which encouraged (and still does) victims to "pardon" offenders from criminal punishment. The offenders then provide the victims with compensatory payments to make up for the injuries (Al-Sagheer, 1994:81, 85). In this country, many Native American nations made restoration the core of their criminal justice systems (Meyer, 1998); early Navajos, for example, relied on the assistance of respected leaders who helped offenders and victims fashion the appropriate response to and restitution in a variety of criminal cases (Yazzie & Zion, 1996:168). In these early legal systems, crimes were considered violations of people's rights, and victims were to be compensated for the intentional and unintentional harms they suffered at the hands of others.

During the first part of the twelfth century, offenses took on a new meaning. Instead of being viewed as offenses against individuals, crimes (in particular, violent crimes) were redefined by King Henry I, through his *Leges Henrici*, to be against the king or government (Jubilee Policy Group, 1992:10-11; Umbreit, 1994:1). Sometimes criminal offenses were referred to as "breaches of the King's Peace," demonstrating the new focus on the punishment of offenders with little input from, or concern about, victims. Fines and estate forfeiture to the crown replaced restitution made to victims; the king's coffers swelled at the expense of victims who had suffered the actual harm. In fact, convicted thieves were ordered to turn over stolen property to the Crown rather than to the victimized owners (Greek, 1991). Victims who wanted compensation were directed to rely on the civil courts (McDonald, 1992:183), and had to incur the expense and unpredictability of this forum. Although his system was transformed over time [e.g., the 1215 Magna Carta limited the Crown's most egregious abuses of due process to seize assets (Spooner 1852:192)], King Henry I began a seemingly irreversible trend toward viewing the state as the central victim in every crime.

As Great Britain's quilt of control spread over other continents, native restorative systems were replaced by punitive Anglo-Saxon systems. Nigeria and Gambia, and other African countries once employed restorative justice paradigms as their primary form of justice before they "received" their current legal system from the British (Adeyemi, 1994:55). Similarly, the before mentioned Native American restorative initiatives were replaced by the dominant white legal system, first in a piecemeal fashion, then by Congressional mandate in 1885 (Meyer, 1998; Pflüg, 1996:192). Even New Zealand's indigenous restorative justice system was "quickly" replaced by one that was more acceptable to the British (Pratt, 1996:139). It is important to recognize that none of these nations felt they were in need of a new justice paradigm. In fact, they were satisfied with their own traditional forms of justice and felt that imposed justice systems were inferior to their own indigenous processes (Adeyemi, 1994:61).

Restoration is now enjoying a gradual comeback. At first, a few programs serving limited numbers of individuals sprung up across the United States (Umbreit, 1994). Then, entire jurisdictions began to formalize their use of restorative justice under at least some circumstances, typically for non-serious offenses or cases involving juvenile offenders (McCold, 1996:89). The state of Vermont is an example of a jurisdiction that has turned to restorative justice as a way to meet its goals. When state policymakers recognized the severity of the overcrowding in and the rising costs of their jails combined with the uncomfortable realization that existing programs were not reducing crime or satisfying the public, they began looking for more effective options and finally adopted a state-wide restorative justice initiative (Lynch, 1997). The United States is not the only country that has begun endorsing restorative justice. Justice systems around the world have recently rediscovered restorative justice and are turning to it as a form of alternative processing for non-serious cases. A few jurisdictions have even successfully employed restorative justice concepts with crimes as serious as manslaughter and attempted murder (Flaten, 1996; Shepard, 1987).

The Ideas Behind Restorative Justice and Restitution

The primary goal of restorative justice is "to address and balance the rights and responsibilities of victims, offenders, communities, and the government" (Van Ness, 1996:28). In other words, restorative justice seeks to return to society a sense of balance and equality whenever it is disrupted through crime. Victims, offenders, and communities are entitled to experience this sense of societal tranquility and harmony, but share responsibility for ensuring that the social fabric remains intact. Government should play an active role in this process by facilitating restorative justice programming.

An important goal of restoration is to hold offenders accountable for their crimes. Retributive sanctions such as incarceration and fines allow offenders to be "passive recipients of punishment" (Van Ness, 1996:27). In reality, retributive sanctions are done *to* offenders regardless of whether they have accepted responsibility for their offenses. Under retributive regimes, it is easy for offenders to continue with their negative actions after completing their sentences, especially if they place blame for their offenses on others (e.g., thieves who claim that their victims can easily afford the losses due to shoplifting and/or that they deserve victimization because they overcharge consumers).

Offenders are forced to accept responsibility when they work together with their victims to design restorative packages that may involve sincere apologies, compensation, participation in counseling programs, community service, or other proposals tailored to the offense, offender, and/or victim. Full participation in restorative justice initiatives prevents offenders from displacing blameworthiness onto other individuals or vague social realities such as unemployment (Yazzie & Zion, 1995:72-77). Restorative justice paradigms force offenders to take responsibility for their wrongs and to play a role in "making it right" (McCold, 1996:87; McElrea, 1996:78).

Another goal of restorative justice is to eliminate the benefits offenders derive from their crimes (Adeyemi, 1994:54). Through solemn meetings with their victims in which the victims are allowed to express their anger and grief, offenders are able to learn the impacts of their actions on others. Victims sometimes need the catharsis granted by these meetings to reassure them that they were not to blame in their offense (e.g., that their home was not burglarized solely because they spent many evenings out of their home or because it appeared to be an easy target due to the owners being elderly) and to help them "restore predictability and order in their lives" (McCold, 1996:87; Van Ness, 1996:23).

Ironically, retributive sanctions do little to restore victims; instead they merely ensure that both the victim and offender have been punished (Van Ness, 1996:27). Rather than elevating victims to their pre-crime status, retributive sanctions instead attempt to impose equality by using punishment to reduce offenders to the level of their victims. This approach is not beneficial for either victims or offenders. Offenders are responsible for their crimes and should be made to acknowledge their actions and the effects of those actions on others. By doing this, they are able to compensate their victims, remind them of their guiltlessness, and return to them a sense of security.

The "rawest" form of restorative justice occurs when an offender undoes the specific harm s/he caused. For example, when a retired police officer on the Navajo reservation caught a group of juveniles spray painting graffiti on his property, he was understandably angry. The young hoodlums had caused a good deal of damage that was going to cost him time and money to repair.

Instead, he asked the juveniles to paint over their graffiti with a message of his choosing: "Stop the violence: unity." The juveniles complied and to this day, the retired officer's property reminds all who drive by about this important message. The victim was pleased with the outcome (he now has an expertly painted mural on his property) and the offenders have the satisfaction of knowing that they did a good deed for a fellow member of their community, were shown that their artwork can be appreciated if it is limited to appropriate situations, and were able to overcome the stigma of being labelled as common criminals. Unfortunately, many offenses cannot so neatly be undone as by painting peaceful messages over hateful ones. In these cases, restoration must be achieved through more indirect means, including restitution and community service.

Restitution involves any form of compensation provided to an injured party. It is common for both crime victims and those who suffer civil wrongs (e.g., someone who incurs medical bills in an accident that is attributed to another person). Restitution has a long history in the United States. We know it was practiced with regularity by Native American nations (Meyer, 1998), but it was also part of the settlers' legal systems. In fact, the first codified laws in this country, the 1636 Plymouth Colony laws, ordered restitution to those who suffered damages by others' livestock (Langdon, 1966:207). Unique because it extended restitution to crime victims, William Penn's 1692 legal code ordered restitution to victims' families in cases of manslaughter and murder; one-third to one-half of offenders' estates were forfeited to the victims' families (Greek, 1991). Although it was rare, restitution did exist.

Due in part to the victims' rights movement in the 1970s, restitution is now an everyday occurrence (Klein, 1988:7). Many misdemeanor and felony courts mandate restitution in cases in which victims have suffered an identifiable loss. Typically, it is imposed as a condition of probation (Glaser & Gordon, 1988:2), or is imposed in addition to other penalties, including incarceration. Federal guidelines even allow restitution as the sole penalty for certain non-serious offenses, and allow it to be a condition of probation or supervised release in more serious cases (Wray, 1994:18). Offenders are often ordered to provide restitution to reimburse their victims for any medical interventions necessary to treat their injuries. When a Hmong man living in Minnesota survived a stabbing, he asked for and received from his attacker $895.00 for a traditional Hmong healing ceremony that involved the ritualistic slaughter of a cow and other animals (Sandok, 1997). More commonly, offenders are ordered to foot the bill for medical treatments or psychological counseling to help their victims recover.

In some cases, the restitution provided by offenders is nearly an exact match, such as replacing one damaged automobile with a similar automobile or repairing a damaged wall to return it to its original condition. More likely, however, the aggrieved party is provided with monetary compensation. This compensation is most sensible when it is property that has been damaged or stolen, so that a victim of a theft is provided with the funds to replace a stolen television or broken window.

One weakness of financial restitution is that it cannot fully address sentimental values attached to property. If a family heirloom is stolen and sold, the victim may receive payments that allow the replacement of a like item, but s/he may feel that the lost property cannot truly be replaced. Jewelry received as gifts from loved ones or passed down from generation to generation, for example, often has much more value to the recipient than it does to others. Having judges or other criminal justice personnel set values for such nostalgic items may make victims feel that they have been cheated out of justice. A second weakness of financial restitution occurs when the crime is violent rather than property-related. How does one accurately place a "value" on assault, battery, rape, or other violent offenses? Does allowing restitution belittle the traumas suffered by victims? These are important questions that are hard to address. A final weakness of restitution is that offenders sometimes fail to make the payments, causing victims even more suffering; one study found that offenders may be less likely to complete restitution payments than they are to pay fines (Gordon & Glaser, 1991:559). Despite these limitations, however, restitution still does a much better job of compensating the victim for the harm s/he has suffered than any of the other four sentencing philosophies.

Restitution does more than return to victims lost property and/or intangibles (e.g., health following medical treatment of an injury). Through restitution, offenders are allowed to "make good" on their crimes and to restore and redefine themselves as non-criminals. While it is hard for some people to imagine, offenders are victimized by their own crimes (Van Ness, 1996:23-24). Consider that committing offenses reminds offenders that they no longer belong to the majority of society who are law-abiding and that this loss of their sense of belonging can further propel offenders into a criminal lifestyle. By returning stolen property or providing the funds with which to replace stolen goods, thieves are permitted to re-enter society without the stigma associated with their offenses. Similarly, other offenders can make significant strides in repairing the harms they have caused. This process lies at the heart of restorative justice. Rather than paying a debt to society, offenders satisfy debts to their victims, and doing so allows them to overcome the shame of and to learn from their offenses.

Another form of indirect compensation is community service. Like restitution, community service has been around for a long time. In Rome, offenders "could be spared worse punishment" if they contributed labor to socially beneficial civic projects such as building roads (McDonald, 1992:184). In this country, drunkards in colonial Boston were sometimes sentenced to chop wood as community service (Klein, 1988:175). Similar to its ancient roots, contemporary community service typically involves working for non-profit or government agencies such as youth and charitable organizations, hospitals and homes for the elderly or handicapped individuals, recycling centers, schools, parks, sports centers, and libraries (Leibrich, Galaway & Underhill, 1986:60; Meeker, Jesilow & Aranda, 1992:200). Sometimes, offenders work for those they have injured, as in the case of youths who break windows or otherwise damage store property. In other cases, the victims designate where offenders will work, that is, in a charity of their choosing. Most often, however, offenders work for whatever agencies the courts have established as valid work sites.

One attraction of community service as a restorative routine is that it serves entire communities by providing valuable labor to organizations that are in need of assistance. Another benefit is that it can be used in cases where offenders cannot afford to make financial payments to victims or where losses are difficult to address through restitution (Harland, 1980:429; Leibrich et al., 1986:58). Finally, restitution may be utilized when no financial loss occurs to victims (e.g., due to insurance coverage), where specific victims cannot be identified (e.g., in cases of public intoxication), or where victims prefer not to participate in other restitutive programs (Pease, 1985:52). While it is no panacea, community service appears to be a solution for many sentencing dilemmas.

Public Support for Restorative Justice

Before restorative justice can be considered as an option, it is important that it be palatable to the public. It makes sense that victims of property crimes would like to be compensated for their lost or damaged possessions, but are they willing to "sacrifice" their interests in punitive sanctions in favor of strictly restorative paradigms? Also, what about the public in general, do they feel that restorative justice has potential in their communities? Researchers have found general public support for restitution and community service (Lee, 1996:339) and for more specific restorative programming such as victims meeting with offenders to ask questions of and express their feelings to offenders (Umbreit, 1994). Some members of the public may see restorative justice as a cost-effective way to pay back victims and keep offenders productive, while others view it as more humanitarian than retributive sanctions (Challeen, 1980:48).

Not unexpectedly, offenders appear to prefer restorative justice programs to retributive sanctions. One research team found that the majority of offenders who were given a choice wanted to meet with those whom they had victimized (Novack, Galaway & Hudson, 1980:65). The team also found high levels of post-sentence satisfaction among offenders who had received community service sanctions in addition to financial restitution (Novack et al., 1980:66). It is possible that offenders derive some enjoyment from participating in constructive sanctions such as community service and restitution that allow them to repay the communities they have harmed. Along these lines, one judge noted that some offenders pay more restitution than they are ordered to provide (Challeen, 1980:8) and several researchers have found that those ordered to complete community service sometimes continue volunteering well past their sentences (Leibrich et al., 1986:61; Novack et al., 1980:66). One reason that offenders may continue working at community service sites is that they see the experience as a way to learn new skills, meet people, and contribute to their communities (Leibrich et al., 1986:61).

Even members of the justice system seem to approve of restorative justice initiatives. One survey found that judges and probation officers are pleased with restorative justice: judges like having community service as an additional option in their sentencing toolbox, while probation officers are supportive of the fact that community service sentences can be flexible and personalized (Leibrich et al., 1986:62). Judge Dennis Challeen (1980:49) is vocal in his support of community service and restitution as "positive" sanctions:

> Our present system neglects most inmates who simply do dead time with no benefit to themselves, their victims, or society. Restitution sentencing saves taxpayers money, it builds self-esteem, and it makes a productive individual out of the offender. It also repays victims and the community and, from all indications, has a much lower [recidivism] rate . . . It makes the offender accountable to, instead of a burden on, society.

Victims, too, seem to appreciate restorative justice paradigms. One researcher found that nearly all (94%) of burglary victims in his study felt that fairness demanded restitution and 90 percent of those individuals wanted to be involved in attending meetings to set the amount of restitution (Umbreit, 1989:53). Ironically, although it was their desires for restitution that lead them to seek victim-offender mediation meetings, actually obtaining that restitution was not in the top three reasons for victims' satisfaction with the meetings; instead, victims were most likely to cite meeting and communicating with the offenders when asked what they found most satisfying (Umbreit, 1989:56). Another research team found that although they were less enthusiastic about restorative justice than offenders, the majority of crime victims wanted to meet with offenders (Novack et al., 1980:65). Researchers in New Zealand found that those who had been victimized by juveniles wanted both restitution and to confront the offenders (Morris, Maxwell & Robertson, 1993:309). Taken together, these studies suggest that victims are not unlikely to request participation in restorative justice programs. There is also some evidence that victims can move beyond their experiences and forgive offenders. An American judge, for example, noted that some victims have actually hired offenders who had been ordered to provide restitution through working for them (Challeen, 1980:8); this demonstrates that victims can be comfortable with these arrangements and are willing to overlook offender's crimes when they have worked to "undo" the harm they caused.

This is not to say that victims endorse restorative justice under all circumstances. Victims of violent offenses may not be ready to meet with offenders until years have passed since the crimes they experienced. For violent offenses, some individuals feel that retribution and restoration should be combined so that offenders are punished but are also given a chance to repay their victims and overcome the stigma of their crimes. Research in Latin America has shown that victims prefer to be compensated for their losses in minor offenses, but want incarceration in addition to restorative justice for serious offenses (Carranza, Liverpool & Rodríguez-Manzanera, 1994:416). Even justice system actors recognize that certain serious offenses "do not fit easily into" restorative justice (Challeen, 1980:9). In response to this general feeling, judges tend to utilize restorative justice elements much like other intermediate sanctions – using them with offenders with little or no prior record who have been charged with low to moderately serious offenses (Leibrich et al., 1986:58).

One issue that proponents of restorative justice often raise is that restorative justice programs cost far less than incarceration, both in terms of financial costs and due to the lost productivity of jailed offenders (Cocks, 1982:31). Although it may mean that fewer costly detention facilities are needed, restorative justice should not be utilized solely as a way to save money; jurisdictions should not design restorative justice initiatives unless they are willing to commit adequate assets to make it an effective option (McElrea, 1996:82-83). Moving to restorative justice to reduce the criminal justice budget rather than provide better justice outcomes does little to advance the treatment of victims.

Conclusion

Rising fear of crime and repeated calls by the public for improvements to the criminal justice system are signals that society is ready for a change. It is now time to overcome our base desires for revenge and return to a system that is both effective and victim-centered. Restorative justice approaches are three-time winners. First, these programs appear to reduce levels of recidivism (Challeen, 1980:49; Griffiths & Hamilton, 1996:183; Moon, 1995:A8; Yazzie & Zion, 1996:170-72). This alone makes restorative justice worth a second look. Then, restorative routines successfully tackle the need to return victims to their pre-crime status. Third, restorative justice serves the communities in which crimes take place by providing reassurance that justice can follow offenses. Restorative justice can fill an important niche in criminal justice by providing a significant intermediate sanction that is beneficial to victims, offenders, and communities. In serious cases, restorative routines can be utilized in addition to retribution-based penalties to provide valuable peace to victims. Victims' cries of "Make me whole" should not go unanswered by a system that appears to be preoccupied with punishing the guilty at the expense of the well-being of victims. There are better alternatives.

CHAPTER 8

Victim Impact Statements:
Fairness to Defendants?

Ida M. Johnson
Etta F. Morgan

Introduction

Historically, the crime victim was the forgotten entity in the criminal justice process. Victims took on passive roles as observers. They were not given an opportunity to voice their opinions or concerns regarding the crime and how the crime impacted their lives. The early 1970s saw a mobilization of action on the part of feminists and rape victims who became the first victims' rights organizers, often under the theme of "Take Back the Night." Victims' rights issues began to appear in law journals proposing that court-reforms be developed to promote the needs of victims and their families. The 1970s can be remembered as the decade when activists developed shelters for battered women, opened rape crisis centers, and established crisis hotlines.

At this same time, victim impact statements were first introduced in Fresno, California, as part of pre-sentence investigations. These statements allow victims to describe the effects of the crime beyond the visible harm. Victims typically describe the emotional and financial harm they experienced as a direct result of the criminal act. Victim impact statements also allow victims an opportunity to outline what they believe is an appropriate punishment for the crime.

Victim impact statements were developed to improve the treatment of crime victims by the criminal justice system, to restore dignity to victims, and to allow victims' input into criminal justice procedures (Kelly & Erez, 1997). At present, victim impact statements are introduced at the sentencing phrase, at plea bargaining hearings, at parole hearings, and at some bail hearings (Clark, 1994).

The purpose of this chapter is to examine victim impact statements. First, the text provides an overview of victim impact statements, including the rationale for introducing victim impact statements in court. Next is a discussion of the arguments for and against using victim impact statements and their constitutional merit. The conclusion draws a discussion of the effect victim impact statements have on sentencing decisions.

Arguments in Favor of Victim Impact Statements

One of the most compelling arguments in favor of victim impact statements is that such statements may have a positive impact upon court dispositions, leading to an increase in the use of restitution and compensation orders. Victim impact statements, at the very least, provide victims with the opportunity to voice their feelings concerning how the crime impacted them socially, physically, mentally, and financially. Such statements will let court officials know that the victim is a real person (Kelly, 1987) with substantial interest in how the case is processed. It is difficult for a judge to evaluate the seriousness of a defendant's conduct without knowing how the crime has burdened the victim and the danger imposed by the defendant (President's Task Force on Victims of Crime, 1982). Recognizing the victim as one whose statements are important will increase the victim's confidence in and satisfaction with the justice system (Erez & Rogers, 1999) while simultaneously reducing any sense of powerlessness over the effects of the crime (Kilpatrick & Otto, 1987).

Favorable support for providing victims with the right to have input into sentencing decisions has been noted by several researchers. The acknowledgement of victim impact statements during the sentencing phrase increases the court's awareness of the loss the victim or/and the victim's family has suffered as a result of the crime (Sumner, 1987), increases victim restitution and compensation (Shapland, Villmore & Duff, 1985), and increases accuracy and proportionality in sentencing (Erez, 1990, 1994; Erez & Rogers, 1999). Victims' right to have input in the sentencing phrase of the trial, however, has not been as widely received by the public and criminal justice officials as has their right to restitution, counseling services, and information updates about their cases. The right to have a voice in the sentencing decision continues to be a debate.

The need to compensate victims or victims' families for the physical, psychological, or/and financial losses incurred as a result of a crime, is one consistent point of reference and is widely accepted. Victims of crime in nine states are eligible to receive more than $25,000 in compensation. Twenty-three states offer $25,000 maximum with 20 states providing up to $10,000 (National Association of Crime Victim Compensation Boards, 1994).

States not only vary in the amount of compensation victims receive but they also vary in terms of victim notification. Forty-three states notify victims when an offender is scheduled for a parole hearing; only 23 states notify the victim when the offender escapes from prison; and 25 states require that the victim be notified when a suspect is up for bail or is released before trial. Currently, 48 states permit victims to make victim impact statements before or at the sentencing hearing.

Arguments Against the Use of Victim Impact Statements

There has been much controversy concerning the use of victim impact statements. One of the major arguments against victim impact statements is the harsh effect that such statements may have on sentencing outcomes. These arguments focus on three areas: (1) legal issues, (2) safety (victim protection) issues, and (3) ideological grounds. It has been suggested that victim impact statements will make the court more susceptible to the outside influences of public pressure (Rubel, 1986), and that the victim's subjective views of his or her victimization process will take precedence over the objective manner in which sentencing decisions are decided in court leading to inconsistency and disparity in sentencing (Grabocky, 1987). Although it was stated in the President's Task Force on Victims of Crime (1982) report that "a judge cannot reach an informed determination of the danger posed by a defendant without hearing from the person he has victimized . . ." (1982:77), such a statement begs several questions. Are we to believe that judges are incompetent to interpret the law based on an individual's prior criminal history as well as considering all of the evidence in a case in order to make an informed decision based on sentencing guidelines? Do we really believe the judge cannot do this absent hearing from the victim?

It should not be forgotten that criminal offenses are crimes against the state and as such, the prosecution of those cases should reflect the public interest as it relates to a particular case, not one individual victim. The state must not lose its ability to provide an acceptable response to crime for its citizenry. In an attempt to maintain consistency in its treatment of offenders, the state may benefit (1) by gaining a reputation for fairness towards its defendants and (2) in the form of increased public confidence (Ashworth, 1993). With the state in control of the punishment instead of the victim, there is an increased likelihood that the sentence will be meted out in proportion to the seriousness of the offense and the protection of society (Ashworth, 1993). Critics of victim impact statements further state that the presence and emotionality of the victim and his or her family may interfere with the defendant's rights to a fair trial and that victim impact statements do not offer new or additional information since victim harm is already built into the judicial system (Hellerstein, 1989). Judges and juries are competent to dispense of justice without victim impact statements. The statements only facilitate a philosophical movement toward a more retributive, punitive approach to justice (Sebba, 1996).

Some arguments against victim impact statements focus on victim protection and the effect that such statements may have on the victim's well being. A victim may experience a level of psychological harm, especially when the victim has been a target of a violent crime, by having the victim re-live the pain and emotional stress that he/she experienced (Reeve, 1993). According to Ashworth (1993), evidence that is presented which suggests or implies unusual physical or mental harm to the victim,

> [R]aises a number of substantive and procedural questions. Among the substantive questions is the issue of chance: is it right that a particular offender should receive a more severe sentence because his victim suffered abnormally serious after-effects, or that another offender should receive a much lower sentence because his victim was counseled successfully and apparently recovered quickly? . . . There are also procedural questions about the victim impact statement and the proper standards of fact-finding. . . . offenders might be subjected to unfounded or excessive allegations by victims, made from the relative security of a victim impact statement (1993:506-507).

Some courts have required the prosecutor's office to release copies of the victim impact statements before the trial date, to support all medical claims with medical evidence, and to disallow new aggravating circumstances to be introduced in victim impact statements (Ashworth, 1993). One issue not clarified by the court is "in what circumstances (may) the prosecutor adduce evidence of this kind?" (1993:507). One must remember that regardless of the source of the evidence, the defense has a right to challenge it.

Victim impact statements may also result in elevating victim psychological stress because the victim often believes such statements will impact the sentencing decision when in actuality the statements may not have a significant impact on sentencing (Fattah, 1986) or may be completely ignored (Henderson, 1985). Historically, the judicial system has sought to render verdicts based on facts and not on human emotions. Thus, the two – the facts of the case and victim impact statements – seem to be in direct competition with each other.

Arguments against the use of victim impact statements are also based upon administrative issues (Miers, 1992). It has been argued that such statements may facilitate delays in trials, cause longer trials, and add expenses to an already overburdened system.

Constitutional Issues: Examining Death Penalty Cases and Victim Impact Statements

One specific argument against supporting victim impact statements is the fear that such statements may lead to racially biased applications of the death penalty. Opponents of victim impact statements are concerned that the emotionalism of victims and their families in court may interfere with the defendant's right to a fair trial, especially in capital murder trials where racial prejudice can surface and affect sentencing outcome. The issue of introducing victim impact statements in the sentencing phrase for death penalty cases has been addressed in three recent United States Supreme Court Cases. During the late 1980s, the Supreme Court heard two cases concerning whether victim impact statements should be permitted in death penalty cases involving a victim or defendant of different races. In *Booth v. Maryland* (1987), the Supreme Court addressed the issue of using victim impact statements in a sentencing jury's determination. In 1983, John Booth and Willie Reed bound and gagged an elderly couple. Fearful that the couple would be able to identify him, Booth stabbed the couple numerous times with a kitchen knife. The trial judge in *Booth* permitted the jury to hear victim impact statements that detailed the impact of the victims' deaths on family members and the respect that the community and family members held for the elderly couple. The Supreme Court held that it was inadmissible to allow a jury to hear victim impact statements during the sentencing phrase of a death penalty case and that such statements lead to an arbitrary imposition of capital punishment. In rendering this opinion, the Supreme Court identified three factors that preclude the prosecution from introducing evidence concerning how the homicide impacted the victim's family.

The first factor raised by the Supreme Court in *Booth* was that the introduction of victim impact statements encourages the jury to focus more on the victim than on the defendant. The Supreme Court stated that:

> While the full range of foreseeable consequences of a defendant's actions may be relevant in other criminal and civil contexts, we cannot agree that it is relevant in the unique circumstances of capital sentencing. In such a case, it is the function of the sentencing jury to express the conscience of the community on the ultimate question of life or death. When carrying out this task the jury is required to focus on the defendant as a uniquely individual bein[g]. The focus of a victim impact statement, however, is not on the defendant, but on the character and reputation of the victim and the effect on his family. These factors may be wholly unrelated to the blameworthiness of a particular defendant (*Booth v. Maryland*, 1987:7).

Second, the Supreme Court held that the imposition of the death penalty should not be contingent upon the ability of the victim's family to articulate their emotions, grief, and anguish of losing a relative. Rather, the focus should be centered on the defendant's characteristics and background and whether the factors warrant the death penalty. The introduction of victim impact statements at the sentencing phrase only shifts attention away from the defendant to the victim's family and friends.

Finally, the Supreme Court held that because victim impact statements include subjective feelings of family members, the defendant has a limited opportunity to rebut the evidence. If an opportunity for rebuttal is allowed, there is a chance that a "mini-trial" on the victim's character and the impact of the homicide on family members and friends will occur – directing the sentencing jury away from its constitutional task of determining whether the death penalty is appropriate in light of the crime committed.

In *South Carolina v. Gathers* (1989), the United States Supreme Court extended the ruling in *Booth*, by stating that any statements made by prosecutors about the victim's character were unconstitutional. In this case, Demetruis Gathers and three companions sexually assaulted and killed Richard Hayes, a man they encountered in a park. During the crime, the perpetrators ransacked a bag the victim was carrying. The bag contained several articles pertaining to religion, including a religious tract titled "Game Guy's Prayer." During the sentencing phrase of Gathers' trial, the prosecution made references to Hayes' character and read "Game Guy's Prayer" in court. The Supreme Court held that references to the victim's qualities were similar to the *Booth* holding, which prohibited victim impact statements and that such statements violated the defendant's Eighth Amendment rights. In a dissenting opinion, Justice O'Connor stated "Nothing in the Eighth Amendment precludes the community from considering its loss in assessing punishment nor requires that the victim remain a faceless stranger at the penalty phase of a capital case." This dissenting opinion set in motion a judicial environment for change.

In *Payne v. Tennessee* (1991), the court reversed itself and held that victim impact statements presented during the penalty phase of a capital murder trial do not violate the constitutional rights of defendants. In 1987, Pervis Tyrone Payne entered the apartment of Charisse Christopher and her two children. Payne stabbed Charisse and the two children numerous times with a butcher knife. Charisse and her daughter died; the boy, a three-year-old, survived the stabbing.

During the penalty phrase of the trial, the prosecution, over the defendant's objection, called the maternal grandmother of the three-year-old boy who survived the stabbing to testify how her grandson continued to cry out for his dead mother and sister. Additionally, the grandmother was allowed to testify about her personal grief over losing loved ones. Stating the Supreme Court's rulings in *Booth* and *Gathers*, the defendant argued that the admissibility of the victim impact statement violated his Eighth Amendment rights.

The Supreme Court ruled that the States have the discretion, in capital cases, as well as in other cases, to determine the admissibility of victim impact statements and that such statements represent another method of informing the court of the harm caused by the crime committed. Therefore, the Supreme Court overruled *Booth* and *Gathers* to the extent that they prohibited statements and evidence that attest to the harm and loss that the victim's families, friends, and community experienced.

In a dissenting opinion, Justices Marshall and Blackmun pointed out that the Court's ruling disregarded the widely accepted judicial standard of *stare decisis*. Justices Marshall and Blackmun stated:

> Today's decision charts an unmistakable course. If the majority's radical reconstruction of the rules for overturning this Court's decisions is to be taken at face value – and the majority offers us no reason why it should not – then the overruling of Booth and Gathers is but a preview of even broader and more far-reaching assault upon this Court's precedents. Cast aside today are those condemned to face society's ultimate penalty. Tomorrow's victims may be minorities, women, or the indigent. Inevitably, this campaign to resurrect yesterday's "spirited dissents" will squander the authority and the legitimacy of this Court as protector of the powerless (*Payne v. Tennessee*, 1991:756).

The majority opinion in *Payne* opened the door for the admission of victim impact statements in courts across the United States. The admissibility of victim impact statements is the prerogative of individual States, and the Supreme Court will not intervene unless "victim evidence is so unduly prejudicial that it renders the trial as unfair" (*Payne v. Tennessee*, 1991:735).

The amount of latitude allowed victims' families in presenting victim impact statements at capital sentencing phases varies from state to state. In some states, the family members can calmly read their victim impact statements in open court. The judge has the discretion to prevent the family members from reading their victim impact statements if they become emotional. Still other states require that the victim impact evidence be pre-approved by the Court. Since *Payne v. Tennessee*, at least 33 of the 38 states using the death penalty have incorporated victim impact statements into capital sentencing procedures.

Effects of Victim Impact Statements on Sentencing

The effects victim impact statements have had on sentencing outcomes have generated ambivalent feelings regarding their use. Arguments in favor of admitting victim impact statements at sentencing are based on the perception that such statements may increase victims' restitution and compensation. Arguments against admitting victim impact statements at sentencing rest upon the assumption that victim impact statements will have a harsh effect on sentencing outcomes.

Some experts have revealed that cases in which victim impact statements were admitted were more likely to result in the offender going to prison than being placed on probation than cases in which no victim impact statements were admitted (Erez & Tontodonato, 1990). However, it was also revealed that even if the sentencing outcome of a case in which victim impact statements were acknowledged resulted in a prison sentence, the statements did not significantly affect the length of the sentence. In cases in which victim impact statements have impacted sentencing outcomes, the impact has been minor, at best, and has not increased the punitiveness of sentencing outcomes, but enhanced sentencing accuracy and proportionality (Erez & Rogers, 1999).

Overall, the evidence regarding victim impact statements has been inconclusive in terms of their impact on increasing victim restitution or compensation. Nevertheless, Shapland et al. (1985) did conclude in their research that using victim impact statements increased victim restitution and compensation.

Phillips (1997) warns that "victim impact statements tend to exaggerate the degree to which juries consider the character of the victim in sentencing by explicitly presenting the jury with these characteristics" (1997:105). Moreover, Justice Sears-Collins of the Georgia Supreme Court noted in *Livingston v. State* (1994) that "clearly some evidence which would fall within the [victim impact statement statute] could also reflect on those factors which this court and our state legislature have already found constitutionally irrelevant to death penalty sentencing" (1994:751). It has also been noted that because of the power of victim evidence, prosecutors may be more inclined to seek the death penalty if the victim is attractive (Phillips, 1997). Other researchers (Luginbuhl & Burkhead, 1995) have found that victim evidence introduced during the penalty phase increases the likelihood of voting for death among those not opposed to capital punishment. Further, when looking at cases with and without victim impact evidence, more subjects vote for death when victim impact evidence is present, then when it is not present.

What Is the Level of Support for Victim Impact Statements Among Criminal Justice Professionals?

Sebba (1996) found that in general victim impact statements are not always taken, that the information provided by victims is often already known to the prosecutor, and that officials have established methods of resistance to victim impact statements. There appears to be conflicting perceptions between the judge and the prosecutor in terms of the role each plays in handling and processing victim impact statements in court (Davis & Smith, 1994). Some judges state that they are interested in seeing that victim impact statements are introduced in court but some prosecutors believe that judges take the admission of such statements lightly and only occasionally consider them in the sentencing phrase. In contrast, prosecutors state that victim impact statements should be introduced on a regular basis in court while judges believe that prosecutors rarely use them (Davis & Smith, 1994). A survey on the use of victim impact statements in California was conducted by the National Institute of Justice during the late 1980s. The study revealed that 69 percent of judges, 48 percent of prosecutors, and 81 percent of probation officers stated that victim impact statements are ineffective (Villmoare & Neto, 1987). These findings were further supported by Henley, Davis, and Smith (1994) in their study of judges' and prosecutors' perceptions of the use of victim impact statements in New York courts. Henley and colleagues (1994) found that judges expressed reservations about the potential of victim impact statements to change in any way the routine dispositions in "quick pleas." Prosecutors, on the other hand, felt that victim impact statements may cause victims to exaggerate the amount of physical, psychological, and financial harm they actually endured. Overall, both judges and prosecutors in New York courts stated that they support victim impact statements, but their action of actually introducing victim impact statements in court did not support their verbal statements (Henley et al., 1994).

Other research on judicial perceptions of the use of victim impact statements in court, including the perception of probation officers, reveals that some court officials favor the input from victims in sentencing decisions (Hillenbrand & Smith, 1989). A telephone survey of judges, prosecutors, and probation officers concerning their perceptions of the use of victim impact statements in court showed that the majority of the judicial personnel in the study supported victim impact statements and did not perceive the statements as creating problems in the criminal justice process (Hillenbrand & Smith, 1989). In fact, most judges and prosecutors thought that victim impact statements improved the quality of a criminal trial.

Victim Satisfaction with Victim Impact Statements

Another area of concern in assessing the effect of victim impact statements is victim satisfaction. Some authorities believe that victim impact statements create a sense of satisfaction among victims when they are able to voice their loss and harm, helping them to emotionally deal with the consequences of the crime. Some authorities, on the other hand, believe that to the extent that victims or their families are allowed to voice their feelings and concerns about the crime, they will be more satisfied with the criminal justice processing of the case.

Victims tend to reach a level of satisfaction if they believe that their statements and evidence influenced the sentencing outcome, even if in actuality their statements have no impact on sentencing decisions (Smith & Hillanbrand, 1981). According to Kelly (1982), allowing victims to give statements about the impact of the crime on their lives was more important to the victims than the severity of the punishment that the defendant received.

Further, some researchers have found that victim participation serves as a therapeutic approach to dealing with victimization (Kilpatrick & Otto, 1987; Wells, 1991). Kilpatrick and Otto, in their study of victim impact statements and its effect on victims of crime, reveal that such statements allow victims to deal with an emotional loss and to regain a level of power and control that was lost when the crime was committed, promoting the psychological recovery of victims (Wells, 1991). Such testimony and evidence serves as a healing modality for victims and sends a strong message that the criminal justice system cares about crime victims.

In contrast, some researchers claim that the impact of victim impact statements on victim satisfaction has been overstated (Davis & Smith, 1994). When examining satisfaction levels of robbery, burglary, and non-sexual assault victims, Davis and Smith (1994) found no supportive data that revealed that victim impact statements result in greater levels of victim satisfaction or greater involvement in the criminal justice processing of the case. Ashworth (1993) also found that there is no apparent increase in victim satisfaction with the criminal justice system when victim impact statements are used. Moreover, Ashworth (1993) found that completing a victim impact statement is not related to future victim cooperation with the criminal justice system.

Conclusion

In an attempt to give victims a sense of participation in the criminal prosecution of their cases, several states have implemented the use of victim impact statements. Advocates supporting the use of victim impact statements believe that these statements have a positive impact upon court dispositions. Perhaps the most important aspect of the victim impact statement is that it offers an opportunity for the victim to present a personal account of the harm caused by the criminal act and to also let the jurors see the humanity of the case.

On the other hand, proponents against the use of victim impact statements argue that these statements merely serve to enhance sentences based on emotions instead of law. Victim impact statements increase the probability that there will be disparity and inconsistency in sentencing among offenders. Additionally, victim impact statements can result in trial delays and further backlog of cases, causing additional expenses for court systems.

The Supreme Court has not settled the issues related to victim impact statements, instead it has first ruled that they were not admissible (*Booth*). In rendering this decision, the Supreme Court stated that the introduction of victim impact statements causes (1) the jury to shift its focus from the defendant to the victim; (2) the jury to ignore the defendant's prior criminal history and background in determining the appropriate sentence; and (3) the defendant to be unable to rebut the (victim impact statement) evidence. In its ruling in *South Carolina v. Gathers*, the Supreme Court added that the introduction of victim's characteristics by the prosecutors were unconstitutional, thereby extending the *Booth* ruling. Yet, in *Payne v. Tennessee*, the Supreme Court reversed itself and ruled that the states have discretion as to the admissibility of victim impact statements and other statements related to the harm suffered by a victim and the victim's family. We should note that this ruling, according to the dissenting opinion, disregarded the widely accepted judicial standard of *stare decisis* and its impact will be far-reaching.

In conclusion, the effects of victim impact statements are a continuing debate. It has been suggested that the introduction of victim impact statements, especially in death penalty cases, increases the vote for a death sentence. There was also a notable increase in the number of persons going to prison instead of being placed on probation after the introduction of victim impact statements. Whether or not these statements are welcomed by the defense, there is some indication that court officials favor input from victims during the sentencing phase. Overall, the real purpose of victim impact statements is to provide a feeling of satisfaction for the victim in the processing of the case, but the actual degree of satisfaction has been inconclusive in previous studies. Perhaps the future of victim impact statements hinges more upon public opinion and public will than it does on perceived or actual fairness to defendants.

CHAPTER 9

Victim-Offender Reconciliation Programs

Michael R. Smith

In recent years, the criminal justice system has begun to respond to the needs of crime victims. Victims' rights legislation and state constitutional amendments have sped the pace of reform. As a result of these changes, and the efforts of restorative justice advocates, more communities have begun developing victim-offender reconciliation programs (VORPs).[1] These programs seek to bring crime victims and offenders together outside of the courtroom in an effort to achieve a just resolution to the case – and perhaps a better outcome than would result from a criminal trial. Participants in VORP (victims and offenders) meet with a mediator who facilitates a discussion of the crime and its consequences and who may assist the parties in reaching a restitution agreement.

Although victim-offender reconciliation programs are found in a variety of forms, they usually have some of the following objectives in mind:

- To improve conflict resolution capacity of the parties involved.

- To help bring closure to the crime victim by allowing for the venting of feelings and the exchange of viewpoints.

- To compensate victims for their losses.

- To help reform offenders by allowing them to observe firsthand the harm caused by their conduct.

- To achieve reconciliation between the victim and offender.

- To relieve the overburdened courts of some of their cases.

- To facilitate a speedier and less costly resolution to the case.

- To improve case outcomes through the implementation of fairer and more just solutions (del Carmen & Smith, 1997).

Most victim-offender reconciliation projects accept only minor criminal cases. Simple assaults, harassment, petty larceny, and vandalism are typical cases resolved through reconciliation programs. A few jurisdictions have extended alternative resolution of criminal cases to more serious offenses, including burglary, robbery, aggravated assault, rape, and even manslaughter (del Carmen & Smith, 1997).

VORPs typically receive their cases through referrals from criminal courts. A smaller number of programs are maintained independently from the criminal justice system and receive their cases from local residents who bring their disputes directly to community dispute resolution centers. Where cases are referred from a criminal court, both the victim and the offender must agree to have the matter heard in an alternative setting. In some jurisdictions, cases are diverted from courts before they are adjudicated. If the victim and offender are able to agree on a resolution of the case, then the criminal charges placed against the offender are dropped if he or she successfully adheres to the agreement. Under another model, victim-offender reconciliation programs receive their cases after an adjudication of guilt but before a sentence is imposed. Under this approach, an offender's sentence may be reduced or suspended if he or she fulfills the terms of the agreement reached with the victim (del Carmen & Smith, 1997).

At first glance, victim-offender reconciliation programs sound appealing, especially to victim's rights advocates who often champion them. However, as these programs begin to proliferate, questions arise concerning their impact on victims, on offenders, and on the basic values upon which the American system of criminal punishment is based. The purpose of this chapter is to raise some of those questions and to provide some answers when they can be found. Some questions, however, remain unanswered and await further research and policy debate. Hopefully, this chapter will serve to help invigorate discussion over the future of alternative dispute resolution in the criminal justice system.

Are Victim-Offender Reconciliation Programs Good for Victims?

Restorative justice takes issue with the traditional view that crimes are primarily offenses against the state. Instead, restorative justice views crimes as offenses against people and communities. Advocates of restorative justice argue that traditional criminal justice processes relegate victims to second-class status and fail to take account of the harm suffered by victims and their families (Umbreit, 1994; Zehr, 1997). Through victim-offender reconciliation, "victims are able to play an active role in holding their offender accountable and receiving both emotional and material assistance" (Umbreit & Bradshaw, 1997:33). Victim-offender reconciliation is more victim-focused than traditional criminal case processing and is thus seen as superior in looking out for the needs of crime victims.

A growing body of research has examined the impact of victim-offender reconciliation on victims. Virtually all of the reported studies to date have
found high levels of satisfaction with VORP among victims (Coates & Gehm,
1989; Galaway, 1988; Gehm, 1990; Umbreit, 1994, 1991). In perhaps the
largest study of victim-offender reconciliation ever conducted, Umbreit
(1994) reported on the experiences of victims with VORPs in Albuquerque,
New Mexico, Minneapolis, Minnesota, Oakland, California, and Austin, Texas.
His evaluation used a quasi-experimental design to compare victims and
offenders who participated in VORP with control groups of those who
were referred to mediation but did not participate and with those who were
never referred to mediation and had their cases handled through traditional court processes.

When asked whether they were satisfied with the way that their cases
were handled by the criminal justice system, victims who participated in
VORP were much more likely to report that they were satisfied then the control groups of victims who did not participate in mediation. Across all four
sites, 79 percent of victims who participated in VORP reported being satisfied while only 57 percent of victims who did not participate stated that they
were satisfied. Victims from Minneapolis, Oakland, and Austin reported satisfaction rates ranging from 83 to 88 percent. Victim satisfaction with VORP
in Albuquerque was considerably lower at 57 percent but still higher than
the 42 and 46 percent satisfaction rates reported by the control groups in
that city (Umbreit, 1994).

In addition to comparing the overall satisfaction of VORP participants
with non-participants, Umbreit (1994) also asked VORP participants how satisfied they were with the actual outcome of the mediation and with their
mediators. Again, satisfaction rates were quite high. Ninety percent of victims reported being satisfied with the outcome of the mediation and 95 percent reported being either satisfied or very satisfied with their mediators.
Umbreit's findings are similar to those of a study by Davis, Tichane, and
Grayson (as cited in McGillis, 1997) that used random assignment to compare mediated criminal cases with control cases processed by the courts in
Brooklyn. They found that 73 percent of complainant-victims in mediated
cases were satisfied with their case outcomes as compared to 54 percent of
complainants whose cases were handled by the courts.

Finally, both Umbreit and Davis, Tichane, and Grayson examined the perceptions of fairness reported by VORP participants versus non-participant
victims. In Umbreit's (1994) four site study, he found that an average of 83
percent of VORP participants stated that they experienced fairness in the
processing of their cases compared with only 53 percent of victims who
were referred but did not participate in VORP and 62 percent of victims who
were never referred. Similarly, Davis, Tichane, and Grayson (as reported in
McGillis, 1997) found that 77 percent of VORP participant-victims in Brooklyn perceived their case outcomes as fair, while only 56 percent of victims
whose cases were handled by the courts reported fair outcomes.

The existing research strongly suggests that victims who participate in VORP are not only satisfied with the mediation process but are more satisfied than victims whose cases are processed by the courts in a traditional manner. Restorative justice advocates appear to be correct in concluding that the VORP alternative for handling minor criminal case offers significant advantages for victims.

Are Victim-Offender Reconciliation Programs Cost-Effective?

Advocates of restorative justice sometimes tout the potential benefits of VORP in reducing court docket overcrowding and in processing cases more efficiently and cheaply than traditional adjudication. Because they typically handle only a fraction of the cases heard by the courts, mediation programs are quite efficient at processing cases. For example, an evaluation of five community mediation projects sponsored by the Florida Supreme Court found that the average time required to process a case from referral to disposition was only 11 days (Bridenback, 1979). Researchers who have calculated the per case costs of processing disputes have likewise found that mediation programs can resolve cases for less than half of the cost associated with traditional adjudication (McGillis, 1997).

A number of studies also have examined the impact that mediation programs (victim-offender reconciliation and civil mediation) have had on reducing the number of cases handled annually by local courts. Most have found that because victim-offender reconciliation programs are both small and few in number, they currently do not have much of an impact on court caseloads (McGillis, 1997). Moreover, in communities where mediation programs exist, they are often underutilized by the courts. A 1992 report by the University of North Carolina's Institute of Government on mediation in North Carolina states that only 22.8 percent of cases that were eligible for mediation were actually referred to local mediation programs (McGillis, 1997).

While it is true that victim-offender reconciliation programs have the *potential* for relieving courts of a meaningful portion of their caseloads and for administering justice more efficiently, it is equally true that they are not currently functioning in this capacity. As Umbreit (1995) puts it, "the practice of mediating conflict between crime victims and their offenders (as part of a larger vision of restorative justice) remains on the margins of how we do justice" (1995:274). Until a sea change occurs in the thinking of policymakers on matters of criminal adjudication and punishment, it is unlikely that VORP will have a major impact on the processing of criminal cases by courts.

Is Victim-Offender Reconciliation Coercive?

The issue of coercion in victim-offender reconciliation programs is frequently ignored by restorative justice adherents, yet a cogent argument is made by some critical criminologists that the feel-good language and approach of VORP may mask some hidden power differentials. Although VORP is designed to be a voluntary process for both offenders and victims, some researchers have found that offenders do not perceive it as voluntary (Coates & Gehm, 1989). Offenders have much to lose in not "agreeing" to participate in VORP. Criminal charges may be held in abeyance or dismissed if they agree to participate, or they may receive reduced or suspended sentences. Thus, it is not surprising that some offenders view VORP as nothing more than an extension of the traditional criminal justice process – a process over which they have little control.

Although Umbreit and Coates (1993) report that 8 out of 10 offenders in their four site evaluation of VORP (discussed previously) stated that their participation was voluntary, 15 percent reported a sense of disempowerment or injustice in the way that their cases were handled (Umbreit, 1994). Common themes of dissatisfaction among offenders in this study included a belief that they were coerced into agreeing to an unjust restitution or that they were wrongly accused. Some offenders also reported being overly criticized by victims and being made to feel worthless (Umbreit, 1994). These findings support the argument by Arrigo and Schehr (1998) that VORP perpetuates stereotypes of juvenile offenders as inarticulate, stupid, and dangerous by privileging the "truths" of victims.

If VORP can be coercive to offenders, Arrigo and Schehr (1998) argue that it can be coercive to victims as well. They point out that VORP sessions are often highly structured, with mediators setting ground rules for communication that prohibit interruptions and clarifications (except by the mediator) and that prescribe who speaks first and how parties are to be addressed. These restrictions prevent victims from fully articulating their often profound sense of fear, loss, pain, and anger. When outbursts do occur, mediators intercede with the typical VORP discourse of healing, resolving, and settling. Thus, "by controlling the method of communication, VOM [victim-offender mediation] initiatives render participants, especially juveniles, passive recipients of a process that is supposed to speak for them (Arrigo & Schehr, 1998:647).

A final way in which VORP can be coercive is by widening the net of criminal justice control. In their article on net-widening and criminal justice reform, Austin and Krisberg (1981) point out that many reform-minded, pretrial diversion programs have the effect of extending court control over cases that otherwise would not have been filed or that would have been dismissed. Minor offenses or cases lacking in evidence that ordinarily would not come under criminal justice control now may have a "home" in new diversion programs such as VORP. Thus, victim-offender reconciliation programs may "serve to strengthen the net [of social control] and to create new nets by formalizing previously informal organizational practices and by creating practices where none had existed" (Austin & Krisberg, 1981:171).

Victim-offender reconciliation may be coercive. Although some studies show that offenders view VORP as voluntary, others indicate that offenders do not feel free to reject a referral to VORP. Restorative justice, of which victim-offender reconciliation is a part, has become a reform movement. It is cloaked with its own jargon, rules, practices, and beliefs, some of which may stifle victims and channel them into the discourse of the movement itself. By creating yet another process for resolving minor criminal offenses, VORP runs the risk of widening the net of criminal justice control. This is particularly true because VORP is viewed as less punitive than traditional adjudication. Cases that would not be worth a prosecutor's or a court's time in the past may now easily be diverted into a "restorative program" that in the end still provides state supervision and control.

Do Victim-Offender Reconciliation Programs Impact Recidivism?

One measure of VORP's success is the rate at which VORP participants re-offend as compared to those whose cases are handled through traditional adjudication. Advocates of VORP contend that it is more "reformative" than adjudication and that VORP participants are less likely than others to recidivate. However, the research on VORP's impact on recidivism is mixed.

As part of a larger study of restitution versus probation in four sites, Schneider (1986) found that juveniles who participated in VORP in Washington, D.C. had lower recidivism rates than those who did not participate. The annual re-offense rate for VORP participants during the follow-up period (between 22 and 36 months) was 53 percent, while the re-offense rate for those who received probation from a court was 63 percent. Although the selection of juveniles for VORP or probation was random, those selected for VORP were allowed to decline participation and did so in large numbers (40%). Thus, a significant methodological weakness in Schneider's study (and others as well) is that it is susceptible to self-selection bias. Juveniles who elected to participate in VORP and who had lower recidivism rates may have been predisposed to lower recidivism rates regardless of the "treatment" that they received.

Because most VORPs operate on the stated premise that participation is voluntary, the findings from studies of participant versus non-participant recidivism are inherently suspect. For example, a study by Nugent and Paddock (1995) found a statistically significant difference in recidivism between VORP participants in Anderson County, Tennessee, and a random sample of juvenile offenders whose cases were adjudicated by the courts. Non-VORP participants were not only more likely to re-offend than VORP participants but were more likely to commit serious violations when they did re-offend. Again, participation in VORP was voluntary, and the researchers were unable to randomize the selection of participants. Random selection of non-participants to make up a control group misses the methodological mark because it cannot account for the possible differences between juveniles who elect to participate in VORP and those who do not.

In one of the more recent studies on VORP and recidivism, Niemeyer and Shichor (1996) evaluated the VORP in Orange County, California. This program accepts both juvenile and adult offenders and handles more than 100 cases per month. As part of their larger evaluation of the Orange County VORP, Niemeyer and Shichor examined the re-offending rates of a group of juvenile VORP participants and a control group of juveniles who were referred to VORP but who did not participate for a variety of reasons. Members of both groups had official contacts with an Orange County law enforcement agency during the study period (2 years) at rates that were similar. Although the difference in average monthly contacts between the two groups (.1 contact per month) was statistically insignificant, participants in VORP actually had a slightly higher rate of contact – by an average of .1 contacts per month – than non-VORP participants.

Finally, Umbreit's (1994) four site VORP evaluation found no statistically significant differences in the recidivism rates of VORP participants and control group offenders who took part in court-administered restitution programs that did not include face-to-face mediations with victims. Overall, however, VORP participants completed their restitution agreements an average of 33 percent more often than non-participants, but again, this difference was not statistically significant.

Basing the expansion of VORP on reduced recidivism rates is questionable at best. As the previous discussion illustrates, methodological problems abound with VORP recidivism studies. Even without the methodological difficulties, the findings from the various studies are mixed and do not support the argument that VORP reduces recidivism rates. Nonetheless, the available research does not suggest that VORP *increases* recidivism, either. At worst, VORP is no better than traditional punishment at preventing future offending. At best, it may produce a group of "graduates" who are less likely to re-offend than those who are sentenced by a court.

Are Victim-Offender Reconciliation Programs Destructive to the Rule of Law?

Persons accused or suspected of a crime in the United States are guaranteed certain procedural rights that are designed to protect individual liberty and ensure due process. Some of those rights are based in the Constitution – the right to counsel, the right against self-incrimination, and the right against excessive bail or fines, to name just a few. Others are judicially or legislatively created and govern, for example, the admissibility of evidence in a criminal trial. VORP has as one of its central goals the privatization of justice and the removal of the interests of the state as the primary goal of criminal justice (Zehr, 1997). In taking criminal adjudication and punishment out of the public realm and delivering it into the hands of victims and mediators, VORP may threaten the rule of law and the constitutional protections afforded to the criminally accused.

To begin with, VORP is not an open forum. Victim-offender mediations are conducted in private and often without the presence of attorneys for either the victim or the offender (Brown, 1994). The public has no way of judging the fairness of either the process or the outcome. In *Richmond Newspapers v. Virginia* (1980), the Supreme Court held that criminal trials may not be closed to the public. In announcing the judgment of the Court, Chief Justice Burger wrote:

> The historical evidence demonstrates conclusively that at the time when our organic laws were adopted, criminal trials both here and in England had long been presumptively open. This is no quirk of history; rather, it has long been recognized as an indispensable attribute of an Anglo-American trial. Both Hale in the 17th century and Blackstone in the 18th saw the importance of openness to the proper functioning of a trial; it gave assurance that the proceedings were conducted fairly to all concerned, and it discouraged perjury, the misconduct of participants, and decisions based on secret bias or partiality (1980:569).

Public trials are an important element in separating the criminal justice systems of democratic nations that respect the rule of law from those of totalitarian states that punish their citizens in secret. Like criminal trials, victim-offender mediations often produce restitution agreements. Unlike criminal trials, however, the agreements produced through VORP cannot be tested for fairness by the observing public. Although VORP advocates speak in glowing terms of the transformative and healing aspects of victim-offender mediation, the process is not open to public scrutiny and so is subject to real and perceived abuses. As the Supreme Court noted in *Richmond Newspapers*, "especially in the administration of criminal justice, the means used to achieve justice must have the support derived from public acceptance of both the process and its results" (1980:570). True public acceptance and accountability cannot occur within a closed system.

In addition to its overall lack of public accountability, victim-offender reconciliation may have the capacity to harm the rule of law and the rights of offenders in other ways. First, statements made and information divulged by offenders (and victims) during the course of a mediation may not be confidential and may be used against offenders if the mediation is unsuccessful. Although some states have confidentiality statutes that apply to VORP, many do not. In some jurisdictions that utilize VORP, offenders' noncompliance with victims' wishes during mediation sessions is routinely reported back to prosecutors and judges. Thus, an offender's failure to reach an agreement with a victim might be used against the offender in a subsequent charging or sentencing decision made by a prosecutor or judge (Brown, 1994).

Secondly, the right of offenders to be represented by counsel is often given short shrift by victim-offender reconciliation. There are no consistent rules in VORP about an offender's right to have an attorney present during a mediation session with a victim or to have a restitution agreement reviewed by counsel. In fact, some programs actively discourage lawyers from attending VORP sessions (Brown, 1994). Yet, the Supreme Court has held that criminal defendants have a Sixth Amendment right to counsel at "critical stages" in the adjudication process (*United States v. Wade*, 1967) and that a sentencing hearing is just such a critical stage (*Mempa v. Ray*, 1967). If an offender's "sentence" (restitution) can, in effect, be determined from a victim-offender mediation session, then a strong argument can be made that VORP violates the Sixth Amendment when it discourages the participation of attorneys in the process. In essence, VORP may weaken "both the procedural rules that protect individuals and the substantive laws that represent society's collective interest in behavioral norms" (Brown, 1994:1291).

Finally, as Professor Brown (1994) notes in her procedural critique of VORP, proponents of victim-offender reconciliation and a restorative justice paradigm argue that "justice should involve victims, offenders, and *community members* in a search to identify needs and obligations, so as to promote healing among the parties" (Zehr, 1997:69-70). The latest iterations of VORP to reach the shores of the United States seek to involve the families and the communities of both victims and offenders in developing an appropriate response to a criminal offense (Bazemore & Griffiths, 1997). These variations on VORP, known as family group conferencing, circle sentencing, or reparative probation, explicitly invoke community norms in the sentencing of offenders. For example, in extolling the benefits of family group conferencing (FGC), Umbreit and Stacey (1996) write that FGC

- Involves more people in the community in the meeting called to discuss the offense, its effects, and how to remedy the harm;

- Acknowledges a wider range of people being victimized by the offense and explores the effects on those people . . .;

- Gets a wider range of participants to express their emotions about the impact of the crime and to be potentially involved in assisting reintegration of the victim and the offender into the community; and

- Makes more deliberate distinctions in the meeting between condemning the offense versus condemning the offender (1996:31).

Family group conferencing has its roots in New Zealand and is based upon the ancient cultural practices of the Maori people. Circle sentencing is an "updated version of the traditional sanctioning and healing practices of Canadian Aboriginal peoples and indigenous peoples in the Southwestern United States" (Bazemore & Griffiths, 1997:26). Brown (1994) argues that in their zeal to hearken back to practices of homogenous aboriginal societies, advocates of these new twists on VORP fail to account for the complexity and heterogeneity of modern, industrialized societies. She points out that "communities" are very difficult to define in urban areas of the United States, much less a set of shared community norms. She maintains that proponents of FGC and circle sentencing fail to offer a clear conceptual framework for identifying and applying community standards. Even Sally Merry (as cited in Brown, 1994), a noted advocate of alternative dispute resolution, recognizes that societies in which mediation is widely practiced are often more homogenous than neighborhoods in America, which lack the shared expectations and values that allow community mediation to work successfully elsewhere.

The argument that VORP can weaken the rule of law and the constitutional protections afforded the criminally accused is compelling and is perhaps its strongest challenge. Brown (1994) suggests several options for maintaining VORP while minimizing its negative impact on the rights of offenders. First, the timing of victim-offender mediation could be restricted to some point after sentencing has occurred. Some programs currently function in this manner, but post-sentencing VORP has drawbacks. Many months or even years may pass before a final sentence is determined, and victims may have difficulty obtaining restitution from offenders after they have been sentenced and possibly incarcerated. As another option, Brown suggests that a "Chinese" wall be constructed that would separate mediation from court processes. Statements made during mediation would be confidential and parties would be legally forbidden from discussing what occurred during mediation with a court or prosecutor. Victims could be deposed prior to mediation so that they would be disinclined to change their stories to an offender's detriment if mediation was not successful.

However the "Chinese" wall is constructed, its purpose is to prevent coercion of offenders and potential recrimination by criminal justice officials if victims are not satisfied with the outcome of the mediation process. Until such safeguards become standard practice, VORP will continue to be attacked as destructive of the rule of law and American constitutional ideals.

Do Victim-Offender Reconciliation Programs Fail to Punish Appropriately?

A related criticism of VORP is that it may fail to adequately punish offenders and thereby undermine the goals of the criminal justice system. Traditionally, criminal punishment has been justified under four theories:

deterrence (specific and general), retribution, incapacitation, and rehabilitation (Regoli & Hewitt, 1996). Of these four, rehabilitation is the only goal of punishment to which VORP may possibly lay claim.

VORP does not support the goal of general deterrence, which is based on the utilitarian notion that citizens will be deterred from committing crime by witnessing the legally sanctioned punishment of others (Zimring & Hawkins, 1973). To begin with, advocates of VORP expressly reject the philosophical notion of general deterrence and disavow its connection with VORP (Brown, 1994). Furthermore, general deterrence is predicated upon publicizing the punishment meted out by the state. As discussed previously, VORP is largely a private affair whose processes and outcomes occur with little public knowledge and oversight.

Whether VORP promotes specific deterrence has already been addressed in this chapter. Research on the recidivism rates of VORP participants versus non-participants is mixed and is fraught with methodological problems. Thus, whether VORP is better than traditional punishment at deterring individual offenders from committing future crimes is questionable, although it does not appear to be any less effective that traditional punishment.

Proponents of VORP and restorative justice explicitly reject retribution as a legitimate basis for punishment (Bianchi, 1994; Cragg, 1992; Van Ness & Strong, 1997). For them, retribution is a failed theory of punishment that causes more harm than good. But retribution is perhaps the most ancient of justifications for punishment. Even Wesley Cragg (1992), a staunch advocate of restorative justice, recognizes that "the principle of desert accords with our deepest intuitions" and that "retributive justice responds to these values" (1992:20). However, the restorative justice paradigm holds that even if punishment should be in accordance with desert, it is nonetheless unjustified (Cragg, 1992). This not only seems puzzling but out of step with many of our democratically passed criminal laws and sanctions that are inherently retributive.

Restorative justice and VORP likewise reject incapacitation as a justification for punishment except in the most extreme cases (Van Ness & Strong, 1997). VORP is viewed as a true alternative to incarceration. Although most VORPs handle only minor assaults and property cases, some include felony cases and even serious violent crimes. In the Washington, D.C., VORP, evaluated by Schneider (1986), more than 60 percent of the offenders were repeat offenders and approximately 60 percent of the referrals were for felony charges. Thus, it appears that in some jurisdictions, VORP offenders who might otherwise be incarcerated and unable to victimize others are being released upon a mere promise to make restitution to their current victims. This practice, particularly in violent or felony cases, makes VORP vulnerable to the argument that it is "soft" on crime and criminals.

VORP advocates emphasis the rehabilitative and transformative aspects of VORP as compared to traditional punishments (Van Ness & Strong, 1997; Zehr, 1997). In its current state of development, the evaluation literature on

VORP contains only two measures of rehabilitation – recidivism and restitution completion. The data on recidivism already have been discussed at length. With respect to restitution completion, Umbreit (1994) found a statistically significant increase in the likelihood of completing restitution by VORP offenders as compared to a matched sample of non-VORP participants. Although they did not compare restitution completion among VORP participants and non-participants in their study of the Orange County, California VORP, Niemeyer and Shichor (1996) found that 96 percent of offenders who reached a restitution agreement with their victims completed their obligations.

The restitution results are susceptible to the same sort of self-selection bias as the recidivism data. Because participation in VORP is voluntary, the treatment and control groups are not randomly assigned and members may differ in their likelihood of providing restitution. Nevertheless, the 96 percent completion rate found by Niemeyer and Shichor is quite high and suggests that the VORP process may indeed have a significant and positive impact on offenders who participate in it. Whether that "transformative" effect is likely to persist beyond the restitution period awaits further illumination.

Conclusion

Victim-offender reconciliation is growing in popularity as the restorative justice movement matures and gains a wider audience. VORP is seen by its advocates as a new paradigm in criminal case processing that offers healing and recompense to victims, as well as transformation and reintegration to offenders. By most accounts, VORP is popular and well-liked where it is in use. Research studies report high satisfaction rates with VORP among victims and offenders. Like any new challenge to the status quo, it is not immune to dispute and criticism. Some VORP evaluations have shown that offenders view it as a less than voluntary process, and critical criminologists have argued that it can be coercive to both victims and offenders. As a new and additional process for handling criminal offenses, it creates expanded opportunities for criminal justice system control over marginal cases that might otherwise have gone unprosecuted.

Solutions to these potential problems may be difficult to achieve. As Brown (1994) points out, the decision by an offender not to participate in VORP or the unproductive outcome of a mediation session should not be allowed to influence the processing of the offender's case. In reality, though, it is difficult to control a prosecutor's charging decision or a judge's sentencing determination, and it is always possible that one or both of these actors will look unfavorably upon an offender who does not work out a solution with his or her victim. Likewise, since prosecutors have almost free reign to file or not file criminal charges, it may be difficult to dissuade a prosecutor from filing a marginal charge just to get an offender into VORP. Perhaps the best solution to these problems is to track the case outcomes (including charges filed and sentences received) of offenders who do not participate in VORP and compare them with the outcomes of VORP participants who achieve agreements with their victims as well as those that do not. Over time, this data will expose patterns of harsher treatment and could be used to evaluate whether a VORP program should continue in its present form or undergo modification.

Although VORP has not been shown to significantly improve recidivism rates among offenders, neither has it been shown to be less effective than traditional, court-imposed punishments. Perhaps the greatest challenge to the expansion of VORP comes from the legal community, which points out that VORP can be destructive to the rule of law and to the rights of the accused. It is a type of private justice that carries with it the risk of abuse and secretiveness. In an effort to tip the delicate balance of rights in favor of victims, it runs the risk of harming the constitutional and procedural rights of offenders. Moreover, as VORP expands beyond the confines of minor criminal cases, it is susceptible to the charge of being soft on criminals and failing to punish those who may truly deserve it.

VORP agreements require careful monitoring by prosecutors and judges to ensure that they are fair to *both* of the parties. States that have not already done so should consider legislation that would require VORP mediators to inform offenders that they have the right to have counsel present during mediation and that an attorney should review any restitution agreement that is reached. In Virginia, for example, both state law and the Virginia Judicial Council's ethical standards governing court-certified mediators require that such information be given to the parties before a mediation session begins (VA Code § 8.01-576.12(3); *Standards of Ethics and Professional Responsibility for Certified Mediators*, 1997, § D(2)(a)). Although VORP advocates may decry the chilling effect of such a requirement, the VORP process should not empower victims at the expense of the constitutional rights of offenders.

Providing attorneys to VORP offenders is not only a good way to safeguard their rights, it helps open up the process to public oversight. On one hand, maintaining the confidentiality of statements made during victim-offender mediation sessions is paramount and some states have passed legislation providing for such confidentiality. On the other hand, communities have a legitimate interest in seeing that offenders receive the appropriate punishment and that the rights of all VORP participants are protected. Like any traditional sentence given by a court, a restitution agreement reached in lieu of a judicially imposed sentence should be read aloud in open court and should become part of the public case file. This will help ensure that VORP does not become a privatized system of criminal justice operating in the shadows of government and public scrutiny. Although some victims may object to this as an invasion of the private nature of VORP, public oversight is crucial to the maintaining the legitimacy of the process. Justice that cannot withstand the light of public scrutiny is questionable justice at best.

Despite the challenges that it faces, VORP and related alternative dispute resolution processes, such as family group conferencing and circle sentencing, will likely expand in the coming years as criminal courts continue to struggle with high case loads, stagnant resources, and repeat offenders. As communities look to develop new approaches to old and intractable problems, they will increasingly look beyond the traditional, criminal adjudication system. As these alternative processes develop, their advocates must strive to shape them in a manner that comports with constitutional requirements and with Americans' deeply held cultural beliefs regarding individual rights and the rule of law.

Note

[1]   Victim-offender reconciliation (VORP) is the traditional name for the process discussed in this chapter and is used here because of its familiarity to most readers. Increasingly, VORP is also being referred to as victim-offender mediation (VOM).

CHAPTER 10

Reconciling Controversies:
Is Education the Panacea?

Laura J. Moriarty

The underlining threads that tie together all the chapters in this reader are (1) a misunderstanding of the criminal justice system; (2) a general lack of knowledge regarding the criminal justice system; and/or (3) too narrow a focus or perspective of victimology.

One clear finding in the victimology literature is that the average citizen really does not understand how the criminal justice system operates. And, perhaps more troublesome is the observation that what the citizen does know about the system, he or she has learned from watching television. What happens in a typical 60-minute police or court drama is not even remotely close to reality. But it often sets the stage for what victims expect from the system.

Most victim and witness assistance programs, at a minimum, provide victims and witnesses with an orientation to the system (Jerin, Moriarty & Gibson, 1995; Moriarty, Jerin & Pelfrey, 1998). This orientation, however, is more practical then theoretical, that is, the advocates typically explain the daily operations of the criminal justice system, leaving out the historical and theoretical underpinnings of the system. Perhaps if the educational process included more of a theoretical orientation, there would be less controversy in the system.

The narrow focus of the discipline includes primarily the conceptualization and operational definition of "victim," and subsequently, the focus of inquiry. Many of the debates or issues discussed in this reader result from pitting the victim (one person) against the offender (one person) or vice versa. Victimology as a field of study relies on a rather narrow definition of "victim" – one that is restrictive. The typical focus of victimology is on victimization that has been defined as the "harming of any single victim in a criminal incident" (Rush, 2000:335). Such a definition excludes harmful events where groups of individuals are injured. Additionally, such a definition ignores groups or entities that harm individuals.

As Eigenberg asserts in Chapter 2, when we focus on this narrow definition of "victim," it makes us, as a discipline, less likely to examine other causes of victimization. In particular, Eigenberg states with such a limited focus, the discipline does not look at societal factors which may explain victimization. She also asserts that such a narrow focus perpetuates old, tired debates, such as blaming victims for their victimization.

Additionally, Toni Dupont-Morales makes a similar argument in terms of domestic violence. The old, standard perspective is too narrow, keeping the focus on one small segment of violence. She maintains that domestic violence must be redefined as "relationship violence" to be reflective of its status as a societal issue, not a gender issue. This societal issue perspective is necessary before the discipline can have an effect on our understanding and knowledge regarding violence. Currently, we do not know much about female-on-male violence – and it is not because such violence does not exist, but simply because the inquiry and interest have not been a primary focus of the discipline.

Moreover, McConnell, focusing on one specific issue, fear of crime, makes a similar argument in terms of measuring this concept. She maintains that fear of crime, as currently measured, is problematic because the perspective used to measure the concept is somewhat limited. Her suggestion to evoke an interdisciplinary measurement requires expanding the focus or perspective of victimology.

Lastly, this narrow focus hinders creative solutions to deal with criminal behavior. As Meyer addressed in her chapter on restoration, in an effort to make the victim "whole" again, or to restore the victim to his or her pre-victimization state, the community must be involved in the process, not just the victim and offender. If the discipline of victimology only focuses on the victim and the offender, then what chances do new programs or initiatives have at succeeding? This is especially true when new programs require a different mindset or perspective.

While all the authors in the reader do not specifically point to these precise reasons for the controversies, they do offer solutions to their individual controversies that might fall into one or more of these categories. As way of illustration, Orvis in Chapter 1 and Johnson and Morgan in Chapter 8 examine two issues that seem to be at the crux of what victims want from the criminal justice system. For example, in Chapter 1, Orvis discusses a federal victims' bill of rights, and in Chapter 8, Johnson and Morgan discuss victim impact statements. Ironically, if a federal victims' bill of rights was passed, victim impact statements would be guaranteed to victims in all states. In both chapters, the authors argue against adding a new amendment to the constitution or using victim impact statements for the same reasons – more than 200 years of distinguished, legal history where the state is the victim. Common law already has evolved a forum for protecting the rights of crime victims, that being the civil courts. Therefore, a federal amendment is redundant. The point is this – does the average citizen – who is likely to become the next victim – know the civil court is an effective remedy for redress? Most likely, the answer is no – thus, it is essential that the general public be educated about the different court systems, including the purposes and basic philosophy of each.

Moreover, Johnson and Morgan use the same fundamental argument but also add that using victim impact statements shifts the focus from the facts of the case to the character and reputation of the defendant – a significant shift in the process – that has no bearing on the blameworthiness of the defendant. Such a focus then is not appropriate or fair given the current philosophy of the criminal justice system.

Furthermore, Mike Smith (Chapter 9) employs similar arguments when he discusses victim-offender reconciliation programs. Relying on his legal expertise, Smith warns that VORPs often are not open forums. Such a process does not allow for public scrutiny in an effort to judge the fairness of the proceedings. Additionally, Smith admonishes that if the mediation does not work, that is, the parties do not come to an agreement, then the information revealed in the session should not be used in any other criminal or civil proceedings. Smith maintains that the rule of law cannot be compromised, therefore, statements made and information divulged during the mediation process should remain confidential. The disclosure of such information has the potential to adversely affect the defendant in terms of subsequent charges or sentence decisions made by a prosecutor or judge.

Other chapters in this reader focus on issues that might be resolved with education. Chapters 3, 4, and 5 address specific topics, including alcohol and victimization, rape victims, and domestic violence. All three topics are related in that the general public is somewhat ignorant or misinformed about the topics. For example, Tewksbury and Pedro discuss alcohol and its relationship to crime, specially focusing on the campus environment. As they assert, the literature clearly indicates that alcohol, *not* illegal drugs, is more likely to be linked to criminal activity. They maintain that societal ignorance regarding alcohol and its relationship to crime contributes significantly to our inability to resolve or curb crime. We tend to focus our attention, energy and resources elsewhere – most typically on illegal drug use and its relationship to crime. Nevertheless, the general public, with its own alcohol-consumption issues, may not be ready to give up the belief that it is illegal drug usage that is most often correlated to crime. Therefore, educating the masses might prove to be quite difficult, especially when the message is one that the general public is unwilling to support and endorse.

In Chapter 4, Grant and Otto recommend that media outlets withhold from publishing the names of rape victims. Some of their arguments in favor of printing such names center on educating the public. However, until the public really understands rape – that it is about power, not sex –

and subsequently demystifies it – including dispelling commonly held myths about rape – they advocate protecting victims by not revealing their identities. Rape myths are particularly imbedded in the socialization process, resulting in dogmatic beliefs about the crime. For example, as Grant and Otto point out, in the year 2000 we are still debating whether rape is a crime of power or a sexual act. What seemed to be resolved many years ago by Brownmiller (1975) and others is once again resurfacing because two evolutionary biologists contend that rape is a sexual act that occurs because men have natural urges to procreate. Clearly, educating the masses is quite a daunting task when it comes to rape and sexual assault.

How Viable Are These Solutions?

While the overarching solutions seem to be education and a change in the focus of a discipline, these are not as easily implemented as we might think. For example, even if we educated the general public about the criminal justice system, including its origins, legal and historical development, as well as the current state of the system, there is no guarantee that the public would view the system in a rational manner instead of an emotional manner. Thus, increasing the awareness or educating the public on a particular issue may result in that information falling on deaf ears. For example, the eloquent arguments made by Greg Orvis as to why we do not need a federal victims' bill of rights may be ignored because the emotionality of actual victimization, along with our increasing levels of fear of crime, may dominate even our most basic ability to understand simple concepts.

To illustrate, victims' rights legislation is found in every state. The rights or services afforded to victims vary slightly by state but the majority of the states provide information about the criminal justice system, allow for victim impact statements, have restitution or compensation plans, provide notification, have separate waiting areas, and provide protection assistance (e.g., retraining orders). As Orvis points out (Chapter 1), with such services or rights being provided on the state level, is there really a need for a federal statute? If the general public understood that the rights afforded to "offenders" have been misidentified as "offenders' rights" as opposed to what they truly are – "rights of the accused," would this make a difference in the public demand for a victims' rights amendment to the Constitution? I believe so.

The general public needs to understand that those arrested are only "accused" of a crime. They are not yet tried and convicted. Too many times, with the media coverage of crime, the general public believes the person identified on the medium is a criminal. This perception promotes fury and anger when it is believed that these "criminals" are provided an inordinate amount of "rights" when the victim is viewed to have none. What needs to be remembered is that these "rights" are safeguards, established in the Constitution, clearly articulated in the Bill of Rights, to make certain citizens are protected.

Still, the average citizen is not aware of this and is not reminded of it when the criminal justice system is being explained. Thus, victims often do not understand why the system operates as it does. They get a thorough overview of how the system works but they are not educated on the basic principles underlying the development and maintenance of the system.

Conclusion

Is education the answer to reconciling these controversies? The answer is a resounding yes. There are different levels within the educational process. As was demonstrated in this reader, there is a clear need to educate the general public regarding the criminal justice system. Not only in terms of its daily operations but also in terms of the foundation and theoretical underpinnings of the system. There also is a great need to counter inaccurate perceptions formed by the media. The public often confuses entertainment with reality. Thus, what victims expect from the criminal justice system is tainted by media. This leads to misunderstandings regarding the criminal justice system and what can actually be accomplished within the system.

On another educational level, the discipline of victimology must grow. In other words, the narrow focus of victimology is hindering any possible advancements that might reconcile the issues. With a narrow focus that pits victims against offenders, there is no opportunity, interest, or inquiry into other areas of explanation, such as examining the role the social structure plays in causing victimization.

References

Abbey, A. (1991). "Acquaintance Rape and Alcohol Consumption on College Campuses: How Are They Linked?" *Journal of the American College Health Association*, 39:165-169.

Abbey, A. & L. Ross (1992). "The Role of Alcohol in Understanding Misperceptions and Sexual Assault." Paper presented at the meeting of the American Psychological Society, Washington, DC.

Adeyemi, A.A. (1994). "Personal Reparations in Africa: Nigeria and Gambia." In U. Zvekiÿ (ed.) *Alternatives to Imprisonment in Comparative Perspective*, pp. 53-66. Chicago, IL: Nelson-Hall.

Adler, J., N.A. Biddle & B. Shenitz (1995). "Bloodied But Unbowed." *Newsweek*, (April 4):54-56.

Agnew, R. (1985). "Neutralizing the Impact of Crime." *Criminal Justice and Behavior*, 12(2):221-239.

Al-Sagheer, M.F. (1994). "Diyya Legislation in Islamic Shari'a and Its Application in the Kingdom of Saudi Arabia." In U. Zvekiÿ (ed.) *Alternatives to Imprisonment in Comparative Perspective*, pp. 80-91. Chicago, IL: Nelson-Hall.

American Association of University Women (1993). *Hostile Hallways: The AAUW Survey on Sexual Harassment in America's Schools*. Washington, DC: American Association of University Women Educational Foundation.

Amir, M. (1971). *Patterns in Forcible Rape*. Chicago, IL: University of Chicago Press.

Arrigo, B.A. & R.C. Schehr (1998). "Restoring Justice for Juveniles: A Critical Analysis of Victim-Offender Mediation. *Justice Quarterly*, 15(4):629-666.

Ashworth, A. (1993). "Victim Impact Statements and Sentencing." *Criminal Law Review*, 477:498-509.

Austin, J. & B. Krisberg (1981). "Wider, Stronger, and Different Nets: The Dialectics of Criminal Justice Reform." *Journal of Research in Crime and Delinquency*, 18(1):165-196.

Balkin, S. (1979). "Victimization Rates, Safety, and Fear of Crime." *Social Problems*, 26(3):343-358.

Bard, M. (1971). "The Study and Modification of Intra-Family Violence." In J.L. Singer (ed.) *The Control of Aggression and Violence: Cognitive Psychological Factors*, pp. 155-163. New York, NY: Academic Press.

Barnes, H. & N. Teeters (1943). *New Horizons in Criminology*. New York, NY: Prentice Hall.

Barajas, R. & S.A. Nelson (1997). "The Proposed Crime Victims' Federal Constitutional Amendment: Working Toward a Proper Balance." *Baylor Law Review*, 49(Winter):1-40.

Baumer, T. (1985). "Testing a General Model of Fear of Crime: Data From a National Sample." *Journal of Research in Crime and Delinquency*, 22(3):239-255.

Baumer, T. (1978). "Research on Fear of Crime in the United States." *Victimology*, 3:258-278.

Bazemore, G. & C.T. Griffiths (1997). "Conferences, Circles, Boards, and Mediations: The 'New Wave' of Community Justice Decisionmaking." *Federal Probation*, 61(2):25-37.

Beatty, D. (1999). "Crime Victims' Right to Privacy in the News Media." *Victim Policy Pipeline*, 5(2):9-14.

Ben-David, N. (1996). "Are Crime Victims Right to Press for Amending U.S. Constitution?" *Broward Daily Business Review*, (July 5):A1.

Benedict, H. (1992). *Virgin or Vamp: How the Press Covers Sex Crimes*. New York, NY: Oxford University Press.

Benedict, J. (1997). *Public Heroes: Private Felons*. Boston, MA: Northeastern University Press.

Berlin, B.J. (1995). "Revealing the Constitutional Infirmities of the Crime Victims Protection Act: Florida's new Privacy Statute for Sexual Assault Victims." *Florida State University Law Review*, 23[Lexis 513].

Bianchi, H. (1994). *Justice as Sanctuary: Toward a New System of Crime Control*. Bloomington, IN: Indiana University Press.

Black, J. (1995). "Rethinking the Naming of Sex Crime Victims." *Newspaper Research Journal*, 16(3):96-109.

Black, J., B. Steele & R. Barney (1995). *Doing Ethics in Journalism: A Handbook With Case Studies*, Second Edition. Needham Heights, MA: Allyn & Bacon.

Borsari, B. & K. Carey (1999). "Understanding Fraternity Drinking: Five Recurring Themes in the Literature, 1980-1998." *Journal of American College Health*, 48(1):30-43.

Bridenback, M. (1979). *The Citizen Dispute Settlement Process in Florida: A Study of Five Programs*. Tallahassee, FL: Florida Supreme Court.

Brooks, J. (1974). "The Fear of Crime in the United States." *Crime & Delinquency*, 20:241-244.

Brott, A.A. (1994). "Special Report: The Lace Curtain." *Nieman Reports*. Boston, MA: Neiman Foundation at Harvard University.

Brown, J.G. (1994). "The Use of Mediation to Resolve Criminal Cases: A Procedural Critique." *Emory Law Journal*, 43:1247-1309.

Brownmiller, S. (1999). *In Our Times: Memoir of a Revolution*. New York, NY: The Dial Press Random House, Inc.

Brownmiller, S. (1975). *Against Our Will: Men, Women and Rape*. New York, NY: Simon and Schuster.

Bureau of Justice Statistics (1999). *National Crime Victimization Survey* (NCJ-176353). Washington, DC: U.S. Department of Justice.

Calvi, J.V. & S. Coleman (1989). *American Law and Legal Systems*. Englewood Cliffs, NJ: Prentice Hall, Inc.

Canterbury, R., C. Gressard & W. Vieweg (1992). "Risk-Taking Behavior of College Students and Social Forces." *American Journal of Drug and Alcohol Abuse*, 18(2):213-222.

Carranza, E., N.J.O. Liverpool & L. Rodríguez-Manzanera (1994). "Alternatives to Imprisonment in Latin America and the Caribbean." In U. Zvekiÿ (ed.) *Alternatives to Imprisonment in Comparative Perspective*, pp. 384-438. Chicago, IL: Nelson-Hall.

Cate, R.M., J.M. Henton, J. Koval, F.S. Christopher & S. Llyod. (1982). "Premarital Abuse: A Social Psychological Perspective." *Journal of Family Issues*, 3:79-90.

Cavanagh, M.E. (1994). "The Myths of Relationship Abuse." *Journal of Religion and Health*, 33(1):45-50.

Cellini, S.A.M. (1997). "The Proposed Victim's Rights Amendment to the Constitution of the United States Opening the Door of the Criminal Justice System to the Victim." *Arizona Journal of International and Comparative Law*, 14:839-879.

Challeen, D.A. (1980). "Turning Society's Losers into Winners." *The Judge's Journal*, 19:4-9, 48-51.

Clarke, A. & M. Lewis (1982). "Fear of Crime Among the Elderly: An Exploratory Study." *British Journal of Criminology*, 22(1):49-62.

Clark, C. (1994). "Crime Victims' Rights." *CQ Researcher*, (July 22):627-643.

Clemente, F. & M. Kleinman (1977). "Fear of Crime in the United States: A Multivariate Analysis." *Social Forces*, 56:519-531.

Coates, R.B. & J. Gehm (1989). "An Empirical Assessment." In M. Wrights & B. Galaway (eds.) *Mediation and Criminal Justice*, pp. 251-263. London: Sage Publications.

Cocks, J. (1982). "The Use of 'Third Sector' Organizations as Vehicles for Community Service Under a Condition of Probation." *Federal Probation*, 46(4):29-36.

Cohen, L.E. & M. Felson (1979). "Social Change and Crime Rate Trends: A Routine Activity Approach." *American Sociological Review*, 44(4):588-608.

Collins, J. (1981a). "Alcohol Careers and Criminal Careers." In J.J. Collins (ed.) *Drinking and Crime,* pp. 152-205. New York, NY: Guilford Press.

Collins, J. (1981b). "Alcohol Use and Criminal Behavior: An Empirical, Theoretical and Methodological Overview." In J.J. Collins (ed.) *Drinking and Crime*, pp. 288-316). New York, NY: Guilford Press.

Collins, J. & P. Messerschmidt (1993). "Epidemiology of Alcohol-Related Violence." *Alcohol Health and Research World,* 17(2):93-104.

Commission on Substance Abuse at Colleges and Universities (1994). *Rethinking Rites of Passage: Substance Abuse on America's Campuses*. New York, NY: Columbia University, Center on Addiction and Substance Abuse.

Conklin, J. (1975). *The Impact of Crime*. New York, NY: Macmillan.

Constitution of Alabama (1999). Amendment 557 (a) [On-line]. Available: http://www.nvc.org/law/alabama.htm.

Constitution of Alaska (1999). Article 2, section 24 [On-line]. Available: http://www.nvc.org/law/alaska.htm.

Constitution of Arizona (1999). Article II, section 2.1(A) [On-line]. Available: http://www.nvc.org/law/arizona.htm.

Constitution of California (1999). Article I, section 28 (d) [On-line]. Available: http://www.nvc.org/law/californ.htm.

Constitution of Colorado (1999). Article II, section 16a [On-line]. Available: http://www.nvc.org/law/colorado.htm.

Constitution of Florida (1999). Article 1, Section 16 [On-line]. Available: http://www.nvc.org/law/florida.htm.

Constitution of Idaho (1999). Article I, section 22 (10) [On-line]. Available: http://www.nvc.org/law/idaho.htm.

Constitution of Indiana (1999). Article 1, section 13 (b) [On-line]. Available: http://www.nvc. org/law/indiana.htm.

Constitution of Kansas (1999). Article 15, section 15(a) [On-line]. Available: http://www.nvc. org/law/kansas.htm.

Constitution of Louisiana (1999). Article I, section 25 [On-line]. Available: http://www.nvc. org/law/louisiana.htm.

Constitution of Mississippi (1999). Section 26A (3) [On-line]. Available: http://www.nvc.org/ law/mississ.htm.

Constitution of Missouri (1999). Article I, section 32 (7) [On-line]. Available: http://www.nvc. org/law/missouri.htm.

Constitution of New Mexico (1999). Section 24 (10) & (11) [On-line]. Available: http://www. nvc.org/law/newmexic.htm.

Constitution of Wisconsin (1999). Article 1, section 9 (m) [On-line]. Available: http://www. nvc.org/law/wisconsi.htm.

Conyers, J. (1997). "Is the United States Constitution a 'Rough Draft'?: An Open Letter to the 105th Congress." *Widener Journal of Public Law*, 6:323-348.

Cooper, C. & V. Whitehouse (1995). "Rape: To Name or Not To Name." *St. Louis Journalism Review*, 24(174):10-12.

Cragg, W. (1992). *The Practice of Punishment: Towards a Theory of Restorative Justice*. London: Routledge.

Crime Control Act of 1968, 18 U.S.C. Sec. 3501 (1968).

Cuklanz, L.M. (1996). *Rape on Trial*. Philadelphia, PA: University of Pennsylvania Press.

Dasgupta, S.D. (1999). "Just Like Men? A Critical View of Violence by Women." In M. Shepard & E. Pence (eds.) *Coordinating Community Responses to Domestic Violence: Lessons from Duluth and Beyond*, pp. 195-222. Thousand Oaks, CA: Sage Publications.

Davis, R.C. & E. Brickman (1996). "Supportive and Unsupportive Aspects of the Behavior of Others Towards Victims of Sexual and Nonsexual Assault." *Journal of Interpersonal Violence*, 11(2):250-262.

Davis, R.C. & E. Brickman (1991). "Supportive and Unsupportive Responses of Others to Rape Victims: Effects on Concurrent Victim Adjustment." *American Journal of Community Psychology*, 19(3):443-352.

Davis, R.C. & B. E. Smith (1994). "Victim Impact Statements and Victim Satisfaction: An Unfulfilled Promise." *Journal of Criminal Justice*, 22:1-15.

DeCrow, K. (1990). "Stop Treating Rape Victims as Pariahs: Print Names." *USA Today*, (April 4):8A.

DeJong, W. & J.A. Winsten (1999). "The Use of Designated Drivers by U.S. College Students: A National Study." *Journal of American College Health*, 47(4):151-156.

de Laguna, F. (1972). *Under Mount Saint Elias: The History and Culture of the Yakutat Tlingit*. Washington, DC: Smithsonian Institution.

del Carmen, R.V. & M.R. Smith (1997). "The Judiciary: The Arbitration of Conflict." In D.H. Chang & M.J. Palmiotto (eds.) *Introduction to Criminal Justice: Theory and Practice*, pp. 117-144. Wichita, KS: Midcontinental Academic Press.

Denno, D.W. (1993). "The Privacy Rights of Rape Victims in the Media and the Law: Perspectives on Disclosing Rape Victims' Names." *Fordham Law School Law Review*, 61[Lexis 1113].

Desiderato, L.L. & H.J. Crawford (1995). "Risky Sexual Behavior in College Students: Relationships Between Number of Sexual Partners, Disclosure of Previous Risky Behavior, and Alcohol Use." *Journal of Youth and Adolescence*, 24(1):55-68.

Doerner, W.G. & S.P. Lab (1998). *Victimology*, Second Edition. Cincinnati, OH: Anderson Publishing Co.

Doerner, W.G. & S.P. Lab (1995). *Victimology*. Cincinnati, OH: Anderson Publishing Co.

Dominick, J.R. (1998). *The Dynamics of Mass Communication*, Sixth Edition. New York, NY: McGraw-Hill.

Dubow, F., E. McCabe & G. Kaplan (1979). *Reactions to Crime: A Critical Review of the Literature*. Washington, DC: National Institute of Law Enforcement and Criminal Justice, U.S. Government Printing Office.

DuPont-Morales, M.A. (1999). "De-Gendering Predatory Violence: The Female Stalker." *Humanity and Society*, 23(4):366-379.

DuPont-Morales, M.A. (1998). "The Female Stalker." In L.J. Moriarty & R.A. Jerin (eds.) *Current Issues in Victimology Research*, pp. 223-238. Durham, NC: Carolina Academic Press.

Dworkin, A. (1997). *Life and Death*. New York, NY: The Free Press.

Editorial (1999). *The New York Times*, (September 30):28.

Elias, R. (1986). *The Politics of Victimization: Victims, Victimology and Human Rights*. New York, NY: Oxford.

Elias, R. (1990). "Which Victim Movement? The Politics of Victim Policy." In A.J. Lurigio, W.G. Skogan & R.C. Davis (eds.) *Victims of Crime: Problems, Policies, and Programs*, pp. 226-250. Newbury Park, CA: Sage Publications.

Elson, J. (1990). "Going Public with Rape: Should Victims Be Identified When Crime Is Sexual Assault?" *Time*, 135(April 15):71.

Engs, R. (1977). "Drinking Patterns and Drinking Problems of College Students." *Journal of Studies on Alcohol*, 38:2144-2156.

Engs, R. & D. Hanson (1994). "Boozing and Brawling on Campus: A National Study of Violent Problems Associated With Drinking Over the Past Decade." *Journal of Criminal Justice*, 22:171-180.

Ennis, P. (1967). *Criminal Victimization in the United States: A Report of a National Survey*. Field Surveys II prepared for the President's Commission on Law Enforcement and Administration of Justice. Washington, DC: U.S. Government Printing Office.

Epstein, L. (1991). "Courts and Interest Groups." In J.B. Gates & C.A. Johnson (eds.) *The American Courts: A Critical Assessment*, pp. 335-371. Washington, DC: Congressional Quarterly, Inc.

Erez, E. (1994). "Victim Participation in Sentencing: And the Debate Goes On." *International Review of Victimology*, 3:17-33.

Erez, E. (1990). "Victim Participation in Sentencing: Rhetoric and Reality." *Journal of Criminal Justice*, 18:9-31.

Erez, E. & K. Laster (1999). "Neutralizing Victim Reform: Legal Professionals' Perspectives on Victims and Impact Statements." *Crime & Delinquency*, 45:530-553.

Erez, E. & L. Rogers (1999). "Victim Impact Statements and Sentencing Outcomes and Processes: The Perspectives of Legal Professions." *British Journal of Criminology*, 39:216-239.

Erez, E. & P. Tontodonato (1990). "The Effect of Victim Participation in Sentencing on Sentence Outcome." *Criminology*, 28:451-474.

Erikson, K.P. (1976). *Everything in its Path*. New York, NY: Simon and Schuster.

Ericksen, K.P. & K.F Trocki (1992). "Behavioral Risk Factors for Sexually Transmitted Diseases in American Households." *Social Science and Medicine*, 34(8):843-853.

Eve, R. & S.B. Eve (1984). "The Effects of Powerlessness, Fear of Social Change, and Social Integration on Fear of Crimes Among the Elderly." *Victimology*, 9(2):290-295.

Eve, S.B. (1985). "Criminal Victimization and Fear of Crime Among the Non-Institutionalized Elderly in the United States: A Critique of the Empirical Literature." *Victimology*, 10(1/2):397-408.

Fagan, J. (1993). "Set and Setting Revisited: Influences of Alcohol and Illicit Drugs on the Social Context of Violent Events." In S.E. Martin (ed.) *Alcohol and Interpersonal Violence: Fostering Multidisciplinary Perspectives*. (Research Monograph-24), pp. 161-191. Rockville, MD: National Institutes of Health.

Fattah, E.A. (1986). *From Crime Policy to Victim Policy*. London: MacMillan.

Fattah, E.A. (1976). "The Use of the Victim as an Agent of Self-Legitimization: Toward a Dynamic Explanation of Criminal Behavior." In E. Viano (ed.) *Victims and Society*, pp. 105-129. Washington, DC: Visage.

Federal Bureau of Investigation (1998). *Crime in the United States: Uniform Crime Reports*. Washington, DC: U.S. Department of Justice.

Federal Bureau of Investigation (1995). *Crime in the United States: Uniform Crime Reports*. Washington, DC: U.S. Department of Justice.

Ferraro, K.F. (1995). *Fear of Crime: Interpreting Victimization Risk*. Albany, NY: State University of New York Press.

Ferraro, K.F. & R. LaGrange (1987). "The Measurement of Fear of Crime." *Sociological Inquiry*, 57(1):70-101.

Fillmore, K. (1985). "The Social Victims of Drinking." *British Journal of Addictions*, 80:307-314.

Fisher, G. (1978). "The Fear of Crime in Public Housing Developments." Unpublished doctoral dissertation, University of Arizona, Tucson, Arizona.

Flaten, C.L. (1996). "Victim-Offender Mediation: Application with Serious Offenses Committed by Juveniles." In B. Galaway & J. Hudson (eds.) *Restorative Justice: International Perspectives*, pp. 387-401. Monsey, NY: Criminal Justice Press.

Fowler, J. & T. Mangione (1974). *The Nature of Fear*. Unpublished manuscript, Survey Research Program, University of Massachusetts, Boston, MA: Joint Center for Urban Studies of M.I.T. and Harvard.

Franklin, C. & A. Franklin (1976). "Victimology Revisited." *Criminology*, 14:125-136.

Friedberg, A. (1983). *America Afraid: How Fear of Crime Changes the Way We Live*. New York, NY: NAL Books.

Friedman, L.M. (1984). *American Law*. New York, NY: W.W. Norton & Company.

Frintner, M. & L. Rubinson (1993). "Acquaintance Rape: The Influence of Alcohol, Fraternity Membership, and Sports Team Membership." *Journal of Sex Education and Therapy,* 19:272-284.

Fuentes, M. & M. Gatz (1983). "Fear of Crime in the Elderly – Its Relation to Leaving One's Abode, Self Reported Health and Sense of Personal Control." *Gerontologist,* 23:296-315.

Furstenberg, F. (1972). "Fear of Crime and Its Effect on Citizen Behavior." In A. Biderman (ed.) *Crime and Justice: A Symposium,* New York, NY: Nailberg.

Furstenberg, F. (1971). "Public Reaction to Crime in the Streets." *American Scholar,* 40(4):601-610.

Galaway, B. (1988). "Crime Victim and Offender Mediation as a Social Work Strategy." *Social Services Review,* 62:668-683.

Gallagher, M. (1998). "The Integration of Women Has Caused Sexual Harassment in the Military." In M.E. Williams (ed.) *Working Women: Opposing Viewpoints,* pp. 119-124. San Diego, CA: Greenhaven Press, Inc.

Gallup, G.H. (1981). *The Gallup Poll,* Princeton, NJ: April 6.

Gallup Report (1985). *Alcohol Use and Abuse in America.* Princeton, NJ.

Gallup Organization (1991b, December). *Public Opinion Online.* Storrs, CT: Roper Center, University of Connecticut.

Gallup Organization (1991a, April). *Public Opinion Online.* Storrs, CT: Roper Center, University of Connecticut.

Gardner, T.J. & T.M. Anderson (1998). *Criminal Law: Principles and Cases,* Sixth Edition. St. Paul, MN: West Publishing Company.

Garofalo, J. (1981). "The Fear of Crime: Causes and Consequences." *Journal of Criminal Law and Criminology,* 72:839-857.

Garofalo, J. (1979). "Victimization and the Fear of Crime." *Journal of Research on Crime and Delinquency,* 16:80-97.

Garofalo, J. (1977). *Public Opinion About Crime: The Attitudes of Victims and Non-victims in Selected Cities.* Washington, DC: U.S. Government Printing Office.

Garofalo, J. & J. Laub (1978). "The Fear of Crime: Broadening Our Perspective." *Victimology,* 13(3/4):242-253.

Garrett-Gooding, J. & R. Senter (1987). "Attitudes and Acts of Sexual Aggression on a University Campus." *Sociological Inquiry,* 59:348-371.

Gartner, M. (1993). "Panel Discussion: The Privacy Rights of Rape Victims." *Fordham Law Review,* 61[Lexis 1133].

Gates, L.B. & W.M. Rhoe (1987). "Fear and Reactions to Crime: A Revised Model." *Urban Affairs Quarterly,* 22(3):425-453.

Gehm, J. (1990). "Mediated Victim-Offender Restitution Agreements: An Exploratory Analysis of Factors Related to Victim Participation." In B. Galaway & J. Hudson (eds.) *Criminal Justice, Restitution, and Reconciliation,* pp. 177-182. Monsey, NY: Criminal Justice Press.

George, W.H., S.J. Gournic & M.P. McAfee (1988). "Perceptions of Postdrinking Female Sexuality: Effects of Gender, Beverage Choice, and Drink Payment." *Journal of Applied Social Psychology,* 18:1295-1317.

Giordano, P.C., T.J. Millhollin, S.A. Cernkovich, M.D. Pugh & J.L. Rudolph (1999). "Delinquency, Identity, and Women's Involvement in Relationship Violence." *Criminology*, 37(1):17-19.

Glascoff, M. & S. Knight (1994). "Designated-Driver Programs: College Students' Experiences and Opinions." *Journal of American College Health*, 43(2):65-77.

Glaser, D. & M. Gordon (1988). "Monetary Versus Confinement Penalties For Misdemeanants." Paper presented at the annual meetings of the Pacific Sociological Association, Las Vegas, NV.

Goldberg, C. (1999). "Spouse Abuse Crackdown, Surprisingly, Nets Many Women." *New York Times*, National News, (November 23):16.

Goodyear-Smith, F.A. & T.M. Laidlaw (1999). "Aggressive Acts and Assaults in Intimate Relationships: Towards an Understanding of the Literature." *Behavioral Sciences and the Law*, (17):285-304.

Gordon, M.A. & D. Glaser (1991). "The Use and Effects of Financial Penalties in Municipal Courts." *Criminology*, 29:651-676.

Governor's Task Force on Sexual Harassment (1993). *Sexual Harassment: Building a Consensus for Change*. Final Report Submitted to Governor Mario M. Cuomo. New York, NY.

Greek, C. (1991). "Drug Control and Asset Seizures: A Review of the History of Forfeiture in England and Colonial America." In T. Mieczkowski (ed.) *Drugs, Crime and Social Policy*, pp. 109-137. Boston, MA: Allyn and Bacon.

Griffiths, C.T. & R. Hamilton (1996). "Sanctioning and Healing: Restorative Justice in Canadian Aboriginal Communities." In B. Galaway & J. Hudson (eds.) *Restorative Justice: International Perspectives*, pp. 175-191. Monsey, NY: Criminal Justice Press.

Grossman, J.B. & R.S. Wells (1980). *Constitutional Law and Judicial Policy Making* (2d ed). New York, NY: John Wiley & Sons.

Gunther, G. (1975). *Constitutional Law*, Ninth Edition. Mineola, NY: The Foundation Press, Inc.

Gwartney-Gibbs, P.A., J. Stockard & S. Bohmer (1987). "Learning Courtship Aggression: The Influence of Parents, Peers, and Personal Experiences." *Family Relations*, (36):276-282.

Hammurabi, King of Babylonia (circa 1780 BC). *Hammurabi's Code of Laws With Commentaries*. Translated by L.W. King (1976). New York, NY: AMS Press.

Hanson, D.J. & R. Engs (1994). "College Students' Drinking Attitudes: 1970-1982." *Psychological Reports*, 54:300-302.

Hanson, D.J. & R. Engs (1992). "College Students' Drinking Problems: A National Study, 1982-1991." *Psychological Reports*, 71(1):39-42.

Hansson, R. & B. Carpenter (1986). "Coping With Fear Among the Elderly." *Clinical Gerontologist*, 4(4):38-40.

Harland, A.T. (1980). "Court-Ordered Community Service in Criminal Law: The Continuing Tyranny of Benevolence?" *Buffalo Law Review*, 29:425-486.

Harris, R. (1969). *The Fear of Crime*. New York, NY: Praeger Publishers.

Haws, D. (1996). "Rape Victims: Papers Shouldn't Name Us." *American Journalism Review*, 18(7):12-14.

Hellerstein, D.R. (1989). "Victim Impact Statements: Reform or Reprisal?" *American Criminal Law Review*, 27:391-430.

Hendy, H., D. Eggen, K. Freeman & C. Gustitus (2000). *Preliminary Results: Predictors of the Quality of Romantic Relationships in College Men and Women*. State College, PA: Penn State University.

Henderson, L.N. (1985). "The Wrongs of Victims' Rights." *Stanford Law Review*, 37:937-1021.

Henley, M., R.C. Davis & B. Smith (1994). "The Reaction of Prosecutors and Judges to Victim Impact Statements." *International View of Victimology*, 3:83-93.

Higgins, R. (1998). "Women Abusing Men: The Violence Ignored." *Boston Globe*, City Edition, (December 6):1.

Hillenbrand, S.W. & B.F. Smith (1989). *Victim Rights Legislation: An Assessment of its Impact on Criminal Justice Practitioners and Victims.* Report of the American Bar Association to the National Institute of Justice. Washington, DC: National Institute of Justice.

Hindelang, M.J. (1975). *Public Opinion Regarding Crime, Criminal Justice and Related Topics.* Analytical Report SD-AD-1. Law Enforcement Assistance Administration, National Criminal Justice Information and Statistics Service. Washington, DC: U.S. Government Printing Office.

Hindelang, M., M. Gottfredson & J. Garofalo (1978). *Victims of Personal Crime: An Empirical Foundation for a Theory of Personal Victimization.* Cambridge, MA: Ballinger.

Holman, J.E. & J.F. Quinn (1996). *Criminal Justice: Principles and Perspectives.* St. Paul, MN: West Publishing Company.

Hotaling, G.T., M.A. Strauss & A.J. Lincoln (1990). "Intrafamily Violence and Crime and Violence Outside the Family." In M.A. Strauss & R.J. Gelles (eds.) *Physical Violence in American Families*, pp. 1-25. New Brunswick, NJ: Transaction Publishers.

House Joint Resolution 64, 106th Congress, 1st Session, Joint Resolution, Section 1 (1999).

Hull, J. & C. Bond (1986)."Social and Behavioral Consequences of Alcohol Consumption and Expectancy: A Metaanalysis." *Psychological Bulletin*, 99347-360.

Hunter, A. (1974). *Symbolic Communities*. Chicago, IL: University of Chicago Press.

Hunter, A. & T. Baumer (1982). "Street Traffic, Social Isolation and Fear of Crime." *Sociological Inquiry*, 52:122-131.

Igra, A. & R. Moos (1979). "Alcohol Use Among College Students: Some Competing Hypotheses." *Journal of Youth and Adolescence*, 8:393-405.

Israel, J.H., Y. Kamisar & W.R. LaFave (1995). *Criminal Procedure and The Constitution*. St. Paul, MN: West Publishing Company.

Jerin, R.A., L.J. Moriarty & M.A. Gibson (1995). "Victim Service or Self Service: An Analysis of North Carolina Prosecution-Based Victim-Witness Program and Providers." *Criminal Justice Policy Review*, 7(2):142-154.

Johnson, L., P. O'Malley & J. Bachman (1997). *National Survey Results on Drug Use From the Monitoring the Future Study* (NIH Publication No. 984140). Washington, DC: U.S. Department of Health and Human Services.

Jubilee Policy Group (1992). *Relational Justice: A New Approach to Penal Reform*, Cambridge, UK: Jubilee Policy Group.

Kaiser Permanente (1995). "*Children Now Survey.*" Portland, OR: Kaiser Permanente.

Kappeler, V.E., M. Blumberg & G. Potter (2000). *The Mythology of Crime and Criminal Justice*. Prospect Heights, IL: Waveland.

Karmen, A. (1996). *Crime Victims,* Third Edition. New York, NY: Wadsworth.

Karmen, A. (1980). "Auto Theft: Beyond Victim Blaming." *Victimology,* 5:161-174.

Keener, J.K. (1999). "How Compuware Mishandled Its Explosive Sexual-Harassment Case." *Business Week,* 3636 (July 5):74-78.

Keller, S.E., J.A. Bartlett, S.J. Schleifer, R.L. Johnson, E. Pinner & B. Delaney (1991). "HIV-Relevant Sexual Behavior Among a Healthy Inner-City Heterosexual Adolescent Population in an Endemic Area of HIV." *Journal of Adolescent Health Care,* 12 (1):44-48.

Kelly, D.P. (1990). "Victim Participation in the Criminal Justice System." In A.J. Lurigio, W.G. Skogan & R.C. Davis (eds.) *Victims of Crime: Problems, Policies, and Programs,* pp. 172-187. Newbury Park, CA: Sage Publications.

Kelly, D.P. (1987). "Victims." *Wayne Law Review,* 34:69-86.

Kelly, D.P. (1982). "Delivering Legal Services to Victims: An Evaluation and Prescription." *Justice System Journal,* 7:62-75.

Kelly, D.P. & E. Erez (1997). "Victim Participation in the Criminal Justice System." In R.C. Davis, A.J. Lurigio & W.G. Skogan (eds.) *Victims of Crime,* pp. 172-187. Thousand Oaks, CA: Sage.

Kelman, S. (1995). *The Enemy Within: Family Violence by Women.* Canada: Maclean Hunter.

Kight, M. (1999). "Enemies of Victims' Rights." *The Washington Post* (August 17):A17.

Kilpatrick, D.G. & R.K. Otto (1987). "Constitutionally Guaranteed Participation in the Criminal Justice Proceedings for Victims: Potential Effects of Psychological Functioning." *Wayne Law Review,* 34:7-28.

Klein, A.R. (1988). *Alternative Sentencing: A Practitioner's Guide.* Cincinnati, OH: Anderson Publishing Co.

Koss, M. & T. Dinero (1989). "Discriminant Analysis of Risk Factors for Sexual Victimization Among a National Sample of College Women." *Journal of Consulting and Clinical Psychology,* 55(22):162-170.

Koss, M. & J. Gaines (1993). "The Prediction of Sexual Aggression by Alcohol Use, Athletic Participation, and Fraternity Affiliation." *Journal of Interpersonal Violence,* 8:94-108.

Koss, M., C. Gidycz & N. Wisniewski (1987). "The Scope of Rape: Incidence and Prevalence of Sexual Aggression and Victimization in a National Sample of Higher Education Students." *Journal of Consulting and Clinical Psychology,* 55(22):162-170.

Koss, M. & C. Oras (1982). "Sexual Experience Survey: A Research Instrument Investigating Sexual Aggression and Victimization." *Journal of Consulting and Clinical Psychology,* 50:455-457.

Lalli, M. & L. Savitz (1976). "Fear of Crime in the School Enterprise and Its Consequence." *Education and Urban Society,* 8:401-416.

Lambeth, E.B. (1986b). "Journalism Looks For Answers To Ethics Problems." *Crime Victims and the News Media, A National Symposium.* Fort Worth, TX: Texas Christian University, Department of Journalism and Arlington, VA: Gannett Foundation.

Lambeth, E.B. (1986a). *Committed Journalism.* Indianapolis, IN: Indiana University Press.

Lamborn, L. (1968). "Toward a Victim Orientation in Criminal Theory." *Rutgers Law Review,* 22:733-768.

Langdon, G.D. (1966). *Pilgrim Colony: A History of New Plymouth, 1620-1691*. New Haven, CT: Yale University Press.

Larson, E. (1998). "The Problem of Sexual Harassment Has Been Exaggerated." In M.E. Williams (ed.) *Working Women: Opposing Viewpoints*, pp. 115-118. San Diego, CA: Greenhaven Press, Inc.

Lasley, J. (1989). "Drinking Routines/Lifestyles and Predatory Victimization: A Causal Analysis." *Justice Quarterly*, 6:529-542.

Lasley, J. & J. Rosenblaum (1988). "Routine Activities and Multiple Personal Victimization." *Sociology and Social Research*, 73:47-50.

Laurence, L. & R. Spalter-Roth (1996). *Measuring the Costs of Domestic Violence Against Women and the Cost-Effectiveness of Interventions: An Initial Assessment and Proposals for Further Research*. New York, NY: Rockerfeller Foundation.

Lawton, M. & S.Yaffee (1980). "Victimization and Fear of Crime in Elderly Public Housing Tenants." *Journal of Gerontology*, 35:768-779.

Lee, A. (1996). "Public Attitudes Toward Restorative Justice." In B. Galaway & J. Hudson (eds.) *Restorative Justice: International Perspectives*, pp. 337-347. Monsey, NY: Criminal Justice Press.

Lee, G.R. (1982). "Residential Location and Fear of Crime Among the Elderly." *Rural Sociology*, 4(3):284-298.

Leibrich, J., B. Galaway & Y. Underhill (1986). "Community Service Sentencing in New Zealand: A Survey of Users." *Federal Probation*, 50(1):55-64.

Lerner, M. (1965). "Evaluation of Performance as a Function of Performer's Reward and Attractiveness." *Journal of Personality and Social Psychology*, 1:355-360.

Levy, S. & L. Guttman (1985). "Worry, Fear, and Concern Differentiated." *Issues in Mental Health*, 7(1):251-264.

Lieberman Research, Inc. (1996). *Domestic Violence Advertising Campaign*. Great Neck: NY: The Advertising Council and the Family Violence Prevention Fund.

Lieberman Research, Inc. (1995). *Domestic Violence Advertising Campaign*. Great Neck, NY: The Advertising Council and Family Violence Prevention Fund.

Lindquist, J. & J. Duke (1982). "The Elderly Victim at Risk: Explaining the Fear-Victimization Paradox." *Criminology*, 20:115-126.

Lo, C.C. & G.A. Globetti (1995). "The Facilitating and Enhancing Roles Greek Associations Play in College Drinking." *International Journal of Addiction*, 30:1311-1322.

Lockart, W.B., Y. Kamisar, J.H. Choper & S.H. Shiffrin (1986). *The American Constitution*, Sixth Edition. St. Paul, MN: West Publishing Company.

Lotz, R. (1979). "Public Anxiety About Crime." *Pacific Sociological Review*, 22:241-253.

Luginbuhl, J. & M. Burkhead (1995). "Victim Impact Evidence in a Capital Trial: Encouraging Votes for Death." *American Journal of Criminal Justice*, 20(1):1-16.

Lurigio, A. (1987). "Are All Victims Alike? The Adverse, Generalized, and Differential Impact of Crime." *Crime & Delinquency*, 33(4):452-467.

Lynch, D.J. (1997). "Restorative Justice: Bridle for Human Passions." Unpublished master's thesis, New Mexico State University, Las Cruces, NM.

MacKinnon, C. (1978). *Sexual Harassment of Working Women: A Case of Sex Discrimination*. New Haven, CT: Yale University Press.

Madison, J. (1961). "The Federalist No. 10." In C. Rossiter (ed.) *The Federalist Papers*, pp. 77-84. New York, NY: Mentor.

Makepeace, J.M. (1986). "Gender Differences in Courtship Violence Victimization." *Family Relations*, 5:383-388.

Marshall, M. (1991). "Values, Customs and Traditions of the Mi'Kmaq Nation." *Micmac News*, (March 15):6-7, 9.

Martin, E. & R. Hummer (1989). "Fraternities and Rape on Campus." *Gender and Society*, 3:457-473.

Maxfield, M. (1984). "The Limits of Vulnerability in Explaining Fear of Crime: A Comparative Neighborhood Analysis." *Journal of Research in Crime and Delinquency*, 21(3):233-250.

Maxwell, G.M. (1994). "Children and Family Violence: The Unnoticed Victims." *Social Policy Journal of New Zealand*, 2:81-96.

McAloon, D.T. (1994). "The Effect of Alcohol Abuse on Academic Achievement on Two-Year Campuses." *Community College Review*, 22:12-18.

McCold, P. (1996). "Restorative Justice and the Role of Community." In B. Galaway & J. Hudson (eds.) *Restorative Justice: International Perspectives*, pp. 85-101. Monsey, NY: Criminal Justice Press.

McConnell, E. (1989). "An Examination of Relationships Among Fear of Crime, Crime Seriousness, Crime Victimization, and Crime Precaution Behaviors." Unpublished doctoral dissertation, Sam Houston State University, Huntsville, Texas.

McCormick, L.K. & J. Ureda (1995). "Who's Driving? College Students' Choices of Transportation Home After Drinking." *The Journal of Primary Prevention*, 16(1):103-115.

McDonald, D.C. (1992). "Punishing Labor: Unpaid Community Service as a Criminal Sentence." In J.M. Byrne, A.J. Luvigio & J. Petersilia (eds.) *Smart Sentencing: The Emergence of Intermediate Sanctions*, pp. 182-193. Newbury Park, CA: Sage.

McElrea, F.W.M. (1996). "The New Zealand Youth Court: A Model for Use With Adults." In B. Galaway & J. Hudson (eds.) *Restorative Justice: International Perspectives*, pp. 69-83. Monsey, NY: Criminal Justice Press.

McGillis, D. (1997). *Community Mediation Programs: Developments and Challenges*. Washington, DC: Office of Justice Programs.

McGinnis, J. & W.H. Foege (1993). "Actual Causes of Death in the United States." *Journal of the American Medical Association*, 270(18):2207-2214.

McIntyre, J. (1967). "Public Attitudes Toward Crime and Law Enforcement." *The Annals of the American Academy of Political and Social Science*, 374:34-46.

McMurry, K. (1997). "Victims' Rights Movement Rises to Power." *Trial*, (July):12-14, 16.

Meeker, J.W., P. Jesilow & J. Aranda (1992). "Bias in Sentencing: A Preliminary Analysis of Community Service Sentences." *Behavioral Sciences and the Law*, 10:197-206.

Meilman, P., P. Riggs & J. Turco (1990). "College Health Service's Response to Sexual Assault Issues." *American Journal of College Health*, 28:145-147.

Mendelsohn, B. (1963). "The Origin of the Doctrine of Victimology." *Excerpta Criminologica*, 3:239-245.

Merry, S. (1981). *Urban Danger: Life in a Neighborhood of Strangers*. Philadelphia, PA: Temple University Press.

Meyer, J.F. (1998). "History Repeats Itself: Restorative Justice in Native American Communities." *Journal of Contemporary Criminal Justice*, 14:42-57.

Miers, D. (1992). "The Responsibilities and Rights of Victims." *Comparative Law Review*, 55:15-30.

Miers, D. (1992). "The Responsibilities and Rights of Victims." *Modern Law Review*, 55:482-505.

Miethe, T. & G. Lee (1984). "Fear of Crime Among Older People: A Reassessment of The Predictive Power of Crime-Related Factors." *Sociological Quarterly*, 25:397-415.

Miller, B. & J. Marshall (1987). "Coercive Sex on the University Campus." *Journal of College Student Personnel*, 28:38-47.

Monahan, J.L. & S.T. Murphy (1999). "When Women Imbibe." *Psychology of Women Quarterly*, 23(3):643-653.

Moon, P. (1995). "Native Healing Helps Abusers." *The Globe and Mail*, (April 8):A1, A8.

Moriarty, L.J. (1988). "A Social Learning Approach to Explaining Fear of Crime." Unpublished doctoral dissertation. Huntsville, TX: Sam Houston State University.

Moriarty, L.J., R.A. Jerin & W.V. Pelfrey (1998). "Evaluating Victim Services: A Comparative Analysis of North Carolina and Virginia Victim Witness Assistance Programs." In L.J. Moriarty & R.A. Jerin (eds.) *Current Issues in Victimology Research*, pp. 111-124. Durham, NC: Carolina Academic Press.

Morris, A., G.M. Maxwell & J.P. Robertson (1993). "Giving Victims a Voice: A New Zealand Experiment." *The Howard Journal*, 32:304-321.

Muehlenhard, C. & M. Linton (1987). "Date Rape and Sexual Aggression in Dating Situations: Incidence and Risk Factors." *Journal of Counseling Psychology*, 34(2):186-196.

Mustaine, E. & R. Tewksbury (1998). "Specifying the Role of Alcohol in Predatory Victimization." *Deviant Behavior*, 19:173-199.

Musto, D.F. (1996). "Alcohol in American History." *Scientific American,* 1.

National Association of Crime Victim Compensation Boards (1994). *Maximum Benefits Paid to Crime Victims*. Washington, DC: National Association of Crime Victim Compensation Boards.

National Center on Addiction and Substance Abuse (1996). *Substance Abuse and the American Woman*. New York, NY: Columbia University Press.

National Center for Victims of Crime (1999). *Statistics: State Legislative Summary* [On-line]. Available: http://www.ncvc.org/state/sls/htm.

National Center for Victims of Crime (1990). *Crime Victims and the Media*. Arlington, VA: National Center for Victims of Crime.

National Council for Research on Women (1994). *Sexual Harassment: Research and Resources*. Washington, DC: National Council for Research on Women.

National Institute on Alcohol Abuse and Alcoholism (1999). *The Economic Cost of Alcohol and Drug Abuse in the United States* (Publication No. 98-4327). Bethesda, MD: Lewin Group.

National Institute on Drug Abuse (1998). *Drug Abuse Cost to Society* (NIDA Capsule Series: Publication No. 98-3478). Washington, DC: U.S. Government Printing Office.

National Institute on Drug Abuse (1995). *Trends in Drug Use Among College Students* (NIDA Capsule Series: C-86-06). Washington, DC: U.S. Government Printing Office.

National Victims' Constitutional Amendment Network (1999). *On to the Senate!* [On-line]. Available: http://www.nvcan.org/home.htm.

National Opinion Research Center. (1991). *General Social Survey*, 1991: Codebook. Chicago, IL: National Opinion Research Center.

National Resource Center on Domestic Violence (1999). *Domestic Violence Awareness Project: Domestic Violence-It IS Your Business.* Harrisburg, PA: National Resource Center.

Niemeyer, M. & D. Shichor (1996). "A Preliminary Study of a Large Victim-Offender Reconciliation Program. *Federal Probation*, 60(3):30-34.

Noell, J., A. Biglan, J. Berendt, L. Ochs, C.W. Metzler, D. Ary & K. Smolkowski (1993). "Problematic Sexual Situations for Adolescents: Alcohol and Unsafe Sex." *Health Values*, 17(6):40-49.

Normoyle, J. & P. Lavrakas (1984). "Fear of Crime in Elderly Women: Perceptions of Control, Predictability, and Territoriality." *Personality and Social Psychology Bulletin*, 10:191-202.

Novack, S., B. Galaway & J. Hudson (1980). "Victim and Offender Perceptions of the Fairness of Restitution and Community Service Sanctions." In J. Hudson & B. Galaway (eds.) *Victims, Offenders, and Alternative Sanctions*, pp. 63-70. Lexington, MA: Lexington Books.

Nugent, W.R. & J.B. Paddock (1995). "The Effect of Victim-Offender Mediation on Severity of Reoffense." *Mediation Quarterly*, 12(4):353-367.

Offen, E.N., J.H. Stein & M.A.Young (1999). "The Victim Advocate's Guide to the Media." Washington, DC: National Organization for Victim Assistance.

Office of the Press Secretary (1996). *Remarks by the President at Announcement of Victims' Rights Constitutional Amendment* [On-line]. Available: http://www.pub.whitehouse.gov/uri-res/I2R?urn:pdi://oma.eop.gov.us/1996/6/26/8.text.1

O'Leary, K.D., J. Barling, I. Arias, A. Rosenbaum, J. Malone & A. Tyree (1989). "Prevalence and Stability of Physical Aggression Between Spouses: A Longitudinal Analysis." *Journal of Consulting and Clinical Psychology*, 57(2):263-267.

O'Neill, T.P. (1984). "The Good, the Bad, and the Burger Court: Victims' Rights and a New Model of Criminal Review." *Journal of Criminal Law & Criminology*, 75:361-387.

Orvis, G.P. (1998). "The Evolving Law of Victim's Rights: Potential Conflicts With Criminal Defendants' Due Process Rights and the Superiority of Civil Court Remedies." In L.J. Moriarty & R.A. Jerin (eds.) *Current Issues in Victimology*, pp. 163-175. Durham, NC: Carolina Academic Press.

O'Toole, L.L. & J.R. Schiffman (1997). *Gender Violence*. New York, NY: New York University Press.

Parker, D.A., T.C. Harford & I.M. Rosenstock (1994). "Alcohol, Other Drugs, and Sexual Risk-Taking Among Young Adults." *Journal of Substance Abuse*, 6(1):87-93.

Parks, K. & B. Miller (1997). "Bar Victimization of Women." *Psychology of Women Quarterly*, 21:509-525.

Patai, D. (1998). *Heterophobia: Sexual Harassment and the Future of Feminism*. Lanham, Maryland: Rowman and Littlefield Publishers, Inc.

Pease, K. (1985). "Community Service Orders." In M. Tonry & N. Morris (eds.) *Crime and Justice: An Annual Review of Research*, Volume 6, pp. 51-94. Chicago, IL: University of Chicago Press.

Pernanen, K. (1991). *Alcohol and Human Violence*. New York, NY: Guilford Press.

Pezza, P. & A. Bellotti (1995). "College Campus Violence: Origins, Impacts, and Responses." *Educational Psychology Review*, 7(1):105-123.

Pflüg, M.A. (1996). "American Indian Justice Systems and Tribal Courts in Rural Indian Country." In T.D. McDonald, R.A. Wood & M.A. Pflüg (eds.) *Rural Criminal Justice - Conditions, Constraints, and Challenges*, pp. 191-213. Salem, WI: Sheffield Publishing.

Phillips, A. (1997). "Thou Shall Not Kill Any Nice People: The Problem With Victim Impact Statements in Capital Sentencing." *American Criminal Law Review*, 35:93-118.

Pratt, J. (1996). "Colonization, Power, and Silence: A History of Indigenous Justice in New Zealand Society." In B. Galaway & J. Hudson (eds.) *Restorative Justice: International Perspectives*, pp. 137-155. Monsey, NY: Criminal Justice Press.

President's Crime Commission on Law Enforcement and Administration of Justice (1967). *The Challenge of Crime in a Free Society*. Washington, DC: U.S. Government Printing Office.

President's Task Force on Victims of Crime (1982). *Final Report*. Washington, DC: US Government Printing Office.

Presley, C., R. Harrold, E. Scouten, R. Lyerla & P. Meilman (1996). *CORE Alcohol and Drug Survey: User's Manual*. Carbondale, IL: Southern Illinois University, CORE Institute.

Presley, C., P. Meilman & J. Cashin (1997). "Weapon Carrying and Substance Abuse Among College Students." *Journal of American College Health*, 46:3-8.

Presley, C., P. Meilman & R. Lyerla (1996). *Alcohol and Drugs on American Campuses: Use Consequences, and Perceptions of the Campus Environment*, Vol. IV. Carbondale, IL: Southern Illinois University.

Prince, A. & A.L. Bernard (1998). "Alcohol Use and Safer Sex Behaviors of Students at A Commuter University." *Journal of Alcohol and Drug Education*, 43(2):1-19.

Pullen, L.M. (1994). "The Relationship Among Alcohol Abuse in College Students and Selected Psychological/Demographic Variables." *Journal of Alcohol and Drug Education*, 40:36-50.

Quigley, L.A. & G. Marlatt (1996). "Drinking Among Young Adults." *Alcohol Health and Research World*, 20(3):185-194.

Regoli R.M. & J.D. Hewitt (1996). *Criminal Justice*. Englewood Cliffs, NJ: Prentice Hall.

Reeve, H. (1993). "Victim Impact Statement." Paper presented at the National Conference of Victim Support. Warwick, England.

Reid, S.T. (1997). *Crime and Criminology*, Eighth Edition. Madison, WI: Brown & Benchmark, Publishers.

Reiss, A. (1982). "How Serious Is Serious Crime?" *Vanderbilt Law Review*, 35:541-585.

Reiss, A. (1967). "Studies in Crime and Law Enforcement in Major Metropolitan Areas." Vol. I, Section II, Field Surveys II. *President's Commission on Law Enforcement and Administration of Justice*. Washington, DC: U.S. Government Printing Office.

Research & Forecasts, Inc. (1980). *The Friggie Report on Fear of Crime: America Afraid*. Part I. Willoughby, Ohio: Research & Forecasts, Inc.

Riger, S. & M. Gordon (1981). "The Fear of Rape: A Study in Social Control." *Journal of Social Issues*, 37(4):71-92.

Riger, S., M. Gordon & R. LeBailly (1978). "Women's Fear of Crime: From Blaming To Restricting the Victim." *Victimology*, 3:274-283.

Riggs, R.O., P.H. Murrell & J.C. Cutting (1993). *Sexual Harassment in Higher Education: From Conflict to Community*. ASHE-ERIC Higher Education Report No. 2. Washington, DC: The George Washington University, School of Education and Human Development.

Roberts, A.R. (1991). "Delivery of Services to Crime Victims: A National Survey." *American Journal of Orthopsychiatry*, 61:128-137.

Roncek, D. & P. Maier (1991). "Bars, Blocks, and Crime Revisited: Linking the Theory of Routine Activities to the Empiricism of "Hot Spot." *Criminology*, 29:725-753.

Roper Center (1993). "Newspaper Journalists Public Opinion Online Survey." Storrs, CT: Roper Center, University of Connecticut.

Rosenfeld, M. (2000). "The Male Animal: Two Scientists Explain Rape as a Natural Behavior and Cause an Unnatural Uproar." *The Washington Post*, (January 28):C-1.

Roth, J. (1994). *Psychoactive Substances and Violence*. Washington, DC: National Institute of Justice.

Roth, R. (1986). "The Impact of Liquor Liability on College Universities." *Journal of College University Law*, 13(1):45-64.

Rush, G. (2000). *The Dictionary of Criminal Justice*, Fifth Edition. Long Beach, CA: Dushkin Publishing.

Ryan, W. (1971). *Blaming the Victim*. New York, NY: Vintage.

Sampson, R.J. (1987). "Personal Victimization by Strangers: An Extension and Test of the Opportunity Model of Predatory Victimization." *The Journal of Criminal Law and Criminology*, 78:327-356.

Sandok, M.R. (1997). "Judge Won't Allow Native Ceremony." *Associated Press Wire*, December 12.

Sarvela, P., E. Taylor, J. Drolet & P. Newcomb (1988). "Indicators of Drinking and Driving Among University Students." *Health Education*, 19(5):72-77.

Saunders, D.G. (1986). "When Battered Women Use Violence: Husband-Abuse or Self-Defense?" *Victims and Violence*, 1(1):47-60.

Schafer, S. (1968). *The Victim and His Criminal*. New York, NY: Random House.

Schmidhauser, J.R. (1984). *Constitutional Law in American Politics*. Monterey, CA: Brooks/Cole Publishing Company.

Schneider, A.L. (1986). "Restitution and Recidivism Rates of Juvenile Offenders: Results from Four Experimental Studies. *Criminology*, 24(3):533-552.

Schwartz, M. & C. Nogrady (1996). "Fraternity Membership, Rape Myths, and Sexual Aggression on a College Campus." *Violence Against Women*, 2(2):148-164.

Scruton, D. (1986). *Sociophobics of Fear: The Anthropology of Fear*. London: Westview.

Scully, D. (1990). *Understanding Sexual Violence: A Study of Convicted Rapists.* Boston, MA: Unwin Hyman.

Sebba, L. (1996). "Victim Impact Statement." Paper presented at the National Conference of Victim Support. Warwick, England.

Senate Joint Resolution 3, 106th Congress, 1st Session, Joint Resolution, Section 1 (1999).

Sheley, J. (1979). *Understanding Crime: Concepts, Issues, Decisions.* Belmont, CA: Wadsworth.

Shapland, J., J. Villmore & P. Duff (1985). *Victims in the Criminal Justice System.* Aldershot, UK: Gower.

Shepard, M. (1987). *Gandhi Today: A Report on Mahatma Gandhi's Successors.* Arcata, CA: Simple Productions.

Shoop, R.J. & J.W. Hayhow (1994). *Sexual Harassment in Our Schools: What Parents and Teachers Need to Know to Spot it and Stop It.* Needham Heights, MA: Allyn and Bacon.

Siegelman, D. (1988). "Crime Victims Rights: Rebalancing the Scales." *The Journal of State Government,* 61:107-109.

Sigmon, S.B. & R. Gainey (1995). "High-Risk Sexual Activity and Alcohol Consumption Among College Students." *College Student Journal,* 29:128.

Silberman, C. (1980). *Criminal Violence, Criminal Justice.* New York, NY: Vintage Books.

Silverman, R. (1974). "Victim Precipitation: An Examination of the Concept." In I. Drapkin & E. Viano (eds.) *Victimology: A New Focus,* pp. 99-110. Lexington, MA: Heath.

Silver, I. (1974). "Introduction." In E. M. Schur & I. Silver (eds.) *The Crime Control Establishment,* pp. 1-15. Englewood Cliffs, NJ: Prentice-Hall.

Simonelli, C.J. & K.M. Ingram (1998). "Psychological Distress Among Men Experiencing Physical and Emotional Abuse in Heterosexual Dating Relationships." *Journal of Interpersonal Violence,* 13(6):667-681.

Skogan, W.G. (1986). "Fear of Crime and Neighborhood Change." In A. J. Reiss & M. Tonry (eds.) *Communities and Crime,* [Vol. 8 of *Crime and Justice: A Review of Research*], pp. 203-230. Chicago, IL: The University of Chicago Press.

Skogan, W.G. & M. Maxfield (1981). *Coping with Crime: Individual and Neighborhood Reactions.* Beverly Hills, CA: Sage.

Smith, B. & S. Hilanbrand (1981). *Nonstranger Violence: The Criminal Courts Responses.* Washington, DC: National Institute of Justice.

Smith, S. (1983). "Public Policy and the Effect of Crime in the Inner City." *Urban Studies,* 20:229-239.

Smith, S. (1987). "Fear of Crime: Beyond a Geography of Deviance." *Progress in Human Geography,* 11(1):1-23.

Sourcebook of Criminal Justice Statistics Online, June 1997, p. 156, Table 2.37 (1995 data).

Sparks, R., F. Glenn & D. Dodd (1977). *Surveying Victims.* London: John Wiley.

Spooner, L. (1852). *An Essay on the Trial by Jury.* Boston, MA: J.P. Jewett and Company.

Stafford, M. & O. Galle (1984). "Victimization Rates, Exposure to Risk, and Fear of Crime." *Criminology,* 22(2):173-185.

Standards of Ethics and Professional Responsibility for Certified Mediators (1997). Richmond, VA: Virginia Judicial Council.

Stanko, B. (1993). *Intimate Intrusions: Women's Experiences of Male Violence.* Boston, MA: Unwin Hyman.

Stein, M.L. (1986) "Covering Sex Crimes." *Editor & Publisher*, 119 (November):16-17, 32.

Steinmetz, S.K. (1978). "The Battered Husband Syndrome." *Victimology*, 2(3/4):499-509.

Steinmetz, S.K. (1971). *The Cycle of Violence: Assertive, Aggressive and Abusive Family Interaction.* New York, NY: Praeger.

Steinmetz, S.K. & J.S. Luca. (1988). "Husband Battering." In V.B. Van Hasselt, R.L. Morrison, A.S. Bellack & M. Hersen (eds.) *Handbook of Family Violence*, pp. 233-245. New York, NY: Plenum.

Strauss, M.A. & R.J. Gelles (1990). *Physical Violence in American Families.* New Brunswick, NJ: Transaction Publishers.

Strauss, M.A. & S. Sweet (1992). "Verbal/Symbolic Aggression in Couples: Incidence Rates and Relationships to Personal Characteristics." *Journal of Marriage and the Family*, 54:346-357.

Strebeigh, F. (1991). "Defining Law On The Feminist Frontier." *The New York Times Magazine*, (October 6):4-6.

Strunin, L. & R. Hingson (1992). "Alcohol, Drugs, and Adolescent Sexual Behavior." *International Journal of the Addictions*, 27(2):129-146.

Substance Abuse and Mental Health Services Administration (SAMHSA) (1999). *1998 National Household Survey on Drug Abuse.* Washington, DC: U. S. Government Printing Office.

Sugarman, D.B. & G.T. Hotaling (1989). "Dating Violence: Prevalence, Context, and Risk Markers." In M.A. Rirog-Good & J.E. Stets (eds.) *Violence in Dating Relationships: Emerging Social Issues*, pp. 3-32. New York, NY: Praeger.

Sumner, C.J. (1987). "Victim Participation in the Criminal Justice System." *Australia and New Zealand of Criminology*, 20:195-217.

Sundeen, R. & J. Mathieu (1976). "The Urban Elderly: Environments of Fear." In J. Goldsmith & S. Goldsmith (eds.) *Crime and the Elderly: Challenge and Response*, pp. 51-66. Lexington, MA: Lexington Books.

Sykes, G. & D. Matza (1957). "Techniques of Neutralization: A Theory of Delinquency." *American Sociological Review*, 22:664-670.

Task Force on Victims of Crime (1982). *Final Report.* Washington, DC: U.S. Government Printing Office.

Taylor, R. & E. Hale (1986). "Testing Alternative Models of Fear of Crime." *Journal of Criminal Law*, 77(1):151-189.

Teske, R.H.C. & N.L. Powell (1978). *Texas Crime Poll.* Huntsville, TX: Criminal Justice Center, Sam Houston State University.

Testa, M. & K. Parks (1996). "The Role of Women's Alcohol Consumption in Sexual Victimization." *Aggression and Violent Behavior: A Review Journal*, 1:217-234.

Thigpen, D.E. (1995). "Confronting the Killer." *Time*, (April 3):50.

Thomason, T., P. LaRocque & M. Thomas (1995). "Editors Still Reluctant To Name Rape Victims." *Newspaper Research Journal*, 16(3):42-50.

Thornhill, R. & C.T. Palmer (2000). "Why Men Rape." *The Sciences*, 40(January):30.

Tobolowsky, P.M. (1999). "Victim Participation in the Criminal Justice Process: Fifteen Years After the President's Task Force on Victims of Crime." *New England Journal on Criminal & Civil Confinement*, 25:21-103.

Toseland, R. (1982). "Fear of Crime: Who Is the Most Vulnerable." *Journal of Criminal Justice*, 10(3):199-209.

Tyler, T. (1980). "Impact of Directly and Indirectly Experienced Events: The Origin of Crime-Related Judgments and Behaviors." *Journal of Personality and Social Psychology*, 39:13-24.

Ullman, S.E. (1996b). "Correlates and Consequences of Adult Sexual Assault Disclosure." *Journal of Interpersonal Violence*, 11(4):554-571.

Ullman, S.E. (1996a). "Social Reactions, Coping Strategies, and Self-Blame Attributions in Adjustment to Sexual Assault." *Psychology of Women Quarterly*, 20:505-526.

Ullman, S.E., G. Karabatsos & M.P. Koss (1999). "Alcohol and Sexual Assault in a National Sample of College Women." *Journal of Interpersonal Violence*, 14(6):603-626.

Ullman, S.E. & R. Knight (1993). "The Efficacy of Women's Resistance Strategies in Rape Situations." *Psychology of Women Quarterly*, 17(1):23-41.

Umbreit, M.S. (1995). "The Development and Impact of Victim-Offender Mediation in the United States." *Mediation Quarterly*, 12(3):263-76.

Umbreit, M.S. (1994). *Victim Meets Offender: The Impact of Restorative Justice and Mediation*. Monsey, NY: Willow Tree Press.

Umbreit, M.S. (1991). "Minnesota Mediation Center Gets Positive Results." *Corrections Today*, (August):194-197.

Umbreit, M.S. (1989). "Crime Victims Seeking Fairness, Not Revenge: Toward Restorative Justice." *Federal Probation*, 53(3):52-57.

Umbreit, M.S. & W. Bradshaw (1997). "Victim Experience of Meeting Adult vs. Juvenile Offenders: A Cross-National Comparison." *Federal Probation*, 61(4):33-39.

Umbreit, M.S. & R.B. Coates (1993). "Cross-Site Analysis of Victim-Offender Mediation in Four States. *Crime & Delinquency*, 39(4):565-585.

Umbreit, M.S. & S. Stacey (1996). "Family Group Conferencing Comes to the U.S.: A Comparison With Victim-Offender Mediation." *Juvenile & Family Court Journal*, pp. 29-38.

U.S. Constitution, Article V.

U.S. Constitution, Article VI.

U.S. Department of Education (1997). *Digest of Educational Statistics*. Washington, DC: National Center of Educational Statistics.

U.S. Department of Health and Human Services (1998). *Driving After Drug or Alcohol Use: Findings from the 1996 National Household Survey on Drug Abuse*. Washington, DC: Substance Abuse and Mental Health Services Administration.

U.S. Department of Justice (1999b). *Sourcebook of Criminal Justice Statistics, 1998*. Washington, DC: Bureau of Justice Statistics.

U.S. Department of Justice (1999a). *National Crime Victimization Survey, 1997-1998.* Washington, DC: Bureau of Justice Statistics.

U.S. Department of Justice (1998). *An Analysis of National Data on the Prevalence of Alcohol Involvement in Crime.* (NCJ-168632). Washington, DC: U.S. Government Printing Office.

U.S. Department of Transportation (1998). *Traffic Safety Facts 1997.* Washington, DC: National Highway Traffic Safety Administration.

Utah Code: Section 77.36-2.3, *Domestic Violence.*

Van Ness, D.W. (1996). "Restorative Justice and International Human Rights." In B. Galaway & J. Hudson (eds.) *Restorative Justice: International Perspectives*, pp. 17-36. Monsey, NY: Criminal Justice Press.

Van Ness, DW. & K.H. Strong (1997). *Restoring Justice.* Cincinnati, OH: Anderson Publishing Co.

Viano, E. (1987). "Victim's Rights and the Constitution: Reflections on a Bicentennial." *Crime & Delinquency*, 33:438-451.

Vicenti, D., L.B. Jimson, S. Conn & M.J.L. Kellogg (1972). *Diné Bibee Haz'áanii: The Law of the People.* Ramah, NM: Ramah Navajo High School Press.

Villmoare, E. & V. Neto (1987). "Victim Appearances at Sentencing Under California's Victims' Bill of Rights." Washington, DC: National Institute of Justice.

Virginia Code § 8.01-576.12(3) (1999).

Von Hentig, H. (1948). *The Criminal and His Victim: Studies in the Sociobiology of Crime.* New Haven, CT: Yale University Press.

Von Hentig, H. (1941). "Remarks on the Interaction of Perpetrator and Victim." *Journal of Criminal Law and Criminology*, 72:742-762.

Wallace, H. (1999). *Family Violence: Legal, Medical and Social Perspectives.* Boston, MA: Allyn and Bacon.

Ward, C. (1995). *Attitudes Toward Rape: Feminist and Social Psychological Perspectives.* Thousand Oaks, CA: Sage.

Warr, M. (1984). "Fear of Victimization: Why Women and the Elderly Are More Afraid." *Social Science Quarterly*, 56:681-702.

Warr, M. & M. Stafford (1983). "Fear of Victimization: A Look at Proximate Causes." *Social Forces*, 61:1033-1043.

Watson, J.B. (1924). *Behaviorism.* New York, NY: Norton.

Wechsler, H., A. Davenport, G. Dowdall, G. Maenner, J. Gledhill-Hoyt & H. Lee (1997). *Binge Drinking on American College Campuses: A New Look at an Old Problem.* Boston, MA: Harvard School of Public Health, Harvard University.

Wechsler, H., A. Davenport, G. Dowdall, B. Moeykens & S. Castillo (1994). "Health and Behavioral Consequences of Binge Drinking in College." *Journal of the American Medical Association*, 272:1672-1677.

Wechsler, H. G. Dowdall, G. Maenner, J. Gledhill-Hoyt & H. Lee (1998). "Changes in Binge Drinking and Related Problems Among American College Students Between 1993 and 1997." *Journal of American College Health*, 47(2):57-69.

Wechsler, H., G. Dowdall, A. Davenport & E. Rimm (1995). "A Gender-Specific Measure of Binge Drinking Among College Students." *American Journal of Public Health*, 85:982-985.

Weis, C. & S. Borges (1973). "Victimology and the Case of the Legitimate Victim." In L. Schultz (ed.) *Rape Victimology*, pp. 91-141. Springfield, IL: Charles C Thomas.

Wells, R. (1991). "Victim Impact: How Much Consideration Is it Really Given? *The Police Chief*, (February):44.

Widom, C.S. (1996). *The Cycle of Violence Revisited*. Washington, DC: National Institute of Justice.

Widom, C.S. (1992). *The Cycle of Violence*. Washington, DC: National Institute of Justice.

Wilkinson, B.A. (1999). "Victims' Rights: A Better Way – The Proposed Constitutional Amendment Could Have Let McVeigh Go Free." *The Washington Post*, (August 6):A21.

Williams, F.P. & R. Akers (1987). "Fear of Crime: A Comparison of Measurement Approaches." Paper presented at the meeting of the Academy of Criminal Justice Sciences, St. Louis, MO.

Williams, M.E. (1998). *Working Women: Opposing Viewpoints*. San Diego, CA: Greenhaven Press, Inc.

Wilson, J.Q. (1986). *American Government: Institutions and Policies*, Third Edition. Lexington, MA: D.C. Heath & Company.

Winokur, L.A. (1998). "Sexual Harassment Is a Serious Problem." In M.E. Williams (ed.) *Working Women: Opposing Viewpoints*, pp. 108-112. San Diego, CA: Greenhaven Press, Inc.

Wolfgang, M.E. (1958). *Patterns in Criminal Homicide*. Philadelphia, PA: University of Pennsylvania Press.

Wray, H.R. (1994). *Restitution, Fines, and Forfeiture: Issues for Further Review and Oversight*. Washington, DC: Government Accounting Office.

Wright, B.F., C.A. Miller & B.T. Cooper (1984). *Federal Practice and Procedure*. St. Paul, MN: West Publishing Company.

Yazzie, R. & J.W. Zion (1996). "Navajo Restorative Justice: The Law of Equality and Justice. In B. Galaway & J. Hudson (eds.) *Restorative Justice: International Perspectives*, pp. 157-173. Monsey, NY: Criminal Justice Press.

Yazzie, R. & J.W. Zion (1995). "Slay the Monsters: Peacemaker Court and Violence Control Plans for the Navajo Nation." In K. Hazlehurst (ed.) *Popular Justice and Community Regeneration: Pathways of Indigenous Freedom*, pp. 67-88. Westport, CT: Praeger.

Yin, P. (1980). "Fear of Crime Among the Elderly: Some Issues and Suggestions." *Social Problems*, 27:492-504.

Zehr, H. (1997). "Restorative Justice: The Concept." *Corrections Today*, 59(7):68-70.

Zimring, F.E. & G.J. Hawkins (1973). *Deterrence: The Legal Threat in Crime Control*. Chicago, IL: University of Chicago Press.

Cases

Adamson v. California, 332 U.S. 46 (1947).

Benton v. Maryland, 395 U.S. 784 (1969).

Bloch v. Ribar, 156 F.3d 673 (6th Cir. 1998).

Booth v. Maryland, 482 U.S. 496 (1987).

Cox Broadcasting Company v. Cohn, 420 U.S. 469 (1975).

Del Valle Fontanez v. Aponte, 660 F. Supp. 145 (D.P.R. 1987).

Duncan v. Louisiana, 391 U.S. 145 (1968).

Florida Star v. B.J.F., 420 U.S. 469 (1989)

Franklin v. Gwinnet County Public Schools, 503 U.S. 60 (1992).

Gary v. Long, 116 S. Ct. 569 (1995).

Gideon v. Wainwright, 372 U.S. 335 (1963).

Guess v. Bethlehem Steel Corp., 913 F.2d 463 (7th Cir. 1990).

Harris v. N.Y., 401 U.S. 222 (1971).

Klopfer v. North Carolina, 386 U.S. 213 (1967).

Livingston v. State, 444 S.E.2d 748 (Ga. 1994).

Malloy v. Hogan, 378 U.S. 1 (1964).

Mapp v. Ohio, 367 U.S. 643 (1961).

Mempa v. Rhay, 389 U.S. 128 (1967).

Meritor Savings Bank FSB v. Vinson, 477 U.S. 57, 65 (1986).

Miranda v. Arizona, 384 U.S. 436 (1966).

Palko v. Connecticut, 302 U.S. 319 (1937).

Payne v. Tennessee, 501 U.S. 808 (1991).

Pointer v. Texas, 380 U.S. 400 (1965).

Robinson v. California, 370 U.S. 660 (1962).

Roe v. Wade, 410 U.S. 113 (1973).

Richmond Newspapers v. Virginia, 448 U.S. 555 (1980).

South Carolina v. Gathers, 490 U.S. 805 (1989).

Title IX of the Educational Amendments of 1972, 86 Stat. 373, as amended, 20 U.S.C. 1681 et seq. (Title IX).

Title VII of the Civil Rights Act of 1991, 78 Stat. 255, as amended 42 U.S.C. 2000e-2(a)(1).

Twining v. N.J., 211 U.S. 78 (1908).

United States v. Wade, 388 U.S. 218 (1967).

United States v. Dickerson, 166 F.3d 667 (4th Cir. 1999).

Washington v. Texas, 388 U.S. 14 (1967).

Whalen v. Roe, 429 U.S. 589 (1977).

Contributors' Biographical Information

M.A. (Toni) Dupont-Morales is an Associate Professor in the School of Public Affairs at Penn State, Harrisburg, and Director, Capital College Honors Program. She received her doctorate at Northeastern University (Boston, MA) in Law, Policy and Society. Her research interests include victimology, predatory violence, stalking, and accountability in corrections. Her published work appears in the *Journal of Contemporary Criminal Justice* and *Journal of Criminal Justice*.

Helen M. Eigenberg is Director and Professor, University of Tennessee at Chattanooga. She received the Ph.D. from Sam Houston State University in 1989. Her research interests include woman battering, sexual assault, male rape in prisons. Her book *Til Death Do Us Part* was recently published by Waveland Press. Her other work appears in *Journal of Criminal Justice*, *American Journal of Policing*, *Criminal Justice Review*, *Women in Criminal Justice*, and *Justice Quarterly*.

Ida M. Johnson is a Professor in the Department of Criminal Justice, and Chairperson of the Womens Studies Department at the University of Alabama. Her earned degrees include the Ph.D. in Criminology and Criminal Justice, Florida State University (1987). Her current research areas include forced sexual intercourse, family violence, women who kill, and school violence. Her published work appears in *Journal of Criminal Justice*, *Journal of Contemporary Criminal Justice*, *Families in Society*, *American Journal of Criminal Justice*, and *Free Inquiry in Creative Sociology*. She is the co-author of the book *Forced Sexual Intercourse in Intimate Relationships* (w/R. Sigler), Darmouth Publishing Company.

Patricia H. Grant is an instructor in the Department of Criminal Justice at Virginia Commonwealth University. Her earned degrees include the Ph.D. in Public Policy and Administrations, VCU (2002). Her research interests include victimology, minorities in the criminal justice system, and juvenile crime. Her published work appears in the *Journal of Contemporary Criminal Justice*. Additionally, Ms. Grant is the co-author of a book chapter.

Elizabeth H. McConnell is Chair and Associate Professor in the Department of Criminal Justice and Director of the Graduate Program at Charleston Southern University. Her earned degrees include the Ph.D. in Criminal Justice, Sam Houston State University (1989). Her research interests include fear of crime, youth gangs, and corrections. Her published work appears in *Prison Journal, Journal of Security Adminstration, The Gang Journal*, and *Youth and Society*. She is the coauthor of *American Prisons: An Annotated Bibliography* (w/Laura J. Moriarty), Greenwood Press.

Jon'a F. Meyer is an Assistant Professor of Criminal Justice in the Department of Sociology at Rutgers University, Camden, NJ. Her earned degrees include the Ph.D. in Sociology, University of California at Irvine. She has published on many aspects of criminal justice, including sentencing, criminal courts, Native American legal systems, prison industry and reform, community oriented policing, and computer crime. She is the author of *Doing Justice in the People's Court: Sentencing by Municipal Court Judges* and *Inaccuracies in Children's Testimony: Memory Suggestibility or Obedience to Authority?*

Etta F. Morgan is an Assistant Professor in the School of Public Affairs at Penn State University. Her earned degrees include the Ph.D. in Interdisciplinary Studies with concentrations in criminal justice and women's studies at the University of Alabama (1999). Her research interests include female criminality, gender and racial disparities in the criminal justice system, sentencing reforms, juvenile justice, and capital punishment. She is the author or co-author of several book chapters.

Laura J. Moriarty is Assistant Dean, College of Humanities and Sciences and Professor of Criminal Justice at Virginia Commonwealth University. Her earned degrees include the Ph.D., Sam Houston State University (1988). Her research areas include victims of crime, victimology, fear of crime, and violent crime. She is the author, co-author, or co-editor of four books: *Victims of Crime* (w/Robert Jerin, Nelson-Hall, 1998), *American Prisons: An Annotated Bibliography* (w/Elizabeth McConnell, Greenwood Press, 1998), *Current Issues in Victimology Research* (w/Robert Jerin, Carolina Academic Press, 1998) and *Criminal Justice Technology in the 21st Century* (w/David Carter, Charles C Thomas, 1998). She has published more than 35 scholarly articles, book chapters, and non-refereed articles.

Gregory P. Orvis is an Associate Professor in the Department of Social Sciences at the University of Texas at Tyler. His earned degrees include the Juris Doctorate, Tulane University (1978) and the Ph.D. in Political Science, University of Houston (1988). He is the current holder of the Bart Brooks Endowed Chair for Ethics and Leadership at UT. His research areas include legal and ethical issues in the public workplace and in the criminal justice process. Dr. Orvis' work appears in *Justice Quarterly*, *American Journal of Criminal Justice*, *Bridges*, and *The Harvard Journal of Law and Public Policy Review*. Additionally, he is the author of many book chapters.

Paula I. Otto is an Associate Professor in the School of Mass Communications at Virginia Commonwealth University. Her earned degrees include the M.A. in Public Communication from American University (1997) and the B.S. in Journalism, summa cum laude, from West Virginia University (1983). She has been in the communications business for more than 15 years as a journalist, public relations director, and college professor.

Diane Pedro is a doctoral student in the Urban and Public Affairs program at the University of Louisville. She holds the Juris Doctorate and is primarily interested in law enforcement ethics and organizational management. She has previously published in *The Justice Professional*.

Michael R. Smith is an Assistant Professor in the Criminal Justice Program at Washington State University—Spokane. His earned degrees include the Juris Doctorate, University of South Carolina (1993) and the Ph.D., Arizona State University (1996). His research interests include police pursuits and police liability, citizen complaints, and alternate dispute resolution. His work appears in *Police Quarterly*, *Policing: An International Journal of Police Strategies and Management*, *South Carolina Law Review*, *Kansas Journal of Law and Public Policy* and *American Journal of Policing*.

Richard Tewksbury is an Associate Professor in the Department of Justice Administration at the University of Louisville. He holds a Ph.D. in sociology from The Ohio State University (1991). His primary areas of interest are victimization risk factors, correctional programming, gender identity construction and management, and men's studies. He is the author of *Introduction to Corrections* (Glencoe, 1997), *The Juvenile Justice System* (Waveland, 1999), *Deviants and Deviance* (Roxbury, 2000) and *Extreme Methods: Innovative Approaches to Social Science Research* (Allyn & Bacon, 2001).

Index

Accountability, restoration and, 85
Actual victimization, 71, 79
Africa, legal systems in, 84
Against Our Will (Brownmiller), 44
Age, alcohol use, crime victimization and, 35, 36
Aggression
  bullying, 67
  stalking, 67-68
  verbal, 67
Agnew, R., 79
Akers, R., 79
Alcohol and alcohol use/abuse, 25-42, 119
  binge drinking, 29-31
  by college students, 28-29
  crime and, x, 32-38
  cycles of popular attitudes and legal responses to, 25
  drinking and driving, 38-39
  economic costs of heavy use, 27-28
  health-related consequences of use/abuse, 27-28, 40-41
  incarceration and, 33
  secondhand binge effects and, 41
  as social problem, 42
  victimization and, x, 25-42
  victims' use of, 33-34
  violent crime and, 34-36
  women and binge drinking, 31-32
Amir, Menachim, on victim precipitation, 16-18
Arrigo, B.A., 107
Ashworth, A., 94, 100
Associated Press Managing Editors Code, 50
Attorneys, for VORP participants, 115
Austin, J., 107
Authoritarian theory, media role in relation to government and, 48

Babylonian Code of Hammurabi, restitution in, 83

Bail, Eighth Amendment and excessive, 6
"Battered Husband Syndrome, The," 61
Battering, defined, 59
Baumer, T., 71, 77
Benedict, H., 54, 55
Benefits from crime, restorative justice and, 85
Bill of Rights
  criminal defendants' rights in, 5-7
  Fourteenth Amendment and, 6
Binge drinking
  by college students, 26
  consequences of, 30-31
  defined, 29-30
  drinkers' perceptions during, 31
  secondhand effects of, 30, 41
  women and, 31-32
Black, Jay, 49
Blackmun, Harry A., 97
Bloch v. Ribar, 46
Blood alcohol concentration levels (BAC), 33
Bohmer, S., 60
Booth v. Maryland, victim impact statements and, 95, 96, 97, 100
Borges, S., 17, 21
Born victims, 15
Bowman, Patricia, 45
Breaches of the King's Peace, 83
Brott, A.A., 62
Brown, J.G., 111, 112, 114
Brownmiller, Susan, 44, 55, 56, 120
Bullying, 67
Burden of proof, in civil and criminal courts, 11
Burger, Warren, 8, 110
Bush, George H. W., 8

Carpenter, B., 77
Cate, R.M., 60
Cavanagh, M.E., 62

Censorship, media identification of rape victims and, 54-55

Central Park jogger rape incident, 45, 52

Cernkovich, S.A., 61

Challeen, Dennis, 89

Challenge of Crime in Free Society, The, 76

Chermerinsky, Erin, on federal victims' rights amendment, 12

Children
aggressive behavior and witnessing family violence, 66
raised in violent families, 63
as victims of female violence, 63

"Chinese" wall, VORPs and, 112

Christopher, Charisse, 96

Christopher, F.S., 60

Circle sentencing, aboriginal societies and, 112, 116

Circular thinking, concept of victim blaming and, 18

Civil courts
historical victim compensation and, 83-84
offender restitution and, 9
procedural and evidentiary rules in, 11
victims and, x, 119

Clarke, A., 75

Clinton, Bill, on victims' rights, 1-2

Coates, R.B., 107

Codes of ethics. *See* Ethics

Coercion, VORPS and, 107-108

Cohn, Cynthia, 47

Colleges
alcohol use by students, 28-29
binge drinking at, 29-33
drinking as health issue at, x, 26, 40-41
Harvard School of Public Health College Alcohol Study and, 29-30
statistics on alcohol drinking at, 25-26
student drinking and driving, 38-39
victimization and alcohol use at, 36-38

Common law
procedural and evidentiary rules for criminal and civil courts and, 11
victims' rights and, 119

Communist theory, media role in relation to government and, 48-49

Communities
benefits of restorative justice to, 90
restoration (restorative justice) and, 82-83, 111

Community service
offenders' post-sentence satisfaction with, 88-89
as restitution, 87-88

Compensation. *See also* Restoration (restorative justice)
civil courts and historical victim, 83-84
indirect, in restorative justice, 87-88
states and, 92
victim compensation fund, 2

Conceptual weakness, in victim precipitation concept, 19-20

Confidentiality, VORPs and, 110-111

Constitution. *See* Bill of Rights; Constitutional amendment(s)

Constitutional amendment(s). *See also* Bill of Rights; Federal crime victims' rights amendment; specific amendments
questions to ascertain need for, 10
for victims' rights, 2, 4-5

Constitutional privacy, 46

Constitutional rights, of defendants and victims' rights, 12-13

Cooper, C., 50-51

Costs
of heavy alcohol use, 27-28
of incarceration vs. restoration programs, 90
of victim-offender reconciliation programs, 106

Counterbalance arguments, for balancing victims' rights with defendants' rights, 10

Court dispositions, victim impact statements and, 92

Courts. *See also* Supreme Court (U.S.)
criminal vs. civil, victims and, x
lobbying by victims' rights movement, 4
offender restitution and, 9
procedural and evidentiary rules in, 11
victims and, x

Courtship aggression, 60

Cox Broadcasting Corp. v. Cohn, 47, 56

Cragg, Wesley, 113

Credibility, media identification of rape victims and, 55

Crime. *See also* specific types
alcohol and, x, 32-38
change from offenses against individuals to offenses against king/government, 83-84
fear of, xi, 71-80
illegal drugs and, 34

limited social reality of, 24
as social problem, victim blaming and, 23
"Crime News Privacy Policy," of *St. Louis Post-Dispatch,* 51
Criminal courts. *See* Courts
Criminal defendants' rights, 5-7. *See also* Rights of the accused
  arguments against balancing with victims' rights, 10-13
  arguments for balancing with victims' rights, 7-10
Criminal justice system
  media, rape victims, and, 45-55
  members' approval of restorative justice initiatives, 89
  of Native Americans, 83
  restoration and, 81-90
  as victim-centered system, 11-12
  victim's active participation in, 3
  victims' statutory rights in, 9
Criminal law, 11
Criminal victimization. *See* Victimization
Criminology, traditional victimology compared to, ix
Crothers, Carl M., 45
Cruel and unusual punishment
  Eighth Amendment and, 6
  Supreme Court on, 7
Culturally legitimate victim, victim precipitation concept and, 20-21

Dasgupta, S.D., 59
Dating violence
  defined, 59
  gender, 60
Davis, 105
Davis, R.C., 99, 100
Death penalty cases, victim impact statements and, 95-97, 98
Deaths, alcohol use and, 27
Defendants. *See* Criminal defendants' rights
Demographic characteristics, alcohol use, crime victimization and, 35-36
Des Moines Register, rape series in, 45
Deterrence, VORPs and, 113
Direct victimization, 79
  fear of crime and, 71
Disposition hearing, rights of juvenile in felony case, 2
Domestic violence, 57-69, 119. *See also* Relationship violence
  defined, 59
  definitional issues, 58-60

lace curtain and, 62
  male victims of, x-xi
  relationship aggression and, 62
  and relationship violence, xi, 60, 118
  research and recommendations, 68-69
  statistics about, 57-58
Domestic Violence Awareness Month, 57
Dominick, J.R., 48
"Do nots" list for media treatment of victims, of NOVA, 51-52
Double jeopardy, Fifth Amendment and, 6
Driving, college students' drinking and, 38-39
Drugs, crime and illegal, 34
Dubow, F., 74
Due process argument, against federal victims' rights amendment, 12-13
Due process revolution, 7
Due process rights, x
  Fourteenth Amendment and, 6
  victims' rights and, 2
Dupont-Morales, M.A. (Toni), x-xi, 57-69
Dworkin, A., 54

Economic costs, of alcohol use, 27-28
Education, victimology controversies reconciled with, 117, 119, 121
Efficiency argument, against federal victims' rights amendment, 12
Eggen, D., 61
Eigenberg, Helen M., x, 15-24, 118
Eighth Amendment, 6
  victim impact statements and, 96
Elias, R., 23, 75
Emotional harm
  caused by family violence, 66
  within context of relationship violence, 60
  verbal aggression and, 66
Engs, R., 40
Ennis, P., 77
Equal standing argument, for balancing victims' rights with defendants' rights, 9
Ethics, guidelines for media identification of rape victims, 49-52, 56
Eve, R., 76
Eve, S.B., 76

Family group conferencing (FGC), 111-112, 116
Family relationships, domestic violence and, 59

Family violence
    aggressive behavior of children
        witnessing, 66
    defined, 59
    included in relationship violence, 66
Fear. *See also* Fear of crime
    interdisciplinary definitions of, 73-74
Fear of crime, xi
    defined, 74-78
    fear of strangers and, 77
    importance of discussion, 71
    interdisciplinary scope of, 73-74
    "national," 73
    pervasiveness of, 72
    problems in measurement of, 80, 118
    restorative justice and, 90
    risk of victimization and, 75-76
    single-item vs. multiple-item indicators
        in measurement of, 78
    as social issue, 72-73
    and victimization, 71-80
    victimization as measurement of, 79-80
    vulnerability and, 77-78
    worry about crime and, 76-77
Federal crime victims' rights amendment,
    2, 4-5, 118, 120
    advocates of, 14
    arguments against, 10-13
    arguments for, 7-10
    counterbalance argument and, 10
    due process argument and, 12-13
    efficiency argument and, 12
    equal standing argument and, 9
    forgotten victim argument and, 8-9
    historical argument and, 11-12
    opponents to, 13-14
Female-on-male relationship violence, x-xi
    emotional harm from, 66, 67
    reality, myths, and contradictions in, 60-
        68
    stalking and, 67-68
    statistical information on, 64-66
Ferraro, K.F., 75, 78, 79, 80
Financial restitution. *See* Restitution
First Amendment, media identification of
    rape victims and, 46, 49, 54
Fisher, G., 76
Florida Star v. B.J.F., 47
Forgotten victim argument, for balancing
    victims' rights with defendants' rights,
    8-9

Fourteenth Amendment, 6
    fundamental rights/ordered liberty
        interpretation of, 6
    total incorporation theory and, 6
Fourth Amendment, 6
Four Theories of the Press, 48-49
Franklin, A., 18
Franklin, C., 18
Fraternities, college drinking and, 28-29, 38
Freeman, K., 61
Friedberg, A., 73
*Friggi Report on Fear of Crime, The:
    America Afraid,* 72
Fuentes, M., 77
Fully responsible victims, 19
Fundamental rights interpretation, of Four-
    teenth Amendment, 6
Furstenberg, F., 75, 76

Garofalo, J., 73, 75, 76-77, 78
Gartner, M., 55
Gates, L.B., 79
Gathers, Demetrius, 96
Gatz, M., 77
Gay, Charles, 54
Gender
    alcohol use, crime victimization, and,
        35-36
    college drinking and, 28
    incarceration, drinking, and, 33
Gender bias, relationship violence and, 63
General Social Survey, fear of crime and, 72
Giordano, P.C., 61
Goldberg, C., 62
Goodyear-Smith, 59
Gordon, M., 75
Grand jury indictment, Fifth Amendment
    and, 6
Grant, Patricia H., x, 43-56, 119, 120
Grayson, 105
Great Britain, native restorative systems vs.
    punitive Anglo-Saxon systems and, 84
Gustitus, C., 61
Guttman, L., 76
Gwartney-Gibbs, P.A., 60

Hale, E., 75
Hammurabi, Babylonian Code of, 83
Hanson, D., 40
Hansson, R., 77
Harvard School of Public Health College
    Alcohol Study, 29

Hayes, Richard, 96
Health problems, college students' drink-
    ing and, 26, 27-28, 40-41
Heavy drinking
    by college students, 26, 28-29
    statistics on, 27
Hendy, H., 61
Henley, M., 99
Henry I
    Leges Henrici of, 83
    Magna Charta and, 84
Henton, J.M., 60
Higgins, R., 62
Historical argument, against federal vic-
    tims' rights amendment, 11-12
HIV testing, for sex offenders, 2
Homicides, victim-precipitated, 16
Hotaling, G.T., 59
Husbands. *See* Domestic violence; Rela-
    tionship violence

Ignored violence, women abusing men as,
    62
Incapacitation, VORPs, restorative justice,
    and, 113
Incarceration costs vs. restoration pro-
    grams costs, 90
Indirect compensation, in restorative jus-
    tice, 87-88
Indirect victimization, 79
    fear of crime and, 71
Inhibitions, alcohol and lowering of, 34
Interpretations, victim precipitation and
    offenders', 17
Islamic law, restoration in, 83

Johnson, Ida M., xi, 91-101, 118, 119
Johnson, Lyndon, 72
Journalism. *See also* Media
    principles of ethical, 50
Judicial perceptions, of victim impact
    statements, 98-99
Justice, VORPs and privatization of, 109-110
Justice Assistance Act, 2

Kaplan, G., 74
Katzenbach, Nicholas B., 72
Kelly, D.P., 99
Kelman, S., 62
Kilpatrick, D.G., 100
Koval, J., 60
Krisberg, B., 107

Lace curtain, domestic violence and, 62,
    63
LaGrange, R., 75, 78, 79
Laidlaw, 59
Lambeth, E.B., 50
Lasley, J., 35
Laub, J., 75, 77
Lavrakas, P., 77
Law Enforcement Assistance Administra-
    tion, victim/witness assistance
    programs funded by, 2
Lawton, M., 77
Lee, G., 75, 77
Levy, S., 76
Lewis, M., 75
Libertarian theory, media role in relation
    to government and, 49
Livingston v. State, 98
Lloyd, S., 60
Lotz, R., 75-76
Lucca, J.S., 61

Madison, James
    constitutional amendments and, 6
    on tyranny of the masses, 13-14
Magna Carta, 84
Maier, P., 35
Males. *See* Men
Marital/relationship status, alcohol use,
    crime victimization, and, 36
Marshall, Thurgood, 7, 97
Mass media. *See* Media
Mathieu, J., 76, 79
Maxfield, M., 76
McCabe, E., 74
McConnell, Elizabeth H., 71-80, 79, 118
    on fear of crime, xi
McIntyre, J., 77
Media
    decisionmaking process in publication
        of rape victims' names, 48-52
    female violence within family and, 63
    Four Theories of the Press and, 48-49
    guidelines, codes of ethics, and news-
        room policy regarding identification
        of rape victims, 49-52
    history of treatment of rape victims by,
        44-45
    and identification of rape victims, 52-53
    and identification of victims, 54-55
    publishing rape victims' names and, x,
        119-120

rape victims and, 43-56
Supreme Court on right to publish rape
    victims' names vs. victims' privacy,
    46-47
and withholding victim names, 53-54
Medical consequences, from alcohol use,
    26, 27-28, 40-41
Men
    binge drinking by, 31
    college drinking and, 28
    female-on-male relationship violence
        and, x-xi, 60-68
    male college students, alcohol use, and
        sexual aggression, 38
Merry, Sally, 112
Meyer, Jon'a F., xi, 81-90, 118
Miethe, T., 75, 77
Mi'Kmaq Nation of Nova Scotia, restitution
    and, 81-82
Millhollin, T.J., 61
Minority publications, Central Park rape
    victim and, 45
Miranda rule, 7
    attempts to reverse, 8
Morgan, Etta F., xi, 91-101, 118, 119
Moriarty, Laura J., ix, 71, 74, 117
Myths
    associated with relationship violence,
        62
    regarding rape, 55-56, 120

National Center for Victims of Crime, and
    ethics code regarding victims and
    media, 51
National Commission on Law Observance,
    2
National Crime Survey (NCS), fear of crime
    assessments by, 78
National Crime Victimization Survey
    (NCVS). *See also* National Crime Sur-
    vey (NCS)
    victimization statistics in 1998, 1
National Household Survey on Alcohol
    Abuse, 25
National Incident-Based Reporting System
    (NIBRS), 32
National Institute on Alcohol Abuse and
    Alcoholism, 27
National Organization for Victim Assis-
    tance (NOVA), "*Do nots*" list for media
    treatment of victims, 51-52
National Resource Center on Domestic
    Violence, 57-58, 64

Native Americans
    restitution practiced by, 86
    restoration in criminal justice systems
        of, 83
    white legal system and, 84
Navajo, restitution and, 82
Net-widening, VORPs and, 107-108
Newspaper Research Journal, 53
New Zealand
    family group conferencing in, 112
    native restorative system vs. British
        legal system in, 84
Niemeyer, M., 109, 114
Nixon, Richard, law and order platform of,
    7-8
Nondisclosure protection, rape victims
    and, 55
Nontraditional victimization, 79
Non-victims, vs. victims research, 18
Normoyle, J., 77
NOVA. *See* National Organization for Vic-
    tim Assistance (NOVA)
Nugent, W.R., 108

O'Connor, Sandra Day, 96
Offender(s)
    attorneys for VORP, 115
    criminology focus on, ix
    interpretations and victim precipita-
        tion, 17
    participation in VORPs, 114-115
    restitution and, 86-87
    restorative justice and, 85
    and restorative justice programs vs. ret-
        ributive sanctions, 88-89
    use of alcohol by, 32-33
    victim blaming and, 21-22
    and VORPs coercive effects, 107-108
Offender restitution, criminal vs. civil
    courts and, 9
Offenders' rights. *See also* Criminal defen-
    dants' rights
    vs. rights of the accused, 120
    victim impact statements and, 93
    vs. victims' rights, ix-x, 1-14
Ordered liberty interpretation, of Four-
    teenth Amendment, 6
Orvis, Greg, ix-x, 1-14, 118, 120
Otto, Paula I., x, 43-56, 119, 120
Otto, R.K., 100
Overholser, Geneva, 45

Paddock, J.B., 108

Payne, Pervis Tyrone, 96

Payne v. Tennessee, victim impact statements and, 96, 97, 101

Pedro, Diane, 25-42, 119

"Penny press" era, crime and violence reporting during, 44

Perpetrators. *See* Criminal defendants' rights; Offender(s)

Phillips, A., 98

Physical aggression, vs. verbal/symbolic aggression in relationship violence, 60

Physical assault, within domestic violence, 59

Plea agreement hearings, victims' rights in, 2

Political power, crime, victimization, and, 23

"Politics of rights," versus "politics of interests," 14

Post-sentence satisfaction, for offenders in restorative justice, 88-89

Poverty, as cause of crime, 23

Poynter Institute for Media Studies, ethical journalism principles of, 50

Predominant aggressor concept, in relationship violence, 65-66

Pregnancy, college drinking and, 41

Prevention, victim and crime, 22-23

Prison sentences, victim impact statements and, 98

Privacy rights
distinct forms under law, 46
media identification of rape victims and, 46
rape victims' rights vs. media right to publish victims' names, 46-47

Probation, restitution and, 86

Property crimes, restorative justice and, 88

Property victimization, 79

Prosecutorial perceptions, of victim impact statements, 98-99

Protective orders, female-on-male relationship violence and, 64, 65

Psychological stress, victim impact statements and victims', 94

Public, restorative justice and, 88-90

Public drinking
crime victimization and, 34
women, crime victimization, and, 35-36

Public law, 11

Public opinion, on media identification of rape victims, 52-53

Public trials, vs. VORPs, 110

Pugh, M.D., 61

Punishment
focus on offenders vs. focus on victims, 83-84
VORPs as adequate, 112-114

Quality of life, fear of crime and, 73

Radio Television News Directors Association (RTNDA), code of ethics, 50, 56

Rape, 119
arguments of advocates for identifying victims, 54-55
arguments of advocates for withholding victim names, 53-54
of college students, alcohol use and, 37-38
history of media treatment of, 44-45
media and victims of, 43-56
myths regarding, 55-56, 120
privacy issue in court and, 45-46
public opinion on identification of victims, 52-53
publishing victims' names and, x, 45-55, 119-120
as sexual act vs. aggressive act, 55
Supreme Court on victim privacy rights vs. media right to publish victims' names, 46-47
UCR definition of, 43
victim blaming and, 43
victim precipitated, 16-17

Rape shield laws, 48

Rape victim privacy laws, 47

Reagan, Ronald, 8

Recidivism
restorative justice approaches and, 90
VORPs and, 108-109, 115

Reconciliation programs. *See* Victim-offender reconciliation programs (VORPs)

Rehabilitation, VORPs and, 113-114

Relationship violence. *See also* Domestic violence
"Battered Husband Syndrome" and, 61
contextualization of female violence and, 66
domestic violence reformed to, xi, 60, 118
emotional harm within, 67
family violence included in, 66
female-on-male violence and, 60-66
forms of female violence in, 62-63

forms of male violence in, 62
myths and misdirected intervention in, 62
predominant aggressor concept in, 65-66
research and recommendations, 68-69
stalking, 67-68
Reporting crime, withholding rape victims' names and, 54
Representation issues, xi-xii
Research
    on effects/consequences of alcohol use/abuse and dependency, 26
    on fear of crime measurement, 78-80
    on relationship between alcohol and crime victimization, 34-36
    on victims vs. non-victims, 18
Responsibility, unwarranted levels on victim and victim precipitation concept, 20
Restitution, 2
    in Babylonian Code of Hammurabi, 83
    criminal courts vs. civil courts and, 9
    described, 86
    occurrence of, 86
    weakness of financial, 87
Restoration (restorative justice), xi, 81-90, 118. *See also* Victim-offender reconciliation programs (VORPs)
    benefits of, 90
    history of, 82-84
    ideas behind, 84-88
    philosophy and goals of, 82-83
    primary goal of, 84-85
    program costs vs. incarceration, 90
    public support for, 88-90
"Rethinking the Naming of Sex Crime Victims" (Black), 49
Retribution
    restorative justice and, 113
    victims and offenders punished in, 85
Revictimization, 8
    media's identification of rape victims and, 49, 53-54
    rape, criminal justice system, and, 43
Rhoe, W.M., 79
Richmond Newspapers v. Virginia, 110
Riger, S., 75
"Rights of Crime Victims" (Alaska), 3-4
Rights of the accused, vs. offenders' rights, 120
Right to confront witnesses
    Sixth Amendment and, 6
    Supreme Court on, 7

Right to counsel
    Sixth Amendment and, 6
    Supreme Court on, 7
    VORPs and, 111
"Right to Truth in Evidence" (California), 4
Ripple effect, spread of fear of crime and, 71
Risk of victimization, vs. fear of crime, 75-76
Roe v. Wade, 46
Roncek, D., 35
Routine activity theory, alcohol-crime link and, 35
Rudolph, J.L., 61
Rule of law, VORPs and, xi, 109-112, 119

Safe sex, college drinking and, 40-41
Sanctions. *See also* Restoration (restorative justice)
    indigenous peoples and, 81-82
Satisfaction
    community service and offenders', 88-89
    victim impact statements and victims', 99-100
    VORPs and victims', 104-106
Saunders, D.G., 61
Scales of balance, victims' rights, defendants' rights and, 13
Schehr, R.C., 107
Schneider, A.L., 108
Scruton, D., 74
Scully, D., convicted rapists study by, 21
Searches or seizures
    Fourth Amendment and, 6
    Supreme Court on, 6
Sears-Collins, 98
Sebba, L., 98
Secondhand binge effects, 30, 41
Second injury, to rape victims, 43
Selective incorporation approach
    to Fourteenth Amendment, 6
    to states and Bill of Rights' guarantees, 7
Sentencing process
    arguments against victim impact statements in, 93-97
    victim impact statements and, 97-98
    victim input, victim impact statements, and, 91, 92-93
Sentimental values, financial restitution and, 87
Sex, women, bingeing, and, 32
Sex offenders
    HIV testing for, 2

registration and community notification of, 3

Sexual abuse, gender and, 63

Sexual assault
  binge drinking and, 31, 32
  of college students, alcohol use and, 37-38

Sexually transmitted diseases, alcohol consumption by college students and, 40

Shapland, J., 98

Shared responsibility, x
  concept of, 15-16
  restoration and, 84-85

Shichor, D., 109, 114

Sibling abuse, 63

Sixth Amendment, 6
  right to counsel, VORPs, and, 111

Skogan, W.G., 73

Smith, B.E., 99, 100

Smith, Michael R., xi, 103-116, 119

Smith, S., 74

Smith, William Kennedy, rape trial, 45, 50, 52, 54

Social issue, fear of crime as, 72-73

Social responsibility theory, media role in relation to government and, 49

Society of Professional Journalists, code of ethics on rape victims' identification, 49-50, 56

Sororities, college drinking and, 28-29

South Carolina v. Gathers, victim impact statements and, 96, 97, 100-101

St. Louis Post-Dispatch, "Crime News Privacy Policy" of, 51

Stacey, S., 111

Stalking, 67-68

Standing doctrine, statutory rights of victims and, 9

Stare decisis standard, Supreme Court, victim impact statements, and, 97, 101

State(s)
  application of Bill of Rights to, 6-7
  capital cases and admissibility of victim impact statements and, 96-97
  victim impact statements and, 93
  victims' rights amendment in, 3
  victims' rights in, x

Steinmetz, S.K., 61

Stockard, J., 60

Strangers, fear of vs. fear of crime, 77

Strauss, M.A., 60

Sugarman, D.B., 59

Sundeen, R., 76, 79

Supremacy clause, federal crime defendants' rights vs. state victims' rights and, 10

Supreme Court (U.S.)
  conservative justice appointed to, 8
  death penalty cases, victim impact statements, and, 95-97, 100-101
  due process revolution and, 7
  interpretations of Fourteenth Amendment by, 6
  on privacy issue in rape cases, 46
  on public criminal trials, 110
  on victim impact statements, 4

Sweet, S., 60

Tautological reasoning, concept of victim blaming and, 18

Taylor, R., 75

Tewksbury, Richard, 25-42, 119

Tichane, M., 105

Tlingit, sanction, restitution and, 81

Total incorporation theory, Fourteenth Amendment and, 6

Totally innocent victims, 19

Traditional victimization, 79

Trial
  Sixth Amendment and rights to, 6
  Supreme Court on rights to, 7
  VORPs vs. public, 110

UCR. *See* Uniform Crime Reports (UCR)

Umbreit, M.S., 105, 106, 107, 109, 111, 114

Uniform Crime Reports (UCR), rape defined by, 43

United States Department of Justice, 32

Verbal aggression, emotional harm caused by, 67

Verbal/symbolic aggression, vs. physical aggression in relationship violence, 60

Vicarious victimization, 71, 79

Victim(s)
  approval of restorative justice initiatives, 89
  benefits of restorative justice to, 90
  early typologies for classification according to degree of responsibility, 15-16
  effect of victim impact statements on, 94
  fully responsible, 19
  goal of "restoring," ix
  male victims of domestic violence, x-xi

media and rape victims, 43-56
narrow definition of, 117-118
research on non-victims and, 18
and retribution/restoration, 89-90
satisfaction with victim impact statements, 99-100
totally innocent, 19
traditional victimology focus on, ix
use of alcohol by, 33-34
victim blaming and creation of culturally legitimate victim, 20-21
VORPS' impact on, 104-106
Victim and Witness Protection Act, 2
Victim assistance programs, 2
   orientation in, 117
Victim blaming, x, 15-24
   conceptual weaknesses and, 19
   creating culturally legitimate victims
      and, 20-21
   development of concept, 16-18
   excusing offenders' behavior and dimin-
      ishing responsibility, 21-22
   historical typologies in, 15-16
   offender motivation, crime prevention,
      and, 22-23
   popularity of, 22-24
   rape and, 43, 55
   rape shield laws and, 48
   societal beliefs, just world, and, 22
   tautological reasoning or circular think-
      ing and, 18
   undue responsibility on victim and, 20
   victim prevention and, 22
Victim compensation fund, 2
Victim facilitation, 15
Victim impact statements, xi, 10, 91-101,
   118, 119
   arguments against, 93-97
   arguments in favor of, 92-93
   criminal justice professionals' support
      of, 98-99
   death penalty cases and, 95-97
   debate over, 101
   effects on sentencing, 97-98
   purpose of, 91
   requirements for, 2
   Supreme Court rulings on, 4, 100-101
   victim satisfaction with, 99-100
Victimization
   alcohol use and, x, 25-42
   categories of, 79
   on college campuses, alcohol and, 36-38
   decrease in, 1

fear of crime and, 71-80
as focus of victimology, 117-118
as measure of fear of crime, 79-80
risk of vs. fear of crime, 75-76
study of causes, ix
vicarious, 71
Victim notification, 2, 92-93
Victim-offender mediation (VOM), 116n.
   See also Victim-offender reconciliation programs (VORPs)
Victim-offender reconciliation programs
   (VORPs), xi, 103-116, 119
   appeal of, 104
   cases referred to, 104
   coercion issues and, 107-108
   cost-effectiveness of, 106
   family group conferencing and, 111-112
   impact on victims, 104-106
   minimizing negative impact of, 112
   monitoring of, 116
   objectives of, 103
   problems with, 114-115
   punishment issues and, 112-114
   recidivism and, 108-109
   rule of law and, 109-112
Victimology
   reconciling controversies in, 117-121
   traditional compared to modern, ix
   victim blaming and, 15-24
Victim-precipitated crimes
   alcohol use and, 34
   homicides, 16
   rapes, 16-17
Victim precipitation, 15. See also Victim
   blaming
   development of concept, 16-18
Victims' Bill of Rights, 4
Victims of Crime Act, 2
Victims' rights
   arguments against balancing with crimi-
      nal defendants' rights, 10-13
   arguments for balancing with criminal
      defendants' rights, 7-10
   vs. offenders' rights, ix-x, 1-14
   trends in, 1-5
Victims' rights amendment(s), 10
   for Constitution, 2, 4-5
   state-level, 3-4
Victims' rights movement, 1
   Constitutional amendment and, 4-5
   growth of, 8
   lobbying courts by, 4
   lobbying state legislatures and, 3-4

Proposition Eight and, 2
restitution and, 86
Violence. *See also* Aggression; Domestic
    violence
    children witnessing, 66
    on college campuses, alcohol use and,
        26
    dating, 59
    domestic, 59
    family, 59
    female-on-male relationship violence,
        60-68
Violent crime
    alcohol and, 34-36
    financial restitution and, 87
    victims of and retribution/restoration
        initiatives, 89-90
Violent Crime Control and Law Enforce-
    ment Act, 2
Violent crime victimization, 79
Von Hentig, H., victim typology of, 15
VORPs. *See* Victim-offender reconciliation
    programs (VORPs)
Vulnerability, vs. fear of crime, 77-78

Wallace, H., 59
Warr, M., 76
Warren Court, x
Watson, B., 73
Wechsler, H., 31, 40
Weis, C., 17, 21
Whalen v. Roe, 46
White, Byron, 47
Whitehouse, V., 50-51
"Why Men Rape" (Thornhill and Palmer),
    55-56

Wilkinson, Beth, federal Victims' Rights
    Amendment and, 12
Williams, F.P., 79
Winston-Salem Journal, rape victims
    named in, 44-45
Witness assistance programs, 2, 117
Witnessing violence, children and, 59, 66
Wives. *See* Domestic violence; Relation-
    ship violence; Women
Wolfgang, Marvin, on victim precipitation,
    16
Women
    bingeing, secondhand binge effects,
        and, 31-32
    as "born victims," 15
    college drinking and, 28
    female college students, alcohol use,
        and sexual assault, 37-38
    female-on-male relationship violence,
        60-68
    public drinking, crime victimization,
        and, 35-36
    rape victims and media, 43-56
    as stalkers, 67
Worry about crime, vs. fear of crime, 76-77

Yaffee, S., 77
Yin, P., 75, 77, 78, 79
Young adults
    consequences of alcohol use, 28
    drinking and driving and, 38-39
    drinking on college campuses by, 26,
        27, 28-32

Ziegenmeyer, Nancy, 45